PLANNING FOR MISSION

Working Papers on the New Quest For Missionary Communities

edited by

THOMAS WIESER

EPWORTH PRESS : LONDON

Published in Great Britain by Epworth Press 1966
Book Steward: Frank H. Cumbers

Printed in U.S.A.

Contents

Introduction

This volume contains a selection of papers and contributions which were produced in the course of the study on "The Missionary Structure of the Congregation." This study was authorized at the Third Assembly of the World Council of Churches in New Delhi in 1961, to be conducted during the period until the next Assembly under the leadership of the Department of Studies in Evangelism. The study has completed the first stage and it seems appropriate to offer some of the fruits to a wider audience. While some of the contributions are the result of sustained research and study on the topic, others are more impressionistic sketches, designed to stimulate thinking along hitherto unexplored lines.

Exciting is not a word which is usually applied to theological investigation—absorbing, interesting, perhaps for those occupied in it: but, *exciting?* Nevertheless, those of us who have been engaged in a comprehensive study of the problem of the congregation in the task of evangelism would be prepared to use this adjective: our work together has been exciting: It is our hope that some of this excitement may be communicated to the reader of this volume of collected papers.

When the Third Assembly of the World Council of Churches at New Delhi gave authority to the Department on Studies in Evangelism to carry out this research programme, it is probable that a majority of the delegates had little inkling how stimulating and provocative an exercise this would prove to be. By no means least among the factors that have made it so is the dialogue between theology and sociology that has formed an essential part of it. There are of course two primary realities with which the congregation must be concerned: the Gospel of God and the world to which it is sent. 'Authentic theology,' it has been rightly said, 'emerges out of the dialogue between the Gospel and the world' (G. M. Webber, *The Congregation in Mission,* 1964, p. 10). We are not suggesting by this quotation that the theologians represent God and the sociologists the world: we are saying that out of the dialogue between the representatives of the two disciplines it is our hope that an authentic theology, meaningful to the man of today, will develop. The words 'will develop' are used advisedly, because none of us would claim that everything is as yet clear; on the contrary, we have more problems than solutions; we have, as in all ecumenical discussions, confessional tensions. Yet we are sufficiently of a common mind to be convinced that the insights, of which we believe we have obtained glimpses, are ones that should be shared with a larger audience than that constituted by the membership of the various international groups and their immediate associates.

This sharing has already taken place between the groups, so that, for example, the papers of the Western European Group were fully available to the North American Group and vice-versa. This has meant that instead of each group having to pursue exactly the same programme, they have been able to develop their own lines of research and to complement them by the work of others. So while there has been some overlapping, there are grounds for saying that the Western European Group has been mainly concerned to develop a new theological understanding of mission and its relation to the world and to the Church, while the North American Group, acutely conscious of certain pressing problems, e.g. the Freedom Movement, has been concerned to face specific practical issues, and this too is largely true of the D.D.R. Working Group in East Germany.

* * * * *

WESTERN EUROPE

The Western Europeans have tended to produce individual papers, which have then been discussed and incorporated into preliminary reports representing the general, although not necessarily the detailed, agreement of all participants. So much of J. C. Hoekendijk's study of the meaning of mission (pp.) underlies the Driebergen paper on mission (pp.). The American Group has not attempted as yet such a drawing together of the separate contributions. In the selection that follows both types of documents are represented, so that the reader can follow for himself some of the detailed thought that is destined eventually to result in a final report. In order to assist the reader further to enjoy this symposium and to comprehend the unity of the individual items, a preliminary survey of the arrangement of the material and a word about some of its chief features may be in order.

The first Christians could describe their new-found faith as 'the Way' (e.g. Acts 19.9), which led through Christ (John 14.6) to the Kingdom of God at its final consummation. 'The Way of the Kingdom,' which is the title of the first main section, is therefore a description and interpretation of the Christian's calling. But this way, as we have come to appreciate, is not one that *we* open up; it is entirely at the disposal of the divine initiative. God is the one who summons us from the world (Wieser pp. 16 ff). To respond to that summons is to participate in mission, which is therefore 'hope in action' (Margull p. 33). For mission is not a function of the Church, but an attribute of God; mission is always *missio Dei* in which we are called to join (Hoekendijk pp. 37 ff). The Church only *is* in mission, although missions may be relative and historical forms of that participation (Driebergen pp. 48 ff). The call then is to historical existence (Bossey pp. 53 ff), not to a timeless adoration; it is a summons to join God in the world and to cooperate with him in the making of history. Our service of Christ therefore is not to be confined to the ecclesiastical structures—the Lord is active *extra muros ecclesiae* (Hollenweger pp. 58 ff). To seek God by involvement in the world now puts to the test our inherited concepts enshrined in our confessional traditions (Wieser p. 61).

The world in which God's will is to be sought and obeyed is a 'World in Change'—the title of the second section. Its one enduring characteristic is its changeability (Schmidt pp. 70 f); the old landmarks are being left behind; unceasing transformation, which is a sign of God working out his purpose (Keller pp. 71 ff), is now the order of the day, for we live in the 'end times,' the times of eschatological crisis to which mission gives meaning. A predominant element in this change is the phenomenon of secularization, which must be both understood sociologically (Matthes pp. 82 ff) and given a positive theological evaluation (Villemétrie pp. 88 ff). It is to this situation that the Church has to adapt its structures (D.D.R. Working Group pp. 118 ff).

But what is the place of the Church in all this? Where is 'The Church in the World?' The Church is a segment of the world and cannot be separated from it (Casalis pp. 122), even the Church's traditional notes—oneness, holiness, catholicity and apostolicity—are to be defined in relation to the world it is called to serve (Williams pp. 128). Sociology enables us to appreciate the relativity of the Church's structures (Hoekendijk, etc. pp. 131) and to acknowledge that to absolutize any of them is to adopt an inflexible attitude which is the opposite of the expectant hope of the mature Christian. Service is the calling of a Church that would accept the pattern of life revealed by its Lord (Villemétrie pp. 138).

The Church's 'Missionary Presence'—our fourth section—must

accordingly assume many forms. Neither Bible nor Church History compels us to accept one structure as sacrosanct (Gager pp. 149; Hollenweger pp. 153). Consequently one cannot provide a blueprint of the ideal congregation, although it is possible to direct attention to numerous contemporary experiments which may reveal, in some measure, the shape of things to come, e.g. in Germany (Simpendörfer pp. 153), at the various levels of a pluriform society (Bossey pp. 156) and in the American Race Struggle (Bossey pp. 164). The key figure in this missionary outreach is the layman (Löffler pp. 168), who is already present in the structures of the world; but he needs assistance and equipment to disclose the ever-present Christ to his neighbour and this raises questions both of the form, content and method of training and the relationship of the ordained ministry to the other ministries in the Church (Vogt etc. pp. 177). It raises too the question of the missionary dimension of worship (Driebergen pp. 185). But the almost exclusive emphasis of the Church upon the residential community makes further advance difficult if not impossible. The gravity of this limitation has to be recognized (Kraemer pp. 193) and the use of community self-surveys, both in terms of the local parish and of the wider area, or zone, of human concern and activity, is to be encouraged as a possible tool which can enable the Church to know itself and its situation (Esslingen pp. 205; Driebergen pp. 208). It is this self-knowledge that can help the Church to participate fully in the *missio Dei*.

This mapping out of the main highway of our study will have enabled the reader to appreciate that we have not proceeded without raising a number of theological issues, and it may be of further help if these are now specified and a few brief comments upon them made.

The first problem is to reach an agreed definition of the relationship of God to the Church and to the world. In the past it has been customary to maintain that God is related to the world through the Church. The sequence is: God-Church-world, and that is understood to mean that God is primarily related to the Church and only secondarily to the world by means of the Church. Further, it has been held that God relates himself to the world through the Church in order to gather everyone possible from the world into the Church. God, in other words, moves through the Church to the world. There is majority, but not unanimous, agreement that this sequence is incorrect and that the last two items in God-Church-world should be reversed so that it reads instead God-world-Church, i.e. God's primary relation is to the world, and it is the world and not the Church that is the focus of God's plan. If this be accepted, then it is wrong to think that God always initiates change from inside out, from inside the Church out into the world. Nor is God's activity to be confined to the Church—his action in the world being no more than that of the Church itself; otherwise the world is apparently bereft of the divine presence, which is then enshrined within and reserved exclusively for the Church.

The second problem, which is closely connected with this, is to define the relationship between the Church and the world. In former times the Church was viewed as the ark, perilously afloat amidst the turbulent seas of this world; outside the safety of this vessel mankind was going down to destruction and the only salvation was to be dragged from the deep into the safety of the ecclesiastical ship. It must be admitted that some support for this way of describing the relationship, i.e. in terms of implacable enmity, may appear to be given by the New Testament, e.g. 'pure religion is to keep himself unspotted from the world' (Jas. 1.27). In our study however we are more inclined to say that the Church is a part of the world and that our thinking about the Church should always start by our defining it as a segment of the world, albeit one which confesses the universal Lordship of Christ. Hence the Church must never separate itself from the world. This apparent contradiction, or rather tension, between defining the relationship of Church and world in terms of hostility or of virtual identity is itself reflected in the New Testament. On the one hand Christians are a community of strangers whose citizenship is in heaven, and yet on the other hand they are to be the salt of the earth and the light of the world. We may say that the Church is only required to be separate in order to be prepared for engagement, i.e. the Church exists for the world.

But what is the distinction between the Church and the world? This is the third issue. The Church is the first fruits of the new creation; it is that place where the world becomes aware of its true destination—it is *pars pro toto*. It lives in order that the world may know its true being. Thus while there is continuity between Church and world, there is also discontinuity, but the nature of this discontinuity is by no means clear.

The next issue turns about the problem whether Christ is primarily to be seen as Saviour or as Lord. Is the message: Repent and be saved, or is it: Christ is risen, you are risen, be what you are? This issue is inseparable from another, viz. the discerning of God's action in the world and the seeking of an answer to the question: what is the nature of that action? Can we distinguish between God's providential action in the world and Christ's redeeming work within the Church? Many would say no, but the question has not been fully examined.

There is further the problem of the relationship of worship and mission. In contemporary thought and practice these two are usually seen as separate activities. If related at all, they are related simply as cause and effect, i.e. we gather in worship in order to be sent out in mission. Many of us would question this. It seems to us that worship and mission are twin aspects of a single totality, that both are concerned, not with man's activity, but with God's initiative. But the fact remains that in the past worship has been interpreted mainly inwards, i.e. as that which builds up the Body of Christ. We believe that the time has come to recognize the missionary dimension of worship and so to develop an understanding of it which is outward-looking.

The overall issue, which we cannot at any time avoid and which impinges upon each of the others, is the meaning of mission itself. But as this is covered in several of the contributions that follow, we need not attempt to go further here.

The study of the missionary structure of the congregation raises not only theological issues but also problems of a practical nature. In particular it poses the question: are we aiming to restore our Church life or are we concerned with its total renewal? It is doubtful if this either/or approach is the correct one. We have to recognize that the sociological context of the Church's engagement in mission differs from continent to continent, from country to country and even within each country from locality to locality, e.g. the situation in some northern country areas in Britain is not the same as that which obtains in the southern conurbations. Depending therefore upon an accurate analysis of the situation, we may say: here we must aim to restore our Church life, or we may say: here total renewal is the only hope. Because the situation is not everywhere the same—although in time it may become so—we cannot produce a single blueprint. Yet there is a general trend in modern western life to be acknowledged, which may issue in the breakdown of the congregation-type based upon residence—the parish is no longer the world of the individual labourer or professional man. In work and leisure he is mobile. Wherever this situation exists the residential congregation may be something of an anomaly. No doubt it has a part to play in ministering to the private sphere of human existence, but the Gospel addresses the *whole* man in the *whole* of his life. This pinpoints the present structural crisis of the Church. If it is truly to participate in mission, it must devise new and multiform structures that will enable it to engage with the new structures of modern society.

The University
Birmingham

J. G. DAVIES
Chairman, Western European Group

NORTH AMERICA

In the North American Working Group the study was taken up at the moment when some experiments in new forms of missionary action had gotten definitely beyond the talking stage and when this development was raising fundamental questions about accepted patterns of thought and action in the churches. Nevertheless, the need was not so much for a new conceptualization of mission as to gain elbow room to let things happen which were not necessarily in the book of home mission boards and church extension committees. Was not God at work in the world in ways which may overthrow our presently held inviolate theological categories of understanding? Could the work of the church continue to be limited to the traditional organized ways of mission and evangelism allowing some exceptions here and there "in case of emergency"? These were the kinds of questions which imposed themselves on the members of the North American Working Group as they began their meetings in 1962.

To these questions was added the sense of urgency in the following year for dealing with issues demanding immediate attention such as the Civil Rights struggle in the United States. This sense of urgency did not generally allow in the meetings the careful delineation of the concepts and understanding and the development to the point where they would be formulated as the thinking of the Group. Rather the urgency pressed the search for, and the development of "parables of missionary action" which might give guidance to thought, and clues for action. This led to the emphasis on newly created task groups, centered in a particular locality or region where a shape of missionary action was either emerging or needed. The work of these task groups is still in process and points to the second stage of the study which will be reported at a later date.

The emphasis on "new forms" of missionary action has incurred the criticism that this study is not living up to its title insofar as it does not show great interest in the work of the existing congregations where, it is said, the church after all carries on its major work. It is true that there has not been made any attempt to describe what would constitute a missionary congregation which could serve as a model toward which one could work. In this respect the formulation of the topic has indeed been misleading and it became soon evident that we were talking not so much about *a* structure for *a* congregation but we were concerned with structures for missionary congregations. For quite apart from the impossibility ever to reach agreement on a model congregation it was recognized early in the study that we do not need a new blueprint for renewal. The renewal which is called for today is a change not from one form to another but to a variety of forms. If there is a new situation today it consists precisely in the fact that people no longer live in one world but in many different worlds, each with its own forms of association and interaction. One of the most dramatic shifts in this respect—sociologically speaking—is represented by the differentiation between the private and the public world, the world of family and residence on the one hand and the world of work and public responsibility on the other. If Christians are enjoined to "gather at the point of mission" (s. below, pp. 159) the multiplicity of sociological localities must be taken seriously just as much as the multiplicity of geographical localities was taken seriously in the earlier missionary expansion of the last hundred years. In distinction or contrast to the geographical multiplicity, however, the sociological multiplicity demands a multiplicity of forms of gathering. The predominant concern with "new" forms in the study, therefore, is not so much a concern for their "newness" as it is in a concern for establishing the notion of *multiple* forms of *relative* value; that is, relative—and hence relevant—to the world in which they emerge. The need for establishing this notion of multiplicity was felt to be a prerequisite for any further discussion and study of the traditional form of the church's gathered life. We should not deny that this in itself involves a challenge to the traditional form but this challenge is misunderstood if it is defined as "new vs. old." Just as the concern for the new is not because of its newness, but because of its implied multiplicity and relativity, the challenge to the traditional is not because of its antiquity but because of its implied uniformity and its normative character.

Obviously the affirmation of the relativity of structures has its dangers. For, one, it might lead to a certain utilitarian attitude toward structures which sees in the question of adequate structures merely a technical problem. Implied in this attitude is the assumption that means can be separated from ends or forms from content. Applied to our study this would mean that only the goals of mission or the content of witness were legitimate subjects for theological discussion and clarification while the question of structures could, and indeed should, be left to technicians trained in organization and management. Some voices were heard at the outset that this study was covering a beaten track in that too much energy was already being wasted in the churches with matters of structure and organization. However, the discussion in the Working Group never was in danger of sliding into such a utilitarian attitude. On the contrary, to the surprise of many, the question of structures soon revealed fundamental theological dimensions, for it was discovered that churches like other social groups speak not only through words or specific actions but also through their structures; that structures are not neutral but are related to the content and goal. Furthermore, it was found that the nature of the relationship between the goal of mission and the structure is not clear and demands thorough examination. Thus the discovery of the relativity of structures did not and need not mean that structures become unimportant. Rather they become more important.

It may also be helpful for an understanding of the documents of this volume and the study as a whole, to point out that while they do not represent a particular type of theology, they reflect a common concern for a certain stance of *theologizing*. This stance is perhaps best captured by the image of the pilgrim or the wandering people of God. "Mission" means sending and involves 'going' and it is therefore only natural that the thought and reflection supporting, surrounding and correcting this 'going' should also have this missionary (going-) quality. A static theology by definition is anti-missionary even if it would claim to be a theology of mission. Precisely the static character of theology, a theology which primarily attempts to work out a *position*, whether biblical, literal, orthodox, neo-orthodox, existentialist, or non-theistic, is not a viable option for a missionary congregation. The excitement felt by some members of the Working Group and the frustration felt by others was to a large extent due to the fact that the meetings and discussions never issued in the delineation of one or several positions on an issue but rather were occasions when people who were 'on the way' in mission could gather for reflection. Thus our discussions in themselves became 'missionary' in the sense that they assumed that the participants were 'on the way' also with regard to their theological thought and that insofar as positions were presented they were properly to be understood as 'way stations.' The main question, therefore, which the reader of these documents should have in mind should not be: where do the authors stand?—but it should be: *where are they going?* For the recovery of the genuine missionary character of Christian and theological thought may well be the main long-range effect of this study long after today's most radically new structures will again be obsolete.

New York

THOMAS WIESER
Secretary to the North American Working Group

First Part

THE WAY OF THE KINGDOM

The Church and the Way of the Kingdom

A Study in Acts

I. THE WAY OF THE CHURCH

The history of events involving the church proceeds, according to Acts 1:8 from Jerusalem to Samaria and to the end of the earth. The central meaning of these events resides in the presence of the risen Lord (Kyrios) in the world. As Luke shows in the case of the church in Jerusalem, the role of the church in this history is to manifest and exhibit the Kyrios' presence in its life as a community as well as in individual—yet representative—acts of witness.

But the mentioning of Jerusalem, Judea, Samaria and the end of the earth is important not only because things come to pass in these places. An account which relates isolated incidents, each connected with a different locale, cannot claim to be 'history.' It would be a series of histories. A book on Christian origins such as Acts might conceivably contain the history of the church in Jerusalem and in Antioch and possibly in Caeserea, followed by Paul's experiences as a travelling missionary. But these would be isolated stories. In fact, Acts is attempting to give a coherent account. The difference between the two types of narratives is more than literary.

For Luke these various places are important not in themselves but as phases in an ongoing history. His concern is to show how this history *moves* from one place to the other. The names in the enumeration in Acts 1:8 signify a *way*. The church exists in order to be on this way. For this reason, too, the disciples become apostles.

It might seem, at first glance, that the way of the church is given by the nature of the circumstances. This impression is most strongly suggested in the first eight chapters of Acts. Here we find that the conviction and enthusiasm of the apostles evoke a favorable response on the part of the Jewish leaders. This is certainly comparable to developments which commonly occur with the rise of a new religious movement. Furthermore, the development in Acts appears to follow a natural and inevitable course: the popularity of the Christians is growing, the apostles become increasingly fearless. On the other hand, the opposition is also stiffening. The aggressiveness of Stephen finally costs him his life. At the same time, it is the signal for a general persecution. This in turn leads to the dispersion of the Christians into the environs of Jerusalem. It is only natural that now attention should be focused on events outside the Holy City. The evangelization of Samaria can therefore be considered as a natural outcome of dispersement.

The emergence of the twelve apostles as leaders could also be considered as a natural development in the early part of the church's history. Their association with Jesus and their experience of the resurrection automatically put them in a position of authority. They were obviously equipped to guide the growing community by their teaching and by watching over its conduct. They were also the authorized persons to defend the new faith over against the outside world.

It is therefore not surprising that this part of Acts has been found to be fairly reliable by scholars who set out to write a history of early Christianity. No doubt Luke has embellished his source and placed the accent somewhat differently, but in principle he has reproduced the historical development as it actually took place.

While an explanation of Acts in terms of a natural historical development might be justified as long as these chapters are considered apart from the rest of the book, this becomes inadequate as soon as we look at the following chapters. Already the latter part of Acts 8 defies such an interpretation. No historical circumstances prompted Philip's meeting with the Ethiopian. The same is true for the conversion of Cornelius. Luke makes it quite clear that this is a most unnatural step for Peter to take.

Paul's conversion appears as an isolated incident which is only subsequently related to the church. His mission is directly connected with his conversion and only indirectly with the church in Jerusalem or the church in Antioch. It is certainly not portrayed as being due to the initiative of these churches. The Council in Jerusalem confirms and in a certain sense authorizes his mission, but it does so only *post factum.*

The Jerusalem church appears in some prominence in chapter 15. But even there it seemingly does not initiate developments. It reacts to a situation. Furthermore, the Council's decree hardly affects Paul's subsequent mission in any fundamental way.

The incidents in Acts which mark decisive turns in the way of the church defy natural-historical explanation. There is no natural transition from one phase to the next in the history of the church. The transition always reflects the view that the new direction which the church is called to pursue is opened up by the Kyrios. The initiative is ascribed either to the Lord, an angel of the Lord, or the Spirit. (Acts 9:3 f; 10:3; 8:29.)

Indications are not lacking in the early chapters of Acts that this perspective is the dominant one from the beginning. The break between the first and second chapter comes again to mind. The door for the church to begin its way in Jerusalem is opened by a divine act, the descent of the Holy Spirit. Later, the growth of the church is not attributed to the effectiveness of the apostles' methods but to the fact that people were being added by the Lord (2:47). On the other hand, the opposition on the part of the Jews is not due to their provincialism which makes them blind to the universal vision of Christianity. The resumption of the theme of opposition at the time of Paul's final visit to Jerusalem shows the Jews as representatives of Israel's refusal to embrace the fulfillment of its destiny. This refusal remains a mystery and no attempt is made to explain it.

The persecution following Stephen's death is surely the occasion for the preaching of the gospel outside Jerusalem, but it is not its cause. Whether the church is experiencing persecution or peace, decimation of its ranks or phenomenal growth, it always can accept it only as the way which at that moment is opened up by the Lord.

Inevitably the question arises as to the reason for this emphasis on divine initiative. It is possible to find here an expression of Luke's interest in divine providence with particular reference to the church: He wants to show how the church enjoys divine guidance and protection. God is watching over his church and at decisive turns in its life and mission he intervenes in its favor through the Holy Spirit. Divine guidance is for Luke the concrete work of the Spirit. Hence Luke's interest can also be defined as showing the Holy Spirit at work in the apostles and in the church.

The concepts of divine guidance, intervention and inspiration as usually understood are essentially static. They presuppose that the church has to take a stand in a given situation, that it receives divine help in order to stand up against Jewish opposition and Roman persecution or to stand for the inclusion of the Gentiles in the church.

This view, however, does not sufficiently take into account the dynamic understanding of divine initiative in Acts. Luke's interest focuses on the question of how the church is enabled to *go forward*, to find its way in the world. The way of the church is not only confirmed, it is determined by divine guidance and intervention. Mere confirmation would imply that the church has already made its choice of a future course and now receives divine sanction. For Luke the divine initiative does not appear at the end of the church's way, as proof of its legitimacy; it stands at the *origin* of this way and at each of its decisive turns. It opens the way, and in so doing it creates it (cf. 14:27). The explanation for this emphasis must therefore go beyond a general affirmation of divine guidance and protection. Examining the reasons for this emphasis in an earlier context, we have come to the conclusion that the way of the church is related to the fact that the Kyrios himself is on his way in the world. Because the Kyrios is on his way, the church has no choice but to follow him who precedes. Consequently, obedience and witness to the Kyrios requires the discernment of the opening which he provides, and the willingness to step into this opening. At this point the three accounts of conversions in Acts 8-10 to which we have already alluded deserve closer attention.

A. Acts 8:2-40

Philip is led by an angel of the Lord on the road towards Gaza. Later, he is moved by the Spirit to approach the chariot of the Ethiopian. In the meantime the Ethiopian is led to read the prophet Isaiah. More particularly, at the moment of Philip's appearance he has just reached the decisive passage of Is. 54:7 ff. No special divine order concerning baptism is issued either to Philip or to the Ethiopian but the presence of the water at the opportune moment may signify divine invitation. Having been brought together, the two men are led down to the water. At the end, divine initiative is superseded by direct divine action: Philip is caught up by the Spirit.

B. Acts 10:1-11:18

The way in which Peter is led to the house of Cornelius is equally dramatic. The momentous importance of the new step in the history of the Kyrios requires more than an order by an angel. Peter needs special preparation in order to serve in the new situation which the Kyrios has created already. This is the meaning of Peter's vision in

10:9 ff. But like Philip, Peter, too, receives a further order by the Spirit which leads to the encounter immediately afterwards. This encounter is here related in several steps until it reaches its climax in the descent of the Holy Spirit upon Cornelius and his house. At each turn of this way Luke is anxious to point out that he is about to undertake the 'unlawful' step of associating with non-Jews only because of the vision. Finally, acceptance of full communion with the Gentiles is based on their having received the Holy Spirit.

The need for Peter to defend himself before his brethren in Jerusalem gives Luke a chance to strengthen his emphasis on divine initiative. The vision and the voice, the order of the Spirit, and the out-pouring of the Spirit upon the Gentiles, all lead Peter on the way where he can only acknowledge that the Kyrios is at work, that he is on his way. Peter's obedience simply consists in not standing in the way of the Kyrios.

Even more clearly than in 8:26 ff Luke shows in 10:1 ff how God is at work on both sides of the encounter. In Acts 8 it can only be assumed that the Ethiopian was led by God to his study of the prophet and to his subsequent openness toward Philip. However, this assumption is strongly enforced by the evidence in 10:1 ff where Cornelius is shown as acting under direct divine order. Furthermore, the vision of Cornelius precedes that of Peter, not only in terms of Luke's composition but chronologically as well. Peter receives his vision 'the next day.' The difference is more than a chronological one; or rather, the chronological difference is of fundamental importance. The kyrios precedes Peter's mission. He is at work even before Peter is prepared for his mission. From the fact of this precedence the nature of Peter's mission can be deduced: the Lord is at work before Peter arrives, but he is not *known,* he is not *manifest.* It is Peter's task to witness, to point to the Kyrios who has arrived and is now present in the house of Cornelius.

In both these accounts the evidence of divine guidance is overwhelming. But again, it is not this guidance as such that counts. It is important because it opens up ways, the way to the Ethiopian for Philip and the road to Caesarea for Peter. The divine order creates the divine opportunity. Now the way is open, now the ground is prepared. On the other hand, as the two visions of Cornelius and Peter in 10:1 ff most clearly show, there is no way apart from that of the Kyrios.

C. Acts 9:1-11

Once more this is evident in the account of Paul's conversion which Luke has placed between the two accounts. The role given in the other stories to Philip and Peter, respectively, is here assigned to Ananias, a Jew in Damascus. Again, he is prepared for his mission by a vision and an order from the Lord. Thus the way is opened. Ananias' reluctance shows that, humanly speaking, no such way exists. The barrier between Ananias and Saul must be overcome by the Lord himself. But now it is overcome on both sides. More than in either the preceding or the following conversion account it is clear in Ananias' case that he is not sent out to accomplish a conversion, that the Kyrios has already done his work on Saul, at least he has begun it. He has thrown Saul off his own course, the course which Saul himself had chosen. Here the mission of Ananias sets in. He is sent to announce a new course to Paul, one which neither Ananias nor Paul have chosen on their own.

Paul is now on a God-given itinerary and not on one of his own choosing. This is strongly emphasized throughout the latter part of Acts. Twice Paul is prevented by the Spirit from pursuing a certain course (16;6 f). On the other hand, the Lord opens the way for him to Macedonia. 'In the Spirit' he resolves to go to Rome, and this decision is confirmed to him by visions. From Ephesus he goes on the road to Jerusalem 'bound in the Spirit,' for he knows that it is part of the 'course' which he has 'received from the Lord Jesus.' Furthermore, in his defense of the course which he has taken as an apostle and which has led him to the deadly opposition of the Jews, his conversion appears twice as the principal evidence that, except for divine intervention, he would not be where he was.

The way which is opened by the Lord is also the ground which he has already prepared so that the labor of his witness may bear fruit. This is true for Philip as he meets the Ethiopian as well as for Peter as he meets Cornelius. It is equally true for Paul as he pursues the course assigned to him. In Philippi the Lord 'opened' the heart of Lydia to give heed to Paul's words (16:14). In Corinth a people is already prepared by the Lord as Paul arrives there (18:10).

The church as an itinerant people on its way staked out by divine will is not an entirely new phenomenon. It has its precedent in the history of Israel under the old covenant. This seems to be the burden of Stephen's argument in his defense before the Jewish accusers.

Stephen is charged with speaking against the Temple and the law. In his reply he does not give a point-by-point rebuttal. He is not concerned with what he may or may not have said in his disputes with the various groups. But his speech is an answer in the sense that it brings to light the fundamental issue which lies between him and his accusers. He recognizes the accusation as the expression of a basic misunderstanding of Israel's history and therefore of Israel's role in the present. Accordingly, the speech has two objectives. On the one hand, it shows forth the nature and purpose of this history, and on the other hand, it demonstrates how this purpose has been resisted from the earliest time until now. Given the atmosphere of controversy, the latter assertion takes on the form of a counter-accusation.

What is the nature of Israel's history? Stephen insists that it is essentially a way whose course depends on God. Abraham is called and is sent on his journey. He is to remain a stranger even in the land into which he is sent. He receives no inheritance but only a promise. The way from promise to fulfillment is subsequently described. Through Joseph, the way leads into Egypt, saving the Patriarchs from starvation. Through Moses, the way leads out of Egypt, saving the people from slavery. The main interest is clearly centered on the latter. For the sending of Moses represents the fulfillment of God's promise to Abraham, and through him Israel is shown its way 'par excellence,' namely the way of deliverance. The paramount significance of Moses emerges in four affirmations (vs. 35-38). (a) He was sent as ruler and saviour of Israel. (b) He led the people out of Egypt. (c) He announced the future prophet whom God will raise and (d) he handed over to the people the 'living word' which he had received through the angel.

The parallelism to Jesus is obvious. This is why the rejection of Moses by the 'fathers' must concern the Jews today. This rejection is first described as idolatry and secondly—and now Stephen comes to the concrete point of the dispute—it is expressed in the shift from the 'tent of witness' to the Temple. The Temple becomes the symbol for Israel's betrayal of the way charted by Moses, the way that leads to its deliverance. It is no longer wandering, it has settled down. The mere existence of the Temple already implies the attempt to set the terms for God's presence in the world. Stephen calls it 'resisting the Holy Spirit.'

This phrase may best be understood in the light of the role of the Spirit in the conversion stories in Acts 8-10. The spirit always commands to *go*. It opens up the way. Consequently, resistance means disobedience toward this command. Rather than risking its position in daring obedience, Israel is bent on consolidating it. 'As the fathers did, so do you.' In the interest of consolidation the fathers persecuted and killed the prophets. The same motivation leads the Jews in Stephen's days to do away with the 'Righteous One' to whom the prophets had pointed.

Stephen's speech virtually amounts to a counter-accusation. This is more than a mere attack for the sake of defense. In fact Stephen is not arguing from any position at all. Of course, the accusation originally impelled Stephen to outline his position. But he is not obliging his accusers. He appears before them as a *witness* in Luke's understanding of the term. He issues the verdict on the Jewish position which they have occupied on their own authority and which is symbolized by the man-made Temple. He pronounces the verdict because he is convinced he stands in the presence of the Lord. He pleads with the Jews to become once more the pilgrim people and to receive their destiny out of the hands of their God. This plea is being heard by those who in the resurrection of Jesus see the fulfillment of Moses' prophecy (Cf. 3:22). A new exodus is taking place.

The interpretation of Acts 7 which we have attempted here receives further support from the consideration of its place in the structure of Acts. Together with the rest of the account concerning Stephen the passage is located at one of the decisive turns in the history recorded by Luke: the outreach of the gospel beyond Jerusalem. This turn seems to coincide with a change of emphasis.

Acts 2-6, while containing the main body of apostolic preaching, also contains the only really descriptive parts of the life of the church. We can interpret these descriptions as Luke's attempt to show the life of the church in relation to the presence of the kingdom. Following the death of Stephen the emphasis shifts to the church as an itinerant people. The question now is how the church will find its way, and when Luke inserts references to the life of the churches, he does so only in the interest of clarifying the way. The church is still seen in relation to the Kyrios and his kingdom. However, it is no longer shown as exhibiting his presence, but rather as following him into the world.

At this important juncture we find Stephen's speech and martyrdom which seems to suggest that the shift of emphasis is quite deliberate and forms an essential part of Luke's composition.

II. CONTINUITY AMIDST CHANGE

The church exists in so far as it is obedient to the way which is opened up for it by the Lord. Stephen's speech and death, followed by persecution and conversions, and later Paul's journeys, stand for the obedience of the church toward this way. In rendering this obedience the church is bound to cross and obstruct other 'ways,' generated by other forces. This is true for the confrontation with the Jews as well as with the Gentiles. The clash over the Temple in Jerusalem is followed by the clash over the Artemis temple in Ephesus. Peter and the Twelve became a threat to the religio-political position of the Jewish leaders in Jerusalem, particularly the Sadducees, while Paul endangered the influence of the leaders at Antioch, Pisidia, Philippe, and Ephesus.

Yet while Acts evinces the dangers which the church faces on its way and the obedience and singlemindedness in which it meets these dangers neither the Twelve nor Paul nor any of the others who emerge as individuals are allowed to clothe themselves in the mantle of religious heroes. The question of whether the Christians will be able to bear the consequences of their witness does not even seem to be a real one for Luke. If the Lord sends them on their way, it is simply assumed that he will guide them to the end. The fundamental task for the church is to watch out for the God-given way, to discern the openings and the new turns, and to be ready to follow.

How can the church fulfill this task? It can most certainly not cope with it in its own strength. The discernment of the way is a gift provided by the Holy Spirit. It is 'in the Spirit' that the church is on its way, that it exists as a pilgrim people (Cf. 19:21). In the Holy Spirit the church discerns the way ahead. Philip, Peter, and Paul, all are commanded and guided by the Spirit. But reference to the Spirit in these instances would be misleading if it were taken to mean that such a discernment is due to special and unique inspirations. The church as Luke pictures it in Acts does not live from momentary revelations of the Spirit, erupting here and there in the ranks of the believers. The Spirit abides with the church and thus witnesses to the *continuity* of its journey. However new and unforeseen a turn might occur in the life of the church, through the Holy Spirit the church is enabled to see, and thereby to witness to, the continuity of its new course with that of the past.

Acts stresses this continuity precisely when the church experiences crucial and dramatic turns in its history. At Pentecost, when the little band of the Twelve expands from a closed group in the upper room to a witnessing community, this is hailed as the fulfillment of God's promise which he had given to the prophets (2:17-21). Stephen's elaborate treatment of Israel's history must, in the last analysis, be understood as a demonstration of the continuity of God's purpose in the light of the impending transformation of the church's way from a way in peace and harmony and numerical growth to a way of persecution. Persecution in no way endangers the continuity of redemptive history. On the contrary, it enhances it. This is evident in two respects. First, persecution as dispersion brings about the preaching of the gospel outside Jerusalem (8:3-40). Second, it prompts conversion of the persecutor (8:3-40).

The prime example cited by Luke to demonstrate the continuity of redemptive history is the turn of the gospel to the Gentiles. There can be no doubt that this is for Luke *the* great event in the history of the church. In Acts it occupies the center stage with everything either leading up to this event or flowing from it. But Luke is not content merely to show how this happened, what were the causes and consequences. The important question for him is that of meaning. What did in fact happen when the gospel began to be preached to the Gentiles? What was the nature of that event? More particularly, was it really the *gospel* that the Gentiles came to hear and are hearing now? Was it really *good news* when they heard about the life, death, and resurrection of Jesus of Nazareth? Luke's answer is an affirmative one, because it is ultimately grounded in the conviction that the great event of the spreading of the gospel to the Gentiles was congruous with the plan and purpose of the God who called Israel to be his people and the apostles to be his witnesses. The line which goes from the calling of the apostles to the preaching of the gospel to the Gentiles is traced in the Cornelius-story, while the turn of the gospel to the Gentiles in its relation to the call of Israel is focused upon in Acts 15.

The main purpose of the story of Cornelius is to show the revelation of God's will that the Gentiles should be received into the church without obligation to the law. The question is, therefore, on what basis this event was recognized by Peter as an expression of God's will. This question calls for a consideration of Peter's defense before his brethren in Jerusalem (11:1 ff). The criticism against his action at Caesarea originates from within the circumcision party which charges that Peter associated with uncircumcised men. Peter answers by first recounting his vision in Joppa. This serves to show that he would not have thought of entering into such an association if it had not really been God's will. How, then, did he recognize God's will in the situation? Here follows the actual reply to the criticism. Peter's acceptance of the Gentiles in Cornelius' house is based on his recognition that 'the Holy Spirit fell on them just as on us at the beginning.' As a result, he realizes that 'God gave the same gift to them as he gave to us.' The importance of this reply lies in the parallelism: what has happened in Cornelius' house is in full continuity with 'the beginning,' i.e. with the event through which Peter and the Eleven were called to be apostles. In his association with the uncircumcized, Peter did not break the continuity, he did not deviate from the path on which he was placed when he, together with the others, 'believed in the Lord Jesus Christ.' The critics of Peter held that the continuity was guaranteed by circumcision. Peter's answer is that it is given in the Holy Spirit.

This continuity is further extended into the past in the first part of the story. Here Peter asserts that the 'word' he has to offer them has been proclaimed throughout Judea, 'beginning from Galilee.' The incorporation of the Gentiles into God's redemptive purpose is in continuity not only with the history beginning at Pentecost, but with the history of Jesus of Nazareth, his ministry, death and resurrection.

Like the Cornelius story, the account of the Apostolic Council is also best understood on the basis of Luke's concern for the continuity of redemptive history.

The issue which brings about the controversy in Antioch and later the debate in Jerusalem is spelled out in a more general way than is the case in 11:18. It concerns the mission of Paul and Barnabas as a whole. If circumcision is necessary for salvation, their work related by Luke in chapters 13-14 has been in vain. After a general remark about the discussion the account in 15:6 ff turns immediately to Peter and Paul. The reason for Peter's prominence is obvious: his experience in Caesarea is vital to the solution of the dispute. In his recapitulation we find again as his principal argument the assertion that God has given them 'the Holy Spirit just as he did to us.' Subsequently this insight is interpreted and applied to the problem under debate. James who takes up Peter's insight, opens up an even wider perspective. What has happened in the conversion of Cornelius and now through the work of Paul and Barnabas is a part not only of the history which began in Galilee after the baptism of John, it is part of the history of Israel to which the prophet testifies. The inclusion of the Gentiles into the history of redemption is part of the fulfillment of Israel's destiny.

Israel's history is not abrogated by the inclusion of the Gentiles apart from the law, it is upheld and fulfilled. Hence, no one has a right to impose conditions on the Gentiles. Furthermore, the continuity of history, assured by the Spirit, becomes the basis for the unity in the Spirit between Jews and Gentiles (15:28). This unity shall be recognized on both sides. On the side of the circumcised it is acknowledged inasmuch as they no longer insist on the circumcision of the Gentiles. The Gentiles in turn are asked to acknowledge it by submitting to four rules proposed by James. The purpose by these rules has been interpreted as a sort of minimal discipline. Discipline is naturally involved in submitting to rules. It is, however, not an end in itself but only a means to the end for Luke. By keeping these rules the Gentiles avail themselves of the opportunity to witness to their unity with the Jews and therefore to the historical continuity of the people which God took out 'for his name,' with the Israel that God called under Moses.

III. CONTINUITY AND AUTHORITY

In Lk. 24 and Acts 1 we find that the 'authorization' of the disciples consists of the promise of the Spirit and the command to be witnesses. Neither of these refer to the past in the sense that they constitute a renewal of an appointment which took place provisionally during the ministry of Jesus. Both refer to the future task of the disciples as witnesses. They are related to the self-designation of the Twelve as witnesses of the resurrection in the course of their mission. This witness is to the present Christ. It carries authority because it testifies to the resurrection as the present reality of the risen Lord.

Furthermore, the term and function of witness is not restricted to the Twelve. It is explicitly applied also to Stephen and to Paul. There are no indications that the term is applied to their mission in a less fundamental sense. Stephen's vision implies his standing in the presence of the Kyrios, and Paul's vision at his conversion and his subsequent visions mark him as a fully authoritative witness. In so far as both Stephen and Paul testify to the resurrection as the presence of the Kyrios, their witness must be considered as no less authoritative than that of the Twelve.

Basically, then, authority for Luke resides in the act of witnessing which depends on the authentication by the Kyrios who is present in the Spirit.

This, however, means that in Acts it is not the 'historia' (the period of Jesus' earthly life) of Jesus which *constitutes* the apostolic authority of the Twelve. In 10:40 ff the witness concerning the past is superseded by the proclamation and affirmation of the one whom God has raised and chosen to be the judge of the living and the dead. Similarly, Matthias is to become a witness to the *resurrection*, not to the 'historia' of Jesus. In any event his authority as one of the Twelve rests in the former, rather than in the handing down of an authoritative past. In what sense, then, can we maintain that the apostles' association with Jesus in the past is a 'conditio sine qua non' for their apostleship?

A clue is given in Luke's description of the past. Acts 1:21 speaks of those 'who walked with us' and in 13:31 the disciples appear as those 'who walked with' from Galilee to Jerusalem. Jesus, it is said, 'went in and out.' All these expressions point to a way. This way 'began' with John's baptism and led to Jesus' death and exaltation. In 13:31 it is described as the way from Galilee to Jerusalem. In so far as the 'historia' of Jesus is part of the witness of the Twelve, it is a witness to the *way* of Jesus.

The same is true for their witness of the resurrection. As witnesses of the resurrection, the apostles point to the way of the Kyrios in the present. Accordingly, when the Twelve in 1:21 f are to point to the way of Jesus in the past, they can do this only in the context of his way in the present. On the other hand, the Twelve *do* point to this way in the past and this sets them apart. For this purpose they receive their particular authority as the Twelve. They are authorized to witness to the resurrection as an event on the continuous way which leads from Galilee to Jerusalem and from Jerusalem to the end of the earth.

The authority of the Twelve is asserted at precisely the same two turning points we have previously singled out in our discussion of the way of the church. The first concerns the confrontation with the Jews. In the witness of the Twelve in Jerusalem the Kyrios who comes to claim Israel as his people is revealed as the Jesus of Nazareth whom the Jews crucified (2:22 ff. 36). The Twelve stand among the people and before the authorities as the sign that it is this Jesus and no other who has now been declared Lord and Christ.

Secondly, the Twelve are called upon to testify to the continuity of the way of the Kyrios at the point where this way turns toward the Gentiles.

The fact that Peter, rather than Paul, is involved in the first and in a sense decisive battle for the mission to the Gentiles may at first seem to run counter to Luke's interest in Acts. It has been suggested that Luke attaches no fundamental significance to the Cornelius story for the mission to the Gentiles. Such a proposition, however, does not do justice to the intimate connection between Act 10-11 and Acts 15 in Luke's composition.

The Cornelius story serves as a background for Peter's authoritative statement in the Council. For the issue in both incidents is for Luke basically the same: the meaning of the new phase in redemptive history which has been opened up in the Gentile mission. The Twelve have a unique role in relation to this new phase. They are not to be the actual carriers of this mission; this responsibility is entrusted to Paul. But they stand at the *threshold* and from this vantage point they give their testimony. Just as in their mission among the Jews they were called upon to witness to the continuity between the pre-resurrection and the post-resurrection period, so they are now to witness to the continuity of the way of the Kyrios among Jews and Gentiles.

Again, the authority for such witness does not rest in the association with Jesus in the past. Peter does not actually recite his experience in Caesarea. He refers to what God has done in 'giving the Spirit to them' (15:8). Peter's authority ultimately consists in pointing to this divine act. James shares this authority with Peter in Acts 15. His authority, too, resides in his witness. This is evident from his summary of Peter's statement that 'God has first visited the Gentiles to take out a people for his name' (v. 14). It is a witness to the way of the Kyrios on which he precedes his people.

James' witness points even further back than the witness of Peter.

He testifies to the continuity of this way with the history of the Israel of old, to the continuity between the old and the new Israel. While Peter points to the continuity of the time before with the time after Easter, James points to the continuity of the time before with the time after the incarnation. Nevertheless, his function as a witness of the continuity of the old with the new way clearly places him in the ranks with the Twelve.

On the other hand, Paul's witness is sharply distinguished from that of the Twelve. The clearest evidence is Paul's speech in Antioch. Here Paul appears as transmitting the witness concerning the continuity of the way of Jesus not on his own authority, i.e. the authority which he received from Christ directly, but on the authority of the Twelve. Before we speak of Paul's subordination to the authority of the Twelve we must recognize the place which Luke assigns him in the context of his understanding of redemptive history.

Paul is called to go to the Gentiles. Luke seems to be more interested in the direction to which the call points than in the circumstances of the call. In the first and second version of his conversion Paul receives the call through Ananias, while in the third version the call comes directly from Jesus. The latter is also true for the version in the Temple. The lack of unity would indicate a lack of interest on Luke's part.

Paul is identified with the phase of redemptive history in which the Kyrios goes on his way to the Gentiles. In this period he emerges as the authoritative witness, going from town to town, preaching and healing, confronting the local authorities and the Greek philosophers, and finally—as a climax—standing before the representatives of the Imperium. The visions which he has on his way serve to underscore the authoritative nature of his witness. These visions never confirm what Paul has already done, but they show him the road ahead: Macedonia, Corinth, Rome. This road is that of the Kyrios.

Thomas Wieser, New York
June 1963

Mission

I.

In a questionnaire sent to a sizeable group of ministers in North America in connection with this study, correspondents were asked to react to the following statement by Hans Margull: "Being called out of the nations, the Church is called to witness to God's own mission to the nations and to partake in His mission. There is no such thing as the Church's own mission. Our mission can only be mission as being included in God's mission." A sizeable number objected on the ground that it is too humanistic to speak of God's mission. As more than one put it :"How can we speak of God as being sent? Who sends Him?" But this is precisely the gospel—that God sent His Son into the world, that the world through Him might be saved; that the Holy Spirit is sent to draw all men to Christ so that He might at last present us whole and entire in the family of God the Father. The heart of the doctrine of the Trinity is that it speaks of the fact that God has a mission. It tells us that it is God "who for us men and our salvation came down."

It is not difficult, however, to see the practical concern that lay behind the objections. There is worry lest in speaking of mission as God's mission, we maye cut the nerve of missionary obedience. In an article by William Stringfellow* this is given direct expression. "Christians are fond of saying that evangelism is the work of God. I suggest that this is not so. Evangelism is the work of the Church."

"Go ye . . . and make disciples of all nations. . . ." (Matthew 28:19) "*Ye* shall be my witnesses in Jerusalem and in all Judea, and Samaria and to the end of the earth" (Acts 1:8). Nevertheless, we must not allow this essential emphasis upon the missionary responsibility of the Church and of all the whole community of God's people, to be taken out of its context within the mission of God. It is only as we see the Church's mission as set within God's mission that we see

a) its full shape . . . "As the Father hath sent me, even so I send you." *Our* mission is shaped by *His* mission. (John 15:12-27; 17:18: Romans 12:1-5.)

b) its true continuing source: "all authority in heaven and on earth has been given to me. Go therefore . . . And lo, *I am with you always to the close of the age*" (Matthew 28:18-20).

*I.J.R.E. Special Issue on Evangelism and Christian Education, November 1963.

Unless the Church is constantly aware that it is not fulfilling its own mission, but is participating in God's mission, it will repeatedly forget that the mission is given its definition by God's missionary activity in Christ and that we are called to work in the framework of the *way* God works ("have this mind among yourselves which you have in Christ Jesus" Phil. 2:5) and of the *goal* towards which God is working ("He has made known to us . . . the mystery of his will according to his purpose which he set forth in Christ, as a plan for the fullness of time, to unite all things in him, things in heaven and things on earth" Eph. 1:9-10). It must not forget also that it can work within this shape and towards this goal, only as it allows itself to be the *instrument* of Christ fashioned for this work by the Holy Spirit (Acts 1:4, 8; 2:1-4).

These three aspects of our participation in the mission of God

a) conformation to the way God works—the *shape* of His mission

b) awareness of the goal towards which he is working—the *end* of His mission

c) participation in the divine life of Christ through the Spirit—the *power* of His mission,

are aspects of one inseparable reality.

From: *Where in the World*, by Colin W. Williams,
New York 1963
p. 22 ff

II.

1. In Mombasa, on the coast of East Africa, I met a young man who had come far from the interior of the country. He was the first of his tribe who had left the home territory. "My people," he said, "did not want to let me go for fear that I would lose God; they thought God was only in our village but not in Mombasa. I told them: 'This is the way your fathers believed when they worshipped the ancestors; now we know that God is everywhere, even in the farthest corners, and therefore I can go there.' "

The fruit of mission is not merely conversion and baptism together with a change of the individual's way of life. The fruit of mission is greater. Christ enters the life of a man as the liberator—and man's relation to the world changes. World is discovered as the world which must be appropriated by transforming it. Hence the fruit of mission is not limited to churches. Once more, it is greater.

2. Walter Freitag used to tell with a certain satisfaction about two Indonesian military chaplains who were Mennonites. They had received the gospel from Mennonite missionaries, had been baptized in a Mennonite congregation, and had thus become part of a Christian community which in Europe and America refuses military service on the grounds of conscience.

The fruit of mission can, therefore, consist not only in a new church but also in a *different* church. This often does not happen in a spectacular way (and when it does, we become terribly nervous), but it does happen. And it happens to a far deeper and wider degree than the evidence might suggest. The development is mostly explained in terms of historical and cultural factors. But it could also be connected with God's way across the worlds and times.

Hans Hoekendijk writes in his essay *On Proselytism:* "We do not continue the old nor do we spread it. We do not pull men over to our side nor do we ask them to join us, to become proselytes. In proclaiming the message we join those who now hear the gospel in the expectation and hope that there men will be gathered anew in the name of Jesus and that we become his witnesses"?

Are we ready to expect, to imagine and to accept as the fruit of mission an ever new kind of church? This question is the test of every understanding of mission. Through this test it will become evident whether we think of mission as involving the mission of the (our) church whose fruit we already know in view of our church (repetition!), or the risk to participate in God's mission, in his movements in the world whose fruits time and again will surprise us.

III

Mission is a matter of faith. That the end of time has come, and therefore, the time for nothing less than mission, that God is calling all nations, that they are reconciled with God in Christ's death and resurrection, that, ultimately, in their missions the churches are not propagating themselves—all this and more is a matter of faith. Going out in mission is only possible in that faith which the Holy Spirit gives and renews.

It is a faith with resources in God's action in the past, in the present, and in the future. Existentially, this faith lives as hope. Evangelism has been defined as "hope in action." The same definition holds true for the wider concept of mission. Mission is hope in action. To be "missionary" is to risk one's hope in challenging man in this world. Mission is *hope* in action, not merely a missionary in action. Mission is not defined by an individual Christian or a Christian community going somewhere or doing something. Mission is defined only by our hope that God will have the last word in this world. This hope must be concretely worked out amidst the manifold temptations to abandon it as hopeless.

A missionary congregation? It would be a congregation praying for this hope, being ready to receive it, living it in concrete action, and accepting its implications. A missionary congregation is a congregation which hopes to be used and is immediately used by God in His epiphany.

Hans Jochen Margull
Geneva, October, 1962

The Crisis of Our Hope

I.

The discussion of structures most often does not clarify the concept of structure. As a rule this concept retains the function of mediating new experiences within the horizon of the old thought patterns. Through this use the thinking remains within the ban of a now questionable Greek-Catholic principle of Western Christendom.

Through this process of mediation the discussion of the structures avoids the prior question of God acting in creation and history; it quickly sidesteps the crisis of *the church's relation to the world* and of *eschatology*, caused by the socio-political and industrial revolution.

But how can the discussion of structures for a missionary congregation lead the way for the church and its witness out of the self-enclosed special world into a contemporary congregational life, conscious of its place and praising God as creator, preserver and perfecter, as long as it does not face the questions which are by-passed by dialectical and critical theology and are not accepted by Orthodox theologians:

—What is the relationship between creation—preservation—consummation?

—Does the hope for the coming world radically transcend the existing world or does it affirm the existing world as *creatio continua* of God, precisely because of its trust in the promises?

—If the congregation waits "*according to his promises* (plural!) for new heavens and a new earth in which *righteousness* dwells," is the congregation of the new covenant bound up with the congregation of the old covenant (cf. the meaning of 'sedaqa' in prophetic eschatology)?

—Does the congregation merely find itself in a pause of redemptive history between resurrection and final return, preoccupied with preparations for x-day? What an apocalyptic affair!

—Does the whole complex of expectations in the old covenant issue in a void in the new covenant, does it dissolve—or does the promise of the land find its unexpected fulfillment in the commissioning of the disciples into the world and in the reasonable worship for the world (Rom. 12:1f)?

—Is Jesus' preaching tied in with Jewish apocalypticism (so Bultmann *and* Pannenberg) or does Jesus not affirm and fulfill prophetic eschatology in contrast to this resigned devaluation of world and history?

God himself is in the midst of the unheard (Amos 5:17; Hos. 5:12ff; Jer. 25:9.). Over against all the piously resigned, the angrily resigned, the cynically resigned the call resounds: He comes, he, God. Even in the destructive blows of the present he comes. He is in their midst! The prophetic word bars on every side man's flight into pious or not so pious despair under the weight of anonymity, the unfamiliar, the foreign . . . This Lord is now to be praised, who in all of this is at work to bring about the triumph of his righteousness, to raise up and to accomplish his 'sedaqa'!

—What, then, is the task of a congregation in the midst of this becoming world, conscious of the promises which in Jesus as the Christ are Yes and Amen?

—What does the congregation have to say *and* to give to the world when in its midst it praises God as creator, preserver and perfecter?

—What is the function of the congregation as the body of Christ for the body of humanity?

—Is the future of humanity involved in the praise of the congregation (cf. Lk. 2:29ff; Rom. 9-11); The present salvation of the world in the presence of the congregation? etc.

—Is the congregation the people of God's elected co-workers in the building of the *oikonomia?* Light of the world! Salt of the earth! The meek to whom the kingdom is promised (cf. Mt. 5:5—Psalm 37:11: promise of the Land!)? Are they in faith freed for history? And what is at stake in the building of the *oikonomia?*

II.

The "Foundations and Perspectives of a Confession," issued by the General Synod of the Dutch Reformed Church where these questions at last are faced demonstrate how much they are still open questions in contemporary discussion.

We find ourselves in a crisis of our eschatology; it is a crisis of our relationship to the world, caused by the problem of *history*.

How easy is it for the missionary church in such a situation *radically to transcend* the world in its "service of witness to humanity" (something which prophetic eschatology never did, cf. recently G. v. Rad, Theol. of the O. T. Vol. II), and thereby to cancel the world as God's creation. How easy is it in this way finally to deny God's work in this world. Of all this we can sadly become conscious by reading the remarkable study by Joh. Blauw on *The Basis of a Biblical Theology of Mission.*

III.

In the present debate the discussion of the structures for a missionary congregation easily tends to overlook the questionable eschatology of the church and its resulting relationship to the world.

And yet we are suffering from *a crisis of our hope.*

But the discussion of the *missionary structure of the congregation* does not need to be determined by the concern to *mediate* between God and a world far from and foreign to him and therefore to find the necessary structures. It could rather begin with the assurance that this changing world already *is* God's work, and that, therefore, a congregation which serves God's work in this world and thereby also constantly equips men anew for the work of service, only needs to be concerned to *correspond* to the structure of God's work which creates the world and moves history. This concern will allow it to remain "missionary," i.e. a congregation sent into this world liberated and called for service to this world, and not to become a pious end in itself.

IV.

Seek first the structure of the kingdom of God and its righteousness, and the missionary structure of the congregation shall be yours as well.

V.

The quest for new and necessary structures is in danger to miss a *necessary "Reformation"* in the heat of reorganization.

If the question of the structure of the congregation is relevant it is identical with the question of the structure of the kingdom of God and its righteousness; and this is the question of the *structure of the history* of this world, because it is the history of God with this world.

The more a congregation, trusting the structure of God's action, is assured of the world as God's work, the freer it is of all rules, the better it can seize upon situations as occasions for praise to God and for the good of man, the more such opportunities will be opened up. Indeed, through it God in a special way furthers his work, continually creating the world.

Hans Schmidt, Hamburg
June, 1962

Notes on the Meaning of Mission (-ary)

I. TERMINOLOGY

A critical history of the term "mission(-ary)" has yet to be written. A few facts in this complex, but so far inadequately explored field are reasonably well established; they might be of some use in clarifying some of the basic concepts of our study-project.

1.

The word group *APOSTOL*—retained for a rather long time its original meaning of "being sent into the world to care for the salvation of mankind." Contrary to a widespread opinion the recent reintroduction of the term APOSTOLATE (apostolê) to indicate *all aspects of the pro-existent nature and ministry of the Church* is *not* a 'modern innovation.'[1] This use of the term is, in fact, as old as the Church and has never vanished completely, although it has often taken 'heretical' movements on the fringe to keep this genuine significance alive.

... *all aspects:* without the arbitrary differentiation between apostolic 'dimension' and 'intention';

... *pro-existence:* a current expression to summarize e.g. what BONHOEFFER has meant with (the Church) living-for-others: für-andere-dasein;

... the *missionary* character of the apostolate has often (esp. in Roman Catholic circles) been blurred; hence the curious desire (and necessity) to create such tautologies as the missionary apostolate: apostolatus missionalis.

2.

Only in a secondary way have the apostles (= 'missionaries') been identified with the TWELVE, who held quite a different and essentially non-missionary office. This brought about (or: was brought about by?) a fateful change of emphasis: The apostles were gradually stripped of (almost all) the dynamic and mobile features of their ministry and turned into static (stabilitas loci!) and residential church leaders: bishops in nuce. In the reflection upon the Church as an Apostolic Body this entailed a shift from a primary interest in expansion (apostolate: participation in the acts of the apostles; keyword: kerygma: missionary proclamation) to a main interest in defining authority (APOSTOLICITY: participation in the representative authority of those, who were now identified as 'apostles'; basic agreement with their teaching; keyword: martyria: faithful witness). This understanding of the apostolic Church in terms of apostolicity has been to a very large extent and is, on the whole, still the main concern in contemporary ecclesiology.

For a new understanding of the Church as the Mission, it may well be essential to understand anew the logical (both chrono- and theological) sequence of apostolate and apostolicity. We shall not understand what the apostles taught, unless we do, what the apostles were

[1]Cf. the evidence in F. KLOSTERMANN, *Das christliche Apostolat* (1962) with interesting corrections cf. the position held by L. M. DEWAILLY, *Envoyés du Père: Mission et Apostolicité* (1960).

commissioned to do and actually did. Only in Mission (apostolate) can the Church be an authentic ('apostolic') Church.

In recent Roman Catholic missiology a similar thesis is sometimes expounded: the pillar apostles (foundation of the Church) ought to be situated in the tradition and *as a function* of the conquest-apostles.[2] This is a far cry indeed from the traditional definitions of 'apostolicity' such as the definition of Vaticanum I: apostolicity: invincible *stability* (stabilitas).

3.

The first evidence of the word group *MISSIO-(-NARIUS)*, in approximately the same sense in which we use these terms now, dates from the XIIIth century and is to be found in the milieu of the Mendiant Orders. Apparently these words served as simple translations of apostle/apostolos in the original meaning of: 'being sent to live the life and to continue the work of an apostle in the world and for the sake of the world.'

Only in the course of the XVIth and XVIIth centuries were these terms adopted in official ecclesiastical vocabulary: a MISSIO is now: and expedition, undertaken for the cause of the Word of God, to a precisely defined 'portion' of the world, i.e. to those regions, where non-Catholics live and where the Church is either not yet (im-)planted or else, not yet sufficiently consolidated and stabilized.

The important point to make here is, that missions are defined by their receiving end, rather than by their divine origin; the 'missionary situation' is determined by the status of the envisaged receptors of the mission; man decides where missionaries shall go. This *anthropocentric conception of missions* was canonized.

There is ample reason to believe that the verbal dissociation of Missio (= apostolate) from apostolicity is both a portent and a sign of an increasing theological dissociation of apostolate from apostolicity. In contemporary missiology the 'theological inadequacy of this canonical view of missions' is increasingly admitted.[3]

4.

Generally speaking, the *Protestants* have taken over exactly this inadequate and anthropocentric conception of missions. Even today, we have not moved very far beyond the classical definition of GUSTAV

---

[2] G. SEUMOIS, Apostolat: *Structure Théologique* (1962), pp. 66 ss.
[3] e.g. A. M. HENRY, *Esquisse d'une Théologie de la mission* (1959), passim.

WARNECK (1890s): missions: "the total activity of Christendom (= all true believers) to plant and organize the Church among Non-Christians." Later attempts at a rethinking of missions are practically all variations on this same theme; they start on the basic assumption that there are 'Christian' and non-'Christian' areas; a 'faith'-locality and an 'unbelief'-locality with a 'frontier' in-between, and missions are then defined as "the crossing of this frontier between faith and unbelief." The only *new* element in this rethinking seems to be that the context is reduced from global to regional dimensions: "The missionary frontier now runs (no longer between continents, but) through every land, where there are communities living without the knowledge of Christ, the Lord."[4] Here again, missions are defined by their receiving end; as frontier-crossing-movements towards "unbelieving' communities.

5.

To sum up: the concept of missions, as expressed in traditional and current terminology is the end-product of a long series of fatal reductions of the apostolate into a more or less peripheral affair. Schematically:

a) the apostles had to yield their central place in the history of the coming Kingdom to the Twelve, the authoritative representatives of a past event;
b) the apostolic Church was increasingly defined in terms of apostolicity to the neglect of the terms of the apostolate;
c) even the verbal reminder of an intrinsic connection between apostolate and apostolicity vanished, as soon as the term Missio and its derivatives came to indicate all aspects of the apostolate;
d) in order to define missions alongside all the other 'activities' of the Church, their *differentium* was stressed: movements (across 'faith'-frontiers) towards the places where the unbelievers are;
e) missions are supposed to begin at the periphery of the faith-area; in missionary thinking spatial (Raum-) categories will rank prior to historical categories. From here on it will be almost impossible to steer clear of a concept of mission = displacement of the community of faith or (and that would be sheer disaster) = a selfrepetition of the Church in an area of unbelief.

---

[4] L. NEWBIGIN, *One Gospel, One Body, One World* (1959).

II. BASIC ISSUES

6.

Out of this brief survey it may have become clear already that we cannot begin any attempt at a study of the Mission from current or traditional terminology. We have to rediscover 'Mission' in its original cluster and in its authentic frame of reference. The decisive setting for any reconception of the Mission can only be the *MESSIANIC PATTERN*, understood as a comprehension of the distinctive character of Israel's God and the nature of His redemptive purpose. It is the business of the Messiah to announce (gospel) and perform the decisive redeeming act of God; in the 'last' (= decisive) days and in a universal context (to all nations, unto the ends of the earth); thus inaugurating the new order of the Spirit by establishing the Kingdom, offering 'peace and salvation.' Mission is the inner dynamic of this cluster, relating the different elements in a meaningful frame of reference; it is THE messianic event, by which history is brought to its destination.

7.

In contemporary missionary thinking we may notice several attempts to correct the traditional anthropocentric conceptions of the Mission by an increasing emphasis upon the *Missio Dei.*[5] Very often, however, this simply means a back-reference to God's prevenient initiative; merely a theocentric preface to an unaltered anthropo- or ecclesio-centric text; God is recognized in an almost deistic fashion as the great Inventor and Inaugurator of the Mission, who has since withdrawn and left the accomplishment of the Mission to His ground personnel.

Before anything else, the *apostolate/Mission is a predicate of God* (cf. in ecumenical documents: "Our God is a Missionary God"). He operates and makes Himself known through an all-encompassing sending-economy: sending His angels, prophets, word, Messiah, Son, Spirit, apostles, Church, etc. The truth about this God can be known only by interpreting the events which are effected by this sending-economy; this involves faith, decision and participation. 'God's revelation has been made known through a life-pattern of missionary service (the messianic pattern, cf. the Servant of the Lord) = this revelation can

[5] e.g. G. F. VICEDOM, *Missio Dei: Eine Einführung in eine Theologie der Mission* (1958).

only be received by men who seek to fashion their own lives in accordance with this pattern.'[6] To believe in this God implies acceptance of the form of the messianic life (election-witness-service-self-indentification-suffering) and this means: to be involved and to partake in his Mission.

Reminders of this over-all sending-economy may still be found throughout doctrinal theology, e.g. in the use of the term missio in the treatise on the Trinity, on Christology, and ecclesiology.

8.

This sending-economy is the expression of God's 'philanthropy,' evidence of His concern to be present in the actual life situation of man, there to deliver man out of every form of "establishment" and to involve him in history. The first effect (and, if rightly understood, this may perhaps be all!) of the Mission will always be that man is brought into a historical process, ready to begin an exodus and to move from promise to fulfilment; 'infected with hope.'

It is essential to recognize *history as the decisive context of the* Mission: the God who is identified and known by His Mission, remains a non-residential God; He is not one of the ba'als. And, strictly speaking, man who is touched by the Mission becomes equally non-residential; he can live on only as a sojourner and pilgrim: his land is historized into a "land of promise,' his community into a 'people of the promise.' Even the world (like it was for Israel, cf. von RAD) is now an *event,* rather than a static entity; simply a stage when history may be lived with God; no longer a rigid and obstinate frame and no longer the intractable status quo, but malleable and transformable; a fluid world-in-process.

One of the most hazardous temptations in carrying out the Mission may well be the ever-recurring attempt to re-ba'alize God; the conspiracy to make Him again the residential god of a well-defined locality; which may be a continent (corpus christianum?), a nation (Volkskirche?) or a more restricted residential area (parish?). And one of the most common failures in the history of missions has been the curious fact that though the Church crossed the frontier between faith and unbelief, it did so *too late.* In Western Europe it has almost

[6]A convincing exposition of this thesis in F. W. DILLISTONE, *Revelation and Evangelism* (1948).

been the rule that the Mission reached the place where people had been at least 50 years before (cf. Industrial Missions!).

9.

As the inner dynamic of the *new* order, the *Mission begins beyond religion.* In the messianic era religion is once and for all outdated and superceded. Without residential gods, there is no need for a fanum, and consequently, nothing can be pro-fane. The quest for security, inherent in all religion, has been overtaken and invalidated by the promise of the Presence. The historical process, in which man has become involved, is, by its very nature the process of secularization,[7] and the history of the Mission is, in fact, the history of a continuous démasqué of the sacred and a continued exit out of the anachronism of religion.

Therefore, in trying to define the *purpose* of the Mission, we must discard all religious categories. We might use the keyword in the messianic pattern: *shalom.* A *secularized* (!) concept, taken out of the religious sphere (= salvation guaranteed to those who have strictly performed the prescribed rites) and commonly used to indicate all aspects of the restored and cured human condition: righteousness, truth, fellowship, communication, peace, etc. (cf. Ps 85). Shalom is the briefest and, at the same time, the fullest summary of all the gifts of the messianic era: even the name of the Messiah can simply be: shalom (Mi. 5:3; Eph. 2:4); the gospel is a gospel of shalom (Eph. 6:15) and the God proclaimed in this gospel can often be called the God of shalom.[8]

Shalom is not a something which can be objectified and set apart; not the *plus* which the haves can serve out to the have-nots; nor is it an intra-human quality ('peace of mind') that someone could enjoy in isolation. Shalom is a *social happening,* an event in inter-human relations, a venture of co-humanity: men may show their proper face (not their masks-persona: 'God is not a respecter of persons') and things can have their proper weight. Therefore shalom can never be reduced to a simple formula, to be applied in all occurring instances: it must be found and worked out in actual situations, relevant shalom (and

[7]Why the history of missions runs parallel to the history of secularization is explained by H. BERKHOF in his: *Der Sinn der Geschichte: Christus* (1962).

[8]A full study of the shalom-concept might be of great importance for our study project: cf. von RAD in Theol. W. NT, II, 398ff; E. BISER *Der Sinn des Friedens* (1960) and: Handbuch theol. Grundbegriffe (1963), I. 419ff; J. COMBLIN, *Théologie de la Paix* (1960).

irrelevant shalom *is* no shalom) can only be discovered, tested and achieved in actual cooperation (cooperation with those for whom shalom is destined).

The Church is a function of the Mission/apostolate and even that only in so far as it will actually let itself be used in God's sending-economy. In no respect can the Church regard itself either as the subject of the Mission or as its sole (and exclusive) institutionalized form.

The Church will be disfunctional in the apostolate, as long as it conceives itself as a 'religious organization' (that would be an anachronism) or as the locality where the deposit of shalom may be found to be dispensed to the outsider (that would imply a false objectivation of shalom). Knowing that shalom must happen cooperatively, the Church will realize that it will never *have* more shalom than it *shares* with those 'outside.' It lives ex-centredly. It has no model of an 'exemplary existence' to show (thus calling attention to itself) but humbly and servingly it searches for those situations in the world that call for loving responsibility, there to offer cooperation in working out shalom concretely and relevantly.

It would be misleading to speak simply of an 'out-going' structure of the Church-in-Mission; the Church that is to serve the Mission and therefore to fashion its life according to the messianic pattern, will have to *empty* itself, to practice kenosis (Phil. 2:5ff, in NEB "to make itself nothing"), mortifying its ecclesiastical stature and status, in order that it may "bear human likeness and be revealed in human shape." In Mission the Church will come closest to being simply a segment of Main Street, Anno 1963; in the esteem of the world it will certainly be the poorest section of it "without form or comeliness": "the segment of Main Street Anno 1963, divested of all its illusions."[9]

III. SOME PRACTICAL INFERENCES

11.

Here are simply a few suggestions for further discussion, esp. on the basis of what has been said about the ex-centric position of the Church.[10]

[9]cf. L. S. MUDGE, *In His Service: The Servant Lord and His Servant People* (1959), p. 123.

[10]P. L. BERGER, *The Noise of Solemn Assemblies* (1961), p. 159 f.

The Church is nothing more than a par-oikia, added to the oikos of the world; and it is completely free to be added unto each and any situation that might arise, precisely because as par-oikia the Church does not 'belong' to the world.

Over and over again we will have to start our thinking about missionary structures at the centre, in the world, or rather in a specific time-conditioned and (far less) space-conditioned 'world-situation.'

This might seem obvious, but in discussions on evangelism we often speak about the world as if it were the Church's frontgarden or the Christian's drill-ground, in short: as if the *world* were the paroikia added unto our ecclesiastical oikos; and we still refer to centri-petal and centri-fugal in such a way as to suggest that the Church is the centre.

To take this ex-centric position of the Church seriously would seem to imply, *negatively:*

A) *That we stop thinking from the inside towards the outside.*

This still is the main train of thought in missionary thinking; the apostolate is conceived of as a repetition outside (in a slightly modernized edition of course) of what happens inside, as an extension or repetition of the pastorate, and we continue to do so, although we have enough evidence that in this way we shall never touch people, beyond the fringes of Church life (those famous Vier-Rad-Christen, conformistes saisonniers, seasonal conformists, etc.) Moreover, this movement from the inside to the outside, from the alleged centre to the periphery (and the real centre) will more often than not distort and pervert the Mission into PROPAGANDA: the attempt to make man in *our* Christian image and after our ecclesiastical likeness; the propagandist, who has taken as normative what he has found at home, and has to impose himself; he tries to make exact copies of himself: "Er macht Wiederholungen dessen, was er selbst ist" (Martin Kähler).

B) *That we refuse to take for granted the Church and its institutions.*

There is a widespread feeling that we already possess the institutions we need (perhaps after some new interior decorating) and that whoever doubts this, should be decried as an 'iconoclast.'[10a] This is a precarious delusion that usually goes along with the dangerous illusion that the Church has a central position. In the face of all the evidence it may be rather doubtful and even highly improbable that we already possess the necessary institutions; at least they all need to be scrutinized and tested in their relevance to the needs of modern man.

C) *That we refrain from the customary mental movement from the ministry towards the laity.*

Only the (non-domesticated!) laity can be really and fully present in the oikos of the world: a missionary structure can only be a lay-centred structure: the task and position of the ministry with regard to the Mission will have to be defined in relation to the concrete needs of the laity. At any rate the function of the ministry will be a very modest one; we should not even accept, without further inquiry, the rather common suggestion that the minister is capable of 'equipping God's people for work in his (missionary) service' (Eph. 4:12): the ministry might well be in too centric a position to do this.

D) *That we do not try to 'integrate' as soon as possible in the Churches, as they are, those who have responded to the Mission.*
There are, of course, the well-known tactical reasons not to hurry any 'incorporation,' because of the closed and non-receiving character of many Churches which one cannot join unless one has endured a painful cultural circumcision. But, apart from these tactical (and quite legitimate) reasons, a more fundamental question is involved: in Mission we expect that a *new* thing will happen: that people will find new, perhaps even unprecedented, forms to express their 'obedience of faith.' "The seed we sow . . . is it not the body that shall be but a naked grain . . . and God clothes it with the body of His choice" (1 Cor. 15:36ff). It may well be (in fact it has happened very often) that the new body of God's choice suffers a premature death because of the missionary's impatience to incorporate those who have accepted the faith, in the old body. Very likely this impatience is an indication of PROSELYTISM which is

[10a] P. L. BERGER, *The Noise of Solemn Assemblies* (1961), p. 159 f.

the very contrast of Mission; the proselyting Church conceives itself as the mediating-centre of salvation and extra ecclesiam nulla salus; it takes itself as the oikos, to where man has to emigrate completely out of his worldly oikos; proselytism is the concomitant of a Church's refusal to accept its paroikia status.

Perhaps we should refuse to 'integrate' altogether, so as not to impose an illegitimate scandal by inviting people to adapt themselves to the pattern of this present Church (cf. Rom. 12:2). It would be more realistic to say that people are invited to adapt themselves to the various patterns of the present chaos of denominations. The communities that might arise as a fruit of the Mission should at any rate have their full opportunity to form their own life as 'independent younger Churches' at our doorstep.[11]

To take the ex-centric positions of the Church seriously will, among many other things, imply *positively:*

E) That we *recognize* honestly and completely, *without any ulterior motives, the existence of the world* with all its own principles of movement, hopes and possibilities . . . and identify ourselves fully with the things and the people of the world."[12]

F) That we *devise missionary structures inductively,* close and relevant to the human situation and therefore in a 'contextual' rather than in an 'absolutistic' fashion.[13]

(for an elaboration of this point I may refer to PAUL KRAEMER's article, pp. 183 ff.)

G) *That we attempt to synchronize the Church's calendar with the (various!) 'secular' calendars:* What does it mean concretely that 'the sabbath is made for man, not man for the sabbath'?[14]

---

[11]The whole question of proselytism, especially in relation to baptism, needs far more investigation; there is a Dutch thesis by A. J. HEBLY, *Het Proselitisme* (with French summary) (1962); for baptism cf. H. MENTZ, *Taufe und Kirche in ihrem ursprünglichen Zusammenhang* (1960) Baptism: *not* an "Initiationsritus : Wer sich taufen lässt, tritt nicht etwas Bestehendem bei" (p. 95).

[12]R. G. SMITH, *The New Man, Christianity and Man's Coming of Age* (1956), pp. 69ff.

[13]A. B. COME, *Agents of Reconciliation* (1960) p. 43f.

[14]The calendar question as a missionary issue: H. STORCK, *Kirche im Neuland der Industrie* (1958).

H) That, in a world-in-flux, we be content with *ad-hoc* (and, consequently, temporary) *structures.*

12.

In any missionary structure the existing confessional denominational differences are completely irrelevant.

J. C. Hoekendijk, Utrecht
September, 1963

Mission in God's Mission

Steadfast love and faithfulness will meet; righteousness and peace will kiss each other. Faithfulness will spring up from the ground, and righteousness will look down from the sky. Yea, the Lord will give what is good, and our land will yield its increase. Righteousness will go before him, and make his footsteps a way (Psalm 85:10-13).

1. *The present discussion about the renewal of the Church begins from the question of mission.*

It has been our task, in our study on "The Missionary Structure of the Congregation," to understand the church in the light of mission. The New Testament talks of the church in various contexts and with various emphases. Today we are discovering anew that it is always a question of the church caught up in mission. The New Testament, we would say, is a missionary document.

The aim of our study is to make mission a fruitful impulse for the renewal of the church. We are after possibilities of discovering and developing structures of missionary congregations.

2. *What does "mission" mean?*

a) Missio Dei—In the mission of Jesus we recognize *God* as a sending God. God's people experience God's Lordship in being sent. The witness and obedience of the church are determined by this experience.[1]

—The *world* is recognized by the church sent in Christ, is experienced and accepted as creation in movement, as the content and the goal of God's act of sending.

—The *church* of Jesus Christ stands in the service of the sending God. This mission is always determining her commission and constantly shaping the forms in which she lives and works.

b) *Missions* These are missionary forms of the church in the past, the present and the future, historically determined and therefore transitory forms of obedience in reference to the *missio Dei.*

3. *The missio Dei is manifest in history*

a) The missio Dei is experienced in both the Old and the New Testament as the epiphany of God. The apostles receive their commission in the event of their exalted Lord's appearance to them.[2] While the church awaits the epiphany that is yet to come

[1]D. Stoodt sums up his article on "Mission in the self-understanding of the early church" (EMZ 21, 1964, 1-21): "How they are to organize themselves, which forms of life and which languages are appropriate, even who God is, who Jesus Christ is, who the Holy Spirit is, these are questions whose answers cannot be known as it were in themselves or of oneself, they can only be discovered in the missionary situation, in regard to it and as a consequence of it. The early church cannot be understood within the history of ideas but only in the history of mission.

The New Testament is a missionary document. Not just because it teaches about mission or because it lets us see into the missionary forms of the early church but because it owes its existence to mission, to the proclamation of Jesus Christ and to the movement of mission that inevitably grow from that. It is witness to the life of the early church, and therefore to the life of every church as life in mission. We correspond to the New Testament when we ourselves are a missionary document."

[2]In a study of "The Passion and Easter Narratives in Matthew" (Basileia. Walter Freytag zum 60, Geburtstag, Stuttgart 1959, 41) H. W. Bartsch reaches the following conclusion: "The missionary commandment is thus not only the the consequence of the epiphany; in his epiphany the Kyrios reveals himself as Lord of the whole world."

in the Parousia of Christ, her life is determined by the tension between the 'already' and the 'not yet.' For the church it is this tension which produces the dynamic of history and brings on historical change. History thus becomes an irreversible process and one directed by its goal. Men are brought out of their isolation from history and are introduced into the multitude of possible ways of taking up their historical responsibilities. Blessing and curse are placed before them (Deut.5).

b) The missio Dei, with the cross and resurrection at its centre, brings world history into a crisis; it is always leading history out of the old and into the new. Hope is thereby created, an active expectation of good in the transforming of the world for Christ's sake, a distinguishing of the good from the evil, of the old from the new.

c) Christians then know and grasp the changes in history in the perspective of the missio Dei, since in faith their actual past and their actual future is presented to them.

—Since faith trusts in *God's promise* it can dare to involve itself in actual history. New forms of responsibility for the world will arise. It becomes urgent for faith to act towards change in the history of the church and of the world.

—Since faith lives from *God's faithfulness* it can dare to expose the inherited and existing forms and contents of church and world to the testing of history. In this the central question will be whether what exists is still serving the missio Dei or not. What is useful can then be constructively taken up; that which is a hindrance can be abandoned. In such a way the necessary process of tradition can be critically carried further.

4) *The missio Dei compels the church to take a historical form*

The church, obedient to the missio Dei, can only realise its commission in the form of missions conditioned by their own age. These forms, if they are to be able to set up signs of '*Shalom*'[3] in the world, must have the form of a servant (Phil. 2.5ff.). This involves a certain proper institutionalisation but demands at the

[3]We would rather say "salvation" but fear that "salvation" could be misunderstood in a narrow, individualistic sense.

same time a constant readiness to abandon institutional forms and replace them with new ones. This leads naturally to the question whether the church is ready in this respect to accept the implications of Jesus' saying "He who loses his life will find it" (Mt. 10:39).

a) If we examine traditional understandings of the aim of mission(s) (and the forms which follow from these) to see how far their purposes can today serve the missio Dei, we can see the following:

—"Mission(s) are really aimed at the conversion of individuals": The gospel demands and brings out the personal response of individuals but forbids all one-sided concern about the salvation of one's own soul because it is after *shalom* as a social event.

—"Mission(s) are really aimed at the "planting of churches": As they respond to the gospel men gather in churches, but these churches are caught up in the further process of mission. Moreover not all the fruits of the gospel are found in the churches—the gospel aims at *shalom* in the transforming of the *world*.

The following other traditional aims of mission would have to be similarly examined—the christianisation of a people, the building of the Kingdom of God, the calling to the obedience of faith, the call to individuals and groups to make decisions and come apart, etc. Since *shalom* is a social and many-sided event, and since modern society leads us into pluralism we shall have to formulate the aim of our mission(s) in such a way that the manifold involvements and various commissions of Christians in the world are recognized as genuine forms of obedience to the missio Dei.

b) "He is our peace." We understand our missions to be movements that participate in the missio Dei, which is to sum up all things in Christ,—and are therefore led to set up many signs of God's *shalom* in the world. *Shalom* is salvation, peace . . .

Today we find examples of the setting up of '*signs of shalom*,' among many other movements, some of which take place quite without notice, in the Freedom Movement in the USA, the

Aktion "Sühnezeichen" in Germany, in the presence of the worker priests in France, in the venture of interconfessional groups in Holland, in the industrial missions of England or America, in the work at Riesi in Sicily, in the Telephone Samaritarians, in the involvement of Academies and lay institutes, in many sorts of service for peace.

5) *The missio Dei embraces both church and world*

The missio Dei is at work beyond the church (and its various missions). It embraces both church and world. The church serves the missio Dei in the world as the basis of the revelation it points to God at work in world history and names him there. The word, baptism and eucharist, prayer and fellowship are not the instrument of ecclesiastical self-preservation but dynamic pre-figurations of that which God intends for all men in his *shalom.* The church exercises therefore the critical function which liberates the world into becoming the kind of world God wills (Rom. 12, 2).

The expectation that God is shaping his church anew[4] compels us to put the following questions; they must be openly and honestly faced.

—How can we accept as genuine forms of church that are new and hitherto unknown to us?

—How can we meet the challenge of other people's view of the church?

—How can we take into the processes of our church life discussion-in-partnership with non-Christians?

—How, when we see a failure or weak point in society, can we fill the gap in an exemplary way?

—How can we gain courage to set up projects shaped to the world, and which are deliberately institutionalised for a limited period?

—How can we be ready for provisional forms, even in the case of church buildings?

[4]Walter Freytag (Reden und Aufsätze II, Chr. Kaiser Verlag München 1961, 121) said: "All preaching of the Gospel is a step towards something new. . . . Of the proclamation of the Gospel something new always comes into being. There always comes into being another church."

—How can we make room for the future in our present decisions and thus arrive at rational planning?

—How can our services of worship, in the light of 1 Corinthians 14, be now at last changed so as to participate in the missio Dei?[5]

Western European Working Group
Driebergen, March, 1965

God in History

1) Our knowledge of God in Jesus Christ leads us to affirm that God is working his purpose out in the midst of the world and its historical processes. This is not to identify him with the flow of events, but to recognize him in his action in events, the significance of which is declared to us through God-given men.

2) When we ask what forms the Church should take in the world of today and tomorrow we cannot find the answer simply in an analysis of human society and history. The true answer can only come from an understanding of what God has done and is doing in and

[5]We recall the questions raised in the Report of Section I of the Montreal Fourth World Conference on Faith and Order:

a) If the Church is the body of the crucified Lord, can it ever expect to be more honored than he?
b) If the glory and victory of the Lord is seen in his being exalted to the cross (Jn. 12, 28-33), can the Church attain a greater glory or exhibit a greater power than by following gladly, even into suffering at the hands of men?
c) If the Church consists of the followers of the Lord who spent his time with publicans and sinners, why does it look so much like a congregation of scribes and pharisees?
d) If the Lord of the Church was crucified outside the camp (Heb. 13:12) why is the Church so often comfortable within its walls and so hesitant to emigrate to new areas to risk bearing its witness within endeavours to establish justice and mercy, and even where the powers of destruction are at work?
e) How can a Church which tolerates the barriers which separate men today, whether east or west or black and white, face its Lord who has broken down the wall of partition (Eph. 2,14)?
f) If Christ has set us free to be truly men, how can we escape solidarity with all men, whether they live as if there were no God, or confess Him, whether they do good works or live beyond good and evil?
g) If Christ was flesh and blood and if he is to be the Lord of all creation, how can we, his followers, so often flee into a spirituality that divorces God from earth and its possibilities?

for the world and of the unique commission and ministry of the Church within that cosmic plan.

3) One of the most determinative of such events was the Exodus, and again and again Israel's confession of her faith in God was related to it. It is not surprising that in the great movements of corporate and personal liberation at various periods in the past, and again on a worldwide scale in our own day, Christians should see another Exodus and learn afresh the character of the God with whom we have to do.

4) But the passion and Resurrection of Jesus Christ is the Exodus for all men. Now the whole of mankind is delivered from bondage and brought into covenant with God. By the raising up of the New Man, Christ Jesus, every man has been made a member of the New Mankind.*

5) We would seriously ask, therefore, whether we should assume that God's ultimate plan is to incorporate all men into the Church. The Church, rather, may have to be seen as the minister of the new covenant, accepting and dealing with man and society as already belonging to the New Mankind, however little they look like it, since faith is the evidence of things not seen. If this is true, it will make a radical difference to the Church's understanding of its relation to the world. We should have then to ask what is the

---

*There was intensive discussion on this paragraph. The following additions were proposed:

"Therefore he is called to live in faith." "Until man becomes aware of this truth he does not enter into the fulness of Christ." "But only in faith can he become what in Christ he is."

"We discover the configuration of this New Mankind in the New Man, Christ Jesus. Here we discover the true meaning of the destiny which God has eternally intended for his people. In Jesus Christ all is summed up and drawn together—the new creation is here begun in fact. We believe that in the urbanization of the world we are enabled to see, albeit ambiguously, the lineaments of that New City which God has promised is the culmination of his new creation. In the increasing interdependence of all men upon each other culturally, politically and economically there is coming into being a *polis,* a city, which requires of us a cosmopolitan approach if we are true to the world and to our God. The network of communications which link us together, the massive exchange of raw materials and products, the cultural interplay—all these can lead to a massive mediocrity. Yet we must dare so to involve ourselves in commitment to this movement of the world that we can testify to and work for its development toward God's city, the city in which dwells the New Mankind. Its consummation will only be in God's time and in his way, but the vision he has granted to us must give the pattern and direction of our present obedience."

message the Church has to preach? If all men are already in the New Mankind in Christ, in what sense do we call them to decide and to come? Is it enough for us to say in effect, "See where you already belong. Commit yourself by baptism to that of which you are already a member. Take the place already reserved for you at the table of the Lord?" This is enough to indicate that a whole set of questions remains unanswered. But until we can be more clear as to what we should believe about the nature of Christ's presence and action within the whole of mankind and the true relation of the Church's function to that action we shall never be able to discover what its forms and structures ought to be. We must undertake a thorough study of these issues.

6) In the meantime there are no grounds for inaction or despair. We know enough about the calling of the Church within the world to be able to see that its forms and structures need to be reshaped.

7) First, we know that Christians are called to be present with Christ in the life of the world and, corporately, to be a vanguard of the new humanity within history. This means at least making ourselves vulnerable to the full onslaught of the struggles which so engage our times. It means that any sort of hiding, either in ecclesiology or doctrine, to protect us from the anguish of decisions in particular problems which affect the lives of our fellowmen is not worthy of Christ.

8) Secondly, it is the mission of the Church, whose only wisdom is the Word of God, to search the events of our time for the hand of the loving and judging God. The Church is called both to agonize with all men in the bewilderments and struggles of contemporary events and to interpret those events so that they may become, for mankind, not overwhelming but creative. The living Lord who revealed himself in the mighty acts of Israel's history still manifests himself in the history which is common to us all in these days, meeting men directly in the living Christ at the same critical points of human sin, repentance and reconciliation. The mass nature of our society makes it imperative for us to take seriously the fact that God in Christ confronts nations and peoples as well as individuals.

It is the commission of the Church to interpret the ferment of movement and tension, proclaiming the coming Lord towards whose triumph it is all tending in order that we with all men may be lifted above despair and nerved for the struggle.

This is a very risky undertaking, for in every event divine and demonic elements are at work. Furthermore, particular situations will elicit different patterns of Christian obedience. The situation in East Germany is different from that in East Asia and from East Harlem in the United States. There can be no *a priori* program of Christian action which can be transported across the world and applied here and there. But the Church must dare to be God's interpreter, both through the insight of its 'prophets' and through the daily struggle of Christian communities seeking to express their obedience to Christ in the decisions of secular society.

9) Experience from many quarters convinces us that wherever the Church, even in the person of an isolated Christian, enters fully into a situation armed with no preconceived idea of what form its ministry should take, but only with a concern for righteousness and a deep compassion, the right pattern emerges for the particular people in those particular circumstances. A fitting structure for the missionary congregation is always being given by the Holy Spirit —who takes and uses the structures of the world. It is this which gives us confidence to go forward with neither maps nor landmarks, yet unafraid.

Enlarged Meeting of the Working Committee
Bossey, April 1964

"Christus extra et intra muros ecclesiae"

I. *What are our criteria for recognizing Christus extra muros ecclesiae?*

(This paragraph inquires into the right attitude of members of the church towards men *extra muros ecclesiae* in whom we believe to discern Christ. Are they an object for mission? Or are they already—unconsciously—members of the church? Part of the questions will be dealt with under II.)

According to the texts of the New Testament our behaviour should not pose any problem. The New Testament stipulates that Christ can be proclaimed in very diverse and obviously also very self-interested and schismatic ways. (Phil. 1.16). At any rate, Paul does not feel obliged to interfere; he even seems to be pleased with the service of the schismatics. The situation described under I b did not exist at the times of the New Testament. I do not want to take recourse to the often quoted passage in Matt. 25 because it is impossible to base such an important theological affirmation on one single passage in the Bible. Stating, however, that our situation is unprecedented in church history, we have already taken into account an important objection. Whoever refuses to acknowledge the necessity of theological reflection on the problems of industrialisation on the grounds that they do not appear in the Bible and in church history, would doubtlessly prove his unbelief in the ongoing eschatological power of *Christus intra muros ecclesiae*. Whoever refuses to take seriously *Christus extra muros ecclesiae* who penetrated through the fissures of the church because the church has never before had a similar experience does not understand that the history which Christ initiated does not repeat things of old but creates new things (kaine ktisis). He who never thinks of discerning Christ where he is not confessed *expressis verbis* does not understand that we find ourselves in a situation without analogy in which a reflection on the history of dogma provides only very indirect enlightenment.

How can we discern *Christus extra muros ecclesiae?* We discern him by the same signs as *Christus intra muros ecclesiae*. Christ *intra muros* differed essentially from the general religiosity of his time by leaving profane things profane. "The Sabbath has been created for the sake of man" and not for the sake of God. The Sabbath is not to be observed as a sacred time, but man and animal are given a pause to breathe so that they are able to experience man as man (Ex. 23.10-12; Mk. 2:27). Contrary to the sectarians of the Dead Sea (Damascus Document X.14-XI, 18) Christ *intra muros* is therefore able to annul an order of God given in former times (Jer. 1.10-17; Mtt. 5.31-35).

If the Colossians thought that certain days, stars, rites and sacramental actions were sacred in themselves, Christ *intra muros* says that all such things are subordinate to Christ, even created by him. On the basis of such knowledge it was possible to strip the powers of physics (Newton) and also of history and society (Marx) of their self-contained and godlike claim and to objectify them as fields for human research.

It became possible to recognize these forces which *Christus intra muros* declared to be created, profane realities and not independent and godlike, as part of the creation which is man's mandate (von Rad, Bonhoeffer). The Christ *intra muros* of the Epistle to the Colossians would admit that the world is sanctified, not *natura sua* but because it is *creatio filii dei,* the creation, the realm of the power ("Gemächte") of Christ *intra muros.*

The Old Testament has already prepared the secularization and objectivation of the world. Genesis 1 supports the idea that the stars are not gods but lamps which God kindles, water is not the god of the chaos, but H_2O with its God-given limitations. And even earlier the prophets taught, neither the stars, nor the moon, nor a sacred hill, nor the Temple, nor the offerings (be they ordered by God or Moses which —by the way—Amos refutes, Amos 5.25) are sacred in themselves. These things are profane. The purpose of the amphyctionic celebrations was to show profane things as sacred things and only in this respect were they divine service. While the peoples surrounding Israel observed the sabbath only out of a fear of gods and demons, Israel changed the sabbath into a day when man and animal could relax. And even in exile when the Sabbath was fixed by the priests it served as a point of orientation to save the people from being drowned in the swamps of Babylonian mythology. The peoples surrounding Israel have always separated part of the world and declared it to be part of God or at least turned towards God, thus necessarily devaluating other parts of the world.

Such a secular view of the world is only possible if God is understood as radically transcendent and at no point confounded with the world. This is a lesson which the people of Israel have learned through many centuries. In Jesus of Nazareth this movement has reached its irreversible goal. He understands the whole world (also and especially the religious world) as profane and therefore sanctified. He shows us his Father as a Father who can only be served if he is not confounded with man's world. (. . . "who art in heaven"). But at the same time we have to understand that he loves and treats this world as his world and above all mankind as *his* mankind ("Our Father"). As this world is God's world (the world of him who has sent us Jesus and whom we get to know through Jesus), all world preserving rites (astrology, fertility rites, our nervous modern efforts to save the world from crashing) and pacification rites are no longer necessary since God is manifest as a God who preserves the world or dooms it to perish upon his own will and decision. He does not want to and must not be pacified. Thus we have been freed for a new relationship towards our neighbour (who is God's creature), for a new relationship towards the world (which is an object, but an object in the hands of God) and for a new relationship towards God (who does not claim our worship for his sake but worship for the sake of man who needs it). These three points can easily be considered as the basic points of our modern tendency towards objectivation in the field of epistemology.

If men today can let the world be the world without confessing Christ, they can do so on the grounds of the irreversible redemptive act of Christ and the pedagogical function of the church. The leaven of the Gospel has penetrated the dough of the world. It would be surprising had the church not changed the whole way of thinking of those who confess Christ. But at this point a danger immediately becomes evident. We content ourselves by stating that man is quite naturally capable of letting the world be the world. We no longer realize that the entire development of epistemology and natural sciences has been made possible only within the radiation field of the Gospel. And wherever we forget that this is a present given to us by God, if in presumptuous ignorance we misunderstand this present as a fruit of our autonomous intelligence we again make the mistake of deifying a part of the world, be this a part of the psychological, scientific or economic world. It seems to be obvious that we need a church in the institutional sense, a church which explicitly reveals the cohesion between the liberation from the demons and the Jesus of evangelical preaching and liturgy and which as such manifests again the liberation from the demons. We need a place in which we hear of a God who is not confounded with (asygehytos) but at the same time not separated from (adiairetos) the world so that the world may not be confounded with God and thus be separated from him. This service can vicariously be rendered for all mankind by the church as a small minority.

Summary: Where the world is left to be the world, things (objects) left to be things (objects), the profane left to be profane, thus being at the free disposal of man, Christ is at work. Where this work of Christ is not confessed or even denied the danger arises that the freedom from the world becomes slavery to the world. Therefore a church is needed in which the freedom from the world is again and again made manifest.

II. *Which consequences can we draw for the structure of the church?*

At the beginning of the communion service of the early church the presents of Christians were piled up on the altar. At the end of the service the presbyter would take some of the presents and distribute them to the congregation as the "body" and "blood" of the Lord. The larger part of this "body" was distributed to the poor and needy *extra and intra muros.* The early Christian church solved the social problem and thus an important part of its mission in Holy Communion. Later on, these presents were replaced by money collections which were placed between the "body" and the "blood" of the Lord. Thus the profane money was sanctified in its profanity, the mammon was released from the demonic power and brought home to its very essence: an instrument of *diaconia.*

Our church should be so structured that its organisation, its administration of the sacraments and its preaching make possible a clear affirmation of its explicit witness (mentioned under I). This does not mean that the church says as many things as possible and whenever possible but that it should always say with clarity that God and the world are "asygchytos" and "adiairetos" not confounded with and not separated from each other. We should for instance speak in this manner about the Holy Spirit and art, love to our neighbour and economy, authority and war, theology and philosophy.

According to what has been said before the church must develop a structure which does not prevent *joint action* (also in the sacramental life) with those who are *extra muros* of the doctrine and organisation of the church. The same redeemer has redeemed those inside and those outside the church without the latter consciously recognising this redemption and their particular participation in it. Therefore we need structures allowing those inside and outside to express their joint concern—(to leave the world to be the world, a desire for objectivity), These common forms of expression must not simply be joint actions (in the sense of activity) nor should they result in common definitions (because a definition does not create a relationship but *ex definitione* —separates). They must be forms of expression which can be understood by those *intra muros* as a theological expression (in a sacramental way) and by those *extra muros* as a human expression. It is a shame that the sacraments have degenerated and lost their New Testament meaning because nowadays we need them so badly. Therefore we are compelled to give them a new power which will create commitment and confession, or we need "profane sacraments," forms of expression which are sacramental for those inside and human for those outside (see the Holy Communion in the early church).

Walter J. Hollenweger, Zurich
April, 1964

The Test of the Tradition

The whole discussion about arguing out of the history and tradition of the church vs. arguing out of the present day involvement has left in my mind the following formulation of the issue: The relationship between tradition (or history) and present day involvement should not be stated in terms of "both-and." This is acknowledged by everybody and really does not get us very much further. We all know that we need the Bible in one way or another, and that it is out of the Bible that we find the truth about the present day world, but we also know that we need to be involved in the present day world in order to meet the God who is acting today. The question is precisely their relationship, and by stating that we need both we have not really stated the relationship between the two. I wonder whether we should not speak of "*testing the tradition*" in the midst of our involvement in the present world. It seems to me what is happening is that we often want to defend the tradition, rather than test it. Defending the tradition, however, presupposes that we don't trust its own power to defend itself, that we really do not trust God to speak to us in His word. If we test the tradition, it presupposes that we trust that whatever God wants to say to us through this tradition, he will certainly say, and this is precisely its test. We trust that God really speaks in the Bible and in the way it has been heard throughout the history of the church. And it can only be God who will maintain ultimately this tradition . . . and not, for example, the teaching office of some in the church . . .

Thomas Wieser, New York
April, 1964

Of the Goal of Mission

In considering the "shape of mission" it is essential that we keep in mind the goal of God's missionary action. This is expressed in many different ways in Scripture. We use three:

i) The vision of the ultimate *reconcilation and unity of the whole of creation in Christ* (Eph. 1:9-10; 2:14; 4:1-5; 4:13, 16; Rev. 21: 1-5).

The letter to the Ephesians gives us a striking picture of the goal of God's mission—the final unity of everything in creation within the one life of Christ. The life of Christ is seen as a powerful force of unity breaking through all the hostile divisions within the human family and within the world of creation. This is now seen to be the secret purpose of creation—a secret which God has at last unveiled in Christ—as we can look forward with certainty to the ultimate unity of all things within Christ's love (3:7-21).

In chapters 4, 5 and 6, the implications of this for the present life of the Christian community are drawn out. The "unity of the Spirit" is manifested in the community life of the Church (4:1-16). We would be wrong to think of this new life as being lived in a churchly institution isolated from the life of the world. In 4:17 following it is made clear that this life in the unity of the Spirit is lived out in everyday human situations within the institutional life of the world. This in fact is what Christian life is meant to be—a breakthrough of Christ's way of unity into the old world of division and hostility. Because the Christian life is a casting away of the sins which cause division (4:22-32) it results in infusing the structures of the world with the unity of life in Christ (in the family 5:22ff and in master-slave relations 6:5ff).

A summary of the meaning of this unity of life in Christ in the face of the divisions and hostilities which mark the life of the world is given in Col. 3:11-15: "Here there cannot be Greek and Jew (the dividing wall of nation and race), circumcised and uncircumcised (the barriers of religiousness), barbarian or Scythian (the clash of cultures), slave, free man (the hostilities of class), but Christ is all in all." The "missionary structure" of the life of the Church should be such as to allow the unifying power of Christ to be manifest at the points where the hostilities of nation, race, culture, religiousness, class, are destroying the unity of God's creation. The missionary structures must serve Christ in such a way that his healing resources shall be released at the points of the world's sorest needs.

The Reflection of the Goal in the Present

What does this say concerning our present structures? Would it not appear that our present congregations based on residence are desperately inadequate to be the avenue of this mission of Christ? Are not modern urbanized residence communities the most subtle devices ever created to separate men from each other along these lines of separation—race, class, culture, nation, religion? Does not a church pattern which structures Christians within residence communities tend to deepen those worldly separations rather than bring the uniting reconciling power of Christ to bear in such a way that these worldly barriers collapse and Christ's ultimate purpose is revealed? Is it not true that in our world in varying degrees men do come together across these barriers in other activities of life—at work, in politics, in health, in mass entertainment—but that church life is related to men at the place of their greatest separation (residence), and takes on very little form at the places where the world gives an opportunity to break through these separations? It would seem then that the Church in modern urban life is denying itself the structures necessary to express the unifying power of life in Christ.[1]

---

[1]A Biblical symbol that lies in close relation to the symbol of unity, is that of peace (Shalom). Ephesians speaks of "the unity of the Spirit in the bond of peace," and the word "peace" provides us with another way of tracing out *the missionary goal* which God has revealed to us in the coming of Christ and in the sending of the Holy Spirit. This is spelled out in "A Theological Reflection on the Work of Evangelism," (WCC, Geneva, 1959) p. 6:

"The Gospel is the story of God's redeeming work in Jesus Christ. The spread of the Gospel is God's chosen way to establish His triumphant rule over man-

ii) *The vision of the realization of the full potentialities of all creation.*

Karl Barth uses two phrases which give clear expression to the inseparable relation of God's work of redemption to his work of creation. "Creation is the external basis of the covenant." "The covenant is the internal basis of creation." The vision of creation given in Genesis is of man, the obedient son of God, exercising dominion over creation by using his creative capacities to bring out nature's full potential and by using this fruitful world of nature as the arena for the development of the full social and personal capacities of the human family (Gen. 1:26-28; 2:15). Because man has turned away from God he has fallen out of true relationship to himself (3:7); out of harmony with God (3:8-9); out of unity with his human partner (3:12); and also into disharmony with the world of nature (3:16-17). But it is precisely these distortions *in the world* with which redemption is concerned.[2]

---

kind. Gospel and man are meant for each other. They belong together. The Gospel of God's Kingdom is a Gospel for the nations.

"This King has willed to rule as Savior. Wherever His Kingship is proclaimed, His saving concern for mankind will be made manifest. The end of this saving concern is the gift of peace, the establishment of 'shalom.' To receive God's shalom is to enter into an inheritance where many things belong together—mercy and truth, righteousness and peace, goodness and plenty, man's salvation and God's glory. In shalom, peace is established between God and man in atonement and reconciliation, so that man is saved from the terrifying presence of an unknown mystery and is made a partner in God's covenant; peace is established between man and his neighbor, so that society is saved from destructive selfishness and men are established in community; peace is established between a man and himself, so that he is saved from dividedness and is restored in his integrity as made in the image of God.

"This shalom is in Jesus Christ in whom God has proclaimed His Gospel. By this proclamation is created a new situation for mankind because, whether acknowledged or unacknowledged, it brings mankind into a decisive relationship with God."

[2]"A Theological Reflection on the Work of Evangelism" p. 13f. expresses this point:

"When it describes the mighty deeds of God, the New Testament uses political, juridical, sociological and other secular terms. Kingdom of God, Son of David, King of the Jews; Redemption, Faith, Forgiveness; Healing, Freedom, Service—all such words by which the person and work of Jesus Christ are described are secular words. This secular terminology of the New Testament is not only a form of speech. For the coming of Jesus Christ in the flesh and in the power of the Spirit is a 'secular' event. It is an event in the world and for the world.

"For many, however, the language and message of the Bible have become merely 'religious.' It is the task of evangelism to discover and to proclaim the Gospel in its specific, concrete, unique and secular sense. The ministry of the evangelist is to announce that all events happen within and take meaning from the Gospel facts. He pronounces that the promised Messiah-King has come, that He is given full power over heaven and earth, and that the Holy Spirit is being poured out over all flesh as an earnest of the final consummation."

In Colossians Paul draws a parallel between Christ's work as creator and redeemer (Col. 1:15-17 and 18-23). It is the same world to which Christ is related in both cases. When Christ comes as "the Second Adam," it is to overcome *all* the divisions expressed in Genesis 3. That is why his *miracles* are concerned not only with man in his inwardness ("Son thy sins are forgiven"); but just as much in his body, in his community, and in his relation to nature. Christ is the Savior of *the world*. He walks on the water as the sign of his Lordship over nature; he feeds the 5,000 by his mastery of nature and heals men's bodies as a sign of his power to heal the wounds of his created world. Wherever there is hurt, there is the Savior.

The Servant Form of the Church

What does this mean for the missionary structure of the Church? How can her life be so ordered that it may bring to visibility the healing power of Christ at those points where the divisive results of our separation from God are most apparent?

It would seem here that if the Church is to be the servant of God's mission, it must (like Christ) be sensitive to the points of disjunction in the world, and be so structured that it focuses the obedience of the Christian community at these points of need, bringing the healing resources of Christ to bear in such a way that his forgiveness and love are thrown across the chasms of separation. It would seem too, that this obliges Christians to use to the full the "secular" means God offers us in the world to discern "the structures of need" and to match them with the structures of Christian community.[3] What, for example, does this mean for the church's "necessary structure" in relation to the problem of race conflict, the nuclear problem, the "youth culture"?

iii) *The awareness that the final goal has already been revealed in Christ, but will not be fully manifest until Christ returns to complete his new creation.* i) and ii) must be kept within this framework

[3] "A Theological Reflection on the Work of Evangelism," p. 6:

"Christian obedience is the result of Christian conversion. But, once the will is surrendered to Christ's obedience, theological reflection can shed light on all that obedience involves. To such theological reflection, in its work of evangelism, the Church is summoned anew today to understand what God is doing in these times through all the changes that are taking place in the ways and circumstances of human life, to penetrate into the significance of the new forms of association in which persons find their social satisfaction, to ask how the Gospel may be related to men in their several needs as they seek to come to terms with life."

provided by iii) or they run the danger of suggesting that we can look forward to a gradual unfolding of God's plan—a progressive rolling back of the shadow side until we emerge into the full light of the sun. Not so. Our place in God's mission in this "time between the times"—the time from Christ's incarnation until his parousia (his return)—is to be witnesses to Christ. By word and deed members of the Christian community are called to be "signs" of Christ's purpose, so that the world can see in our word and deed what God's purpose is, and so will be ready when he comes at last to "give us the Kingdom," and create the "new heaven and a new earth." The final goal suggested in i) and ii) has already been revealed by Christ. Now in this time of delay before he establishes this Kingdom in open victory, time is given for men to hear the truth (how can they hear unless we preach), and to learn to practice Christ's way (how can they do that unless they see Christ the light as reflected light in the community life of disciples in the world). Life in the Spirit is an "earnest," a "downpayment," on the final gift of the perfect life of Christ which he shall give us when he returns. In the meantime the task of the Church is to be used by Christ to set up "signs" in the world by word and deed—signs which make visible Christ's ultimate purpose at the places where the world seems most separated from the life of God.

> "There can be no distinctive witness where there is no distinctive life. Christians are, therefore, called to repentance. They must come to Christ the Servant and let Him put His distinctive form upon them. They must care that the Church which evangelizes must also give visible evidence of the credentials for its work. But besides these credentials, men will also ask for signs. Signs there will be. Sick people will be healed, prisoners will be visited, lonely men will find fellowship, estranged people will be reconciled, worthless people will get a new value. However, neither herald nor hearer must forget that these signs only point to God and His presence with His Church. As it is written: 'And they went forth and preached everywhere, while the Lord worked with them and confirmed the message by the signs that attended it.' Therefore must the evangelist always seek to press for a faith beyond all signs in the faithful Giver Himself. His command and His promise are, 'Seek His Kingdom and these things shall be yours as well.' "[4]

[4] "A Theological Reflection on the Work of Evangelism," pp. 18-19.

This eschatological perspective has important implications for our understanding of the Church's life in the present. The fact that our present life is not a final expression of victory, and that here we have "no abiding city," but that we seek one still to come, means that no structure of church life either in the realm of church *order* or of church *thought* (theology) can claim eternal validity. Just as Christ took form within the changing structures of history, and put on a particular garb, spoke a particular language, and related himself to a particular government and particular social problems, so he requires of his people that they take on similar particularity.

It is important for us to remember that this is not only true of church order—congregational forms; ways of ministry—but is also true of church thought. A Christian theology, to be Christian, must be a reflection on what God is doing.[5] The "past" character of Christian theology because of the fact that it is rooted in God's deeds and words, often misleads us into assuming that we can formulate theology in such a way that it will be just as "true" 100 years from now as it will be today. To think this way is to forget that the "past" revelation speaks to us of a living God who is continuously at work in history and calls us to respond to his work in the world. It is for this reason that we must resist the common tendency to separate theology from worldly disciplines such as sociology and psychology. Just as we must reject the tendency to treat Church and world as though they were separate entities, so we must reject the separation of the theological task from the sociological. It is within this world that the theological task must be carried on.[6]

From *Where in the World*
By Colin W. Williams, New York, 1963, pp. 27ff.

---

[5]See "A Theological Reflection on the Work of Evangelism," p. 6, as quoted above.

[6]What this means for theological education is an urgent question. There has been too great a tendency to separate the "theological" and "practical" disciplines; and to separate the seminary world from direct responsibility for the Church's mission in the world. However, the oft-heard sneers from parish ministers concerning the ivory-tower character of seminary education is a false expression of the problem. Both *parish* and *seminary* share in the false separation of the Church from the world; and both are called to repentance.

The problem for the seminary is made more acute by the dissatisfaction of so many students with the present "parish ministry." For the most part the seminary curriculum assumes that the structures in which theological students will work can be taken for granted. The seminary's task is assumed to be mainly that of giving the students mastery over

i) the "given" content of the Christian faith.

ii) the practical techniques for a traditional type ministry—Christian education for the local parish; preaching in monologue form from the pulpit; church administration in the parish setting. Even the new practical disciplines like counselling do not question the adequacy of the witnessing forms of the church's life.

This view of seminary training is viable only when the forms of witness in the church are considered to be viable and therefore not requiring reflection. But when there is apparent need for major reformation of the witnessing relation of the church to the world, what then is the task of the seminary? If it is meant to give theological guidance to the church as she seeks to fulfill her mission, then her present curriculum and relation to church and world would appear to be inadequate.

It would seem to be required of seminaries that they accept the theological responsibility of carrying on the present training of ministers in dialogue with the present re-assessment of the witnessing forms of the church's relation to the world. What form this dialogue will need to take is a major question. It may mean that seminaries will need to be involved in experimental forms of mission. It may mean an interweaving of "content" and "practice" in the curriculum to an extent not previously attempted. It may mean a new relation to "lay" training centers. One can only plead that seminaries accept some real responsibility in this rethinking. If the church has "mission" as the central "mark" of her life, the seminary must allow that mission to control her training of the ministry; and if that missionary relationship must now be radically re-assessed, the seminaries must see that her structures are no less in question than those of the local residence congregation. Moreover, her responsibility for leading in the reappraisal is integral to her calling.

In an unpublished article on "The Problem of Education for the Ministry," Gibson Winter, after stating his belief that "seminaries can only be viable structures of training if they participate in the missionary task for which they are educating their students," goes on to suggest some of the necessary elements for "a dialogic framework of preparation." He suggests e.g.,

i) "Theological reflection and ministering can no longer be insulated from one another—the one in the seminary precincts and the other in the parochial institutions of another age."

ii) There needs to be faculty involvement, "at crucial points with the men whom they are preparing for the ministry and focused around the specific role of their own discipline in the mission of the Church."

iii) "The development of the Church's ministry cannot be confined any longer to a training of clergy in isolation from laity. . . . There can and should be, of course, periods of theological work in the quiet of an academic situation, but such reflection becomes integral to training for the ministry when it is set in the larger context of such objective involvement in mission and ministry."

iv) "Training for the ministry is training in apostolate and servanthood. It can no longer be conducted in isolation from that context; in fact, ministry and mission are actually to be developed in the process of training, and this is the joint task of faculty, students, pastors and laymen."

Gibson Winter suggests that just as clinical training has developed in the area of pastoral care, so we need similar dialogue settings in the framework of the church's mission—e.g., urban training centers.

We would suggest that Winter has raised the right questions. Now we must press upon seminaries the need to search for workable answers.

Second Part

THE WORLD IN CHANGE

Continuous Change

1.

It is not the task with which Christians are faced today merely to recognize that the world in which they live is no longer the world of 1920. Nor are they called simply to discard beloved conceptions and entrenched customs in order to make themselves at home in a changed world. The task reaches further.

2.

We shall have to face up to the fact that change is part of our situation in the world and that, as far as we can see, there will never be stable conditions anymore.

3.

We shall have to understand how in the midst of a continually changing world to keep faith, to exercise love and to walk humbly, to the praise of God and to the pleasing of men.

4.

Through the biblical witness the world is opened up to us as the field of service for faith combined with hope and love. The biblical witness proclaims that God opens up ways even in the desert on which he can be found in order that in the places of apparent hopelessness fountains of joy may spring up (Ps. 84:6). It is to be expected of the Christians that they trust these promises and accordingly involve themselves in the world (cf. Rom. 12:1f). For they are to confess and witness that all of God's promises have found their Yes in Jesus Christ (2 Cor. 1:20) and are, therefore, available to us as our heritage (Gal. 4 and 5).

5.

The orders of the church, therefore, should be much more like a marching order than a camping order (cf. Hebr. 13:12-14). It would be dangerous for us to become guilty of confusions, to confuse the "God of peace" with the "God of order" (cf. 1 Cor. 14:33), to speak of "hope in God" and to mean "hope in stable conditions," to speak of "God's faithfulness" and thereby try to save the status quo instead of discerning the oncoming.

6.

God is a God of Abraham, Isaak and Jacob; he is not to be likened to the God of the fathers but he is a God of the grandfather, the father and the son, a God of the generations who calls himself a people to walk with him. God is the creator who elects persons for the purpose of involvement in the world as the history of the covenant; people called and liberated in the service of God to take co-responsibility for the world.

7.

Jesus Christ is the man who has truly fulfilled the office of man in a changing world; the firstborn among many brothers (Rom. 8:29), the second Adam (Rom. 5:12ff.), the son of God, obedient unto death on the cross, in whom God Himself spoke when in dealing with man and world he totally conformed to the will of God for man and world. In him it has been ultimately revealed what God intends for man and the world: that he has intentions of peace! Therein Jesus as the Christ is the Lord of the world and of his congregation. Thus the congregation lives from the task to discern Christ as the Lord of the changing world. For this witnesses are sought who through their witness liberate men in the world for their God-given promising worldly service.

Hans Schmidt, Hamburg
November 1963

The World in Transformation

This expression, the truth of which is evident to sociology, political economy and common sense, presents a problem in theology. These very schematic notes, put together following the work of certain groups (especially in the Commission d'Action Chrétienne of the 12th Region of the Eglise Réformée de France) are concerned to raise questions rather than to provide the answers: in the process they take particular note of a remark of J. C. Hoekendijk to the effect that sound theology should not fear to flirt with heresy . . .

1. So-called orthodox theological thinking—equally within Protestantism—takes no notion of the contemporary transformation or chang-

ing of the world: the great acts of God, creation and redemption, have taken place and, for 2,000 years, sacred history is, as it were, in suspension awaiting the final act. God came into the world in Christ; he left the earth at the Ascension; "he ascended into heaven," says the Creed, whence "he will come again" for the Last Judgment and the commencement of his reign which has been postponed until then. Between the Ascension and the Parousia nothing real is taking place in the world; it is a period marked by an absence, by an emptiness which leaves a place only for an act of witness to the past event of the Son's incarnation and to the future event of his manifestation in glory. The work of Christ seems to be not so much the redemption and transformation of the world as the offer of salvation.

2. The main thing then is to put man into relationship with Christ. But once the hiddeness of Christ in the world is understood as his absence, everything goes on as if the main thing were to withdraw man from the realm of perdition, where the history of the world continues to take place, in order to enable him to enter the realm of eternity and salvation.

—According to Catholicism the Church is the essential link by the objective means of the sacraments whereby men and institutions must be baptized.

—According to Protestantism, the Bible alone occupies a mediating role through subjective means of a personal faith in sola scriptura, sola fide.

On all sides—despite declarations which allow God freedom, and because of a lack of doctrine of the Holy Spirit—Christ is only seen to act in the world today by these links of Church or Bible, of sacrament and faith, so that the institutions themselves become mediators, as guardians of the sacraments or the Book. The Church is not "a segment of the world" but a radically different element. Clericalism is the consequence and expression of this fact.

3. As far as Protestantism is concerned, its desire to purify and to set the Gospel free from the weight of history and of humanity which risks hiding or crushing it, has issued in bringing into play a dimension of faith which stretches directly from eternity to the present moment. This vertical dimension of faith, a giddy Jacob's ladder which leads each one to seek for God on his own little Sinai, is a short-cut by means of which human history is left on one side. So the Church in

its oversimplified concern to incarnate the biblical message, moment by moment, fixedly forgets where she came from and where she is going and rejects the history in which she starts. Congregationalism is by no means the least of the evils produced by this attitude.

Further, the fact of tying Christ exclusively to the Bible and to an eternity which is an absence from the world and from history, has made us incapable of recognizing him where he is active within the world today and to receive his call to join him, to incarnate him at that very place whither he has gone before us.

4. "All is accomplished." We have understood Jesus' saying at Golgatha as if he said: all is finished, ended; there is nothing left to take place when "tetelelestai" really means "everything has reached its fulfilment." This saying refers to and comprehends the world and its destiny. On the Cross, the salvation, for which Christ came, "is fulfilled," reaches its telos, and the whole creation is delivered from the fatality of evil: a promise of fulfilment is given to it. In order to be personal, salvation need not be anything less than universal and precedes anything I can say or do. After Jesus Christ, history, after a fashion, starts again in pursuit of its telos, but it is history with a dynamic, like a seed cast into the ground (Mk. 4), like yeast which a woman puts into three measure of flour (Mat. 13:33).

5. When yeast is put into dough, the whole lump becomes engaged in an immense activity, in a transformation. Jesus Christ is the yeast who has been put into the dough of the world. The Church is not the yeast. Henceforth the dough is worked by him. Because of that yeast, the world is in transformation: the destiny of the dough is now linked with that of the yeast. The movement of the world is history directed towards its end, the Kingdom already inaugurated in the world and acting in it because Christ is there. For the Ascension does not speak to us of the absence of Christ, but of the universality of his presence and of his still hidden reign.

6. Just as this presence of Christ remains hidden, an object of faith not sight, so the transformation of the world cannot be measured nor its continuity laid bare. We even lack the words to talk about it: whether we say progress, evolution, growth, maturation—all our words have overtones which make them suspect and thus inappropriate.

For we are dealing with a secret of which Jesus could only talk in parables: the world is living its history—which is positive—because of Jesus Christ.

7. The transformation of the world proceeds through the humiliation and death of Christ, through his incarnation. The Gospel makes the necessity of this clear by insisting on the indissoluble link between death and resurrection: "Now is the hour when the Son of Man must be glorified" (Jn. 12:23; 17:5; Mt. 16:21) If the seed does not die. . . . Right up to the Parousia, it is in the incognito of his humiliation that Christ is present and active in the world. It is by this poverty that we are enriched (2 Cor. 8:9).

8. The Church hereby is also dependent upon this presence, this action, as a "part of the world." She is distinguished from it by having been entrusted with God's secret, and with the mission of discerning the where and the how of the active presence of Christ at any time, in order to call it by its name where it is service given by non-Christians, and explicitly to announce Christ, his judgment and his grace, where he is struggling against the powers of sin, as in the past.

9. Thus the Church will resolutely participate in the world's history, always being aware of what she has learned: that the world's movement into the future and its transformation are not primarily to be seen as self-affirmation (whether of individuals, of nations or of churches), but as the humiliation of Jesus Christ incarnate, as a message and as a gift. Here one must take seriously the Christological hymn given in Phil. 2, not only in the sense of the Good News which is given to all men but also in the sense of a demand made on all who have received it. "Let your bearing towards one another arise out of your life in Christ Jesus. For the divine nature was his from the first; yet he did not think to snatch at equality with God, but made himself nothing, assuming the nature of a slave . . . . he humbled himself. . . . . Therefore God . . . . ."

It is these qualities (spiritual qualities, and therefore practical as well as intellectual ones) which St. Paul calls upon all Christians, and all congregations, to have. They must not be interested in acquiring privileges, but must be ready to take the form of a servant, so that God (and God alone) can manifest His glory among the men who recognise Christ as Lord. At the principal points of its change, at the critical moments of its development, the Church will stand, like her Lord, "available," vulnerable and hazarded. Thus she will both "be not conformed to this present age" and be best "present" in the world, standing beside the Christ she discerns and serves (Rom. 12:1,2).

10. For today, just as in the apostolic age, our job—whether as individuals or as institutions—is not only to invoke Jesus Christ, to call on him to come and meet us where we are. For rather it is our job in a world that is in change and crisis because of him, to "follow" him where he is, on the paths of his present mobile and diverse ministry.

The church must, on the one hand, learn to recognize in the world the Christ she knows from the Scriptures, and on the other go beside him at his pace, not more slowly nor yet faster.

Paul Keller, Grenoble
October, 1963

The World in the Setting of Historical Change and Eschatological Hope

1. From the biblical point of view the "world" appears primarily and almost exclusively in the context of the "sent" community. Because in Abraham "all the generations of the earth" are blessed (Gen. 12:3), those who come after him will share a unique experience of the world. As Christians are called to the sacrifice of their bodies (Rom. 12:1) and are obedient to this call, they encounter the world—the concrete world of Rome and Corinth, of Greeks and heathen. The experience of mission precedes experience of the world; the former is the basis of the latter.[1] The vitality of our communication with the world is determined by the vitality of our task.

This insight allows us to establish the following consequences:

a) The world as such (as an abstract or metaphysical entity) cannot be an object of theology of the missionary congregation.

[1]Theologically our experience of being commissioned precedes our experience of the world, but as a matter of concrete fact the process is more complicated. There is an intimate interaction between our worldly experiences and the experience of commissioning which, because it comes from the incarnate Christ, comes also from within the world, but from something recognized as authoritative also beyond the world. Our mature, critical understanding of our commission and of the world grows from this interaction, but at a mature level our commission is seen to be the basis of our approach to the world.

The object of theology is rather the relationship of Christians to the entire world, as we meet it in fact.

b) Therefore the secular sciences (e.g. sociology as well) are given the freedom, within their respective fields of inquiry, to examine their respective worlds and to make authoritative judgments about them. The results of such examination and judgment must be seen on one level of explanation which complements the theological statements and judgments of another level. Not that theology can presume to dictate to sociology, but that it must take up the findings of sociology—and vice versa. The theologian will therefore be concerned for the proper secularity both of sociology and of his own discipline.

2. Because Christians are called to mission, i.e., sent to specific men of a specific time, the experience of a changed and constantly changing world will not be strange to them. On the contrary, they are able to recognize and realize God's task only within the context of the concrete situation. The congregation, then must move and change in a changing world. It is precisely by rejecting a metaphysical understanding of the world and by affirming the mission to the world that Christians are able to be alert and present within the changes of their respective worlds. This is true in a twofold way:

a) By understanding the changed and changing world on the basis of faith. But as we understand our changed and changing world on the basis of faith we must make a complex response—e.g., first a Yes to what happens (dynamic society) because the world is created and sustained by God; then a No because it is in the grip of the evil one; then a more profound Yes again, because in spite of the evil the new creation is inaugurated. Every individual change is thus to be evaluated on the whole possible variety of levels of understanding.

b) By sharing actively and hopefully in the changes of an existing world (and thereby critically examining conservativism within the churches).

3. To understand the world on the basis of faith means to understand it on the basis of Jesus Christ. Missionary theology looks to the sending of Jesus. According to the New Testament the mission of the son of God produces a very specific kind of change. In the person of

Jesus the rule of God is present in power (Matt. 12:28). His word and deed bring unrest into the world (Mark 2:22; Matt. 13:33); they begin a movement, they introduce a new beginning in a dynamic way. The phrase *post Christum natum,* has more than a simply calendric significance.[2]

The New Testament sees the change instituted through Christ in a twofold way:

a) It is a change which has *already* taken place. "The old has passed away, the new is come" (2 Cor. 5:17). This fact finds expression in talk of the change of the eons, in baptism, in the indicative mood of the proclamation ("you are") etc.
b) It is a change which is *still* taking place. The salvation which has come in Christ has appeared fully, although not finally (Rom. 8:19 ff.; 1 John 3:2). It is open to the future. A characteristic expression of this fact is the word of promise, the imperative mood in early Christian preaching, etc.

4. The tension between "already" and "not yet" cannot be overcome dialectically; rather it must be understood historically (*geschichtlich*). The interim indicated by the "not yet" and "already" is the place of history.

a) The New Testament describes this "interim" realm as the *regnum Christi* (the realm of his Lordship). From the biblical point of view, history can be understood properly only in the perspective of the Lordship of Christ. Christ *is* the ruler of the world, in so far as the congregation (Church) already belongs to him as his body (1 Cor. 6:13)—that is in the "reality of its being world" (Kaesemann). And he *will* be the ruler of the world to the extent that the final "redemption of the body" (Rom. 8:23) has been promised to Christians and to all creation.
b) Christ's continuing seizure of this power to rule (against all principalities and powers) is the theological foundation of both future and history. The certainty that Christ is Lord today and tomorrow opens up the future and makes history possible. Because the Lordship of Christ is a defeat of the world's principalities and powers, this history has a worldly and world-wide di-

[2]All the same this movement must not be understood in an "enthusiastic" way. The coming of Christ introduces also a sharpening polemic and polarity between the role of Christ and the power of the "old world."

mension. The Lordship of Christ over the "whole body of the congregation" (Church) is not simply the Lordship over individuals. Consequently Christ's continuing seizure of the power to rule goes beyond the limits of an individualistic soteriology and reaches the realm of cosmology. This means that men *and* world are placed under the promise of a future hope. Consequently both man *and* world exist in the tension between changes which have already taken place and changes which have not yet taken place.

c) For the Bible, history can only be prophetic history. "See I am creating a new thing" (Isa. 43:19, cf. Acts 21:5). God works with the mystery of surprise. His saving activity is, of course, profoundly continuous, but it does not necessarily correspond to (divine) historical order. Thus man is deprived of the opportunity to construct schemes of history. On the other hand, he is given the freedom for an open and active encounter with change in the historical realm (which may be pointed out by sociology).[3]

5. There can be no doubt: the new thing which is the goal of change finds its centre in man. In Jesus a new human existence is revealed. According to the creed confessed in the congregation (Church) he is himself the new man (Rom. 5:12 ff.; 1 Cor. 15:22. 45 ff.). He is the new man in such a way that his existence has consequences for mankind (Rom. 5:15-19). The change which proceeds from Christ does not concern man as an abstraction but rather man in his worldly existence. This was already true for the Old Testament: for Israel, the history of the Covenant always involved God, man and the world. Thus the world, when seen in terms of the Bible, is basically a *human* world. It is the world of man which has been changed and set into movement through the Christ event.

This recognition must also be taken seriously in our view of past and present history. The revelation of the Gospel of Jesus Christ (Rom. 1:17) marks not only a decisive point but also a series of irreversible steps and an irresistible movement in human history. In fact this

[3]As the Christian looks back over history he may hope to be aware of at least signs of the continuity of God's action, but these can never at all simply become criteria for action in the present and towards the future. God's action in no way detracts from the freedom of men, but men are promised the gift of the Holy Spirit in their discriminating research for the best possible use of the range of choices that lie open to them.

revelation reveals God's purpose for man in general, beyond the limit of confessing Christians. The Christ event has consequences for all, for Jews and Greeks and Barbarians, for those true to the law and the heathen, for the circumcised and the uncircumcised (Rom. 1:14; 3:23-30). All are challenged to awake to consciousness of their responsibility (Rom. 1:21; 2:14 f. 28 f.). Actually, some will respond to the challenge; others will fail to, but even this failure is to be seen as a negative *response*. For none can avoid the command of the divine task which is encountered in history. Since the time of Christ, a humane structure has been given to the world. Christ has altered it for the better. The gift and power of the righteousness of God has released the Humane and introduced it into history in such a way that no historical consideration can overlook it.

The Church has been a primary agent of this, but no Christian understanding of human history must fail to take into account the profound dynamic interaction between the Church and its environment. Sometimes the Church has been the introducer of change towards the Humane; sometimes she has had it imposed on her from outside.

Moreover, the introduction of the Humane into history has led and is still leading history into an ever more universal reality. Less and less can any of us avoid the questions that are facing our fellowmen in other parts of the world; more and more we are learning that we have to face them together. This is not to say that as Christians we can detect *the* direction of history; it is to say that the assertion that history is moving in *a* direction is unavoidable.

To be sure, important questions arise here:

a) On the one hand the question of a quite new and Christian estimation of the process of secularisation, and

b) The concrete and pressing question concerning the relationship between responsibility for the world in science and technology on the one hand and "*missio Dei*," on the other, between *dominium terrae* and *regnum Christi*, etc.[4]

---

[4]Perhaps this relationship is to be worked out in terms of the different levels of mandate accepted by, say, the scientist, sociologist and theologian respectively (cf. the levels of explanation mentioned in 1.b.). Within the sent community all have their differing but complementary mandates. The question then becomes: Who composes this sent community? As for example many scientists who would not call themselves Christians nevertheless feel themselves entrusted with the same mandate as their Christian colleague professes on the basis of his faith.

6. We must speak more precisely about the renewal of human existence. According to Rom. 12:2 it concerns the personal centre of man: understanding, consciousness, critical sense. Renewal does not simply affect heart and soul. Thought is renewed. Changed is the faculty of understanding which plays a primary role in all affairs concerning the world. Thereby Christians are called into a highly active responsibility for the world. Seen from Christ, history is no longer a fateful process. Rather it is mediated through men, who, on the basis of their renewed understanding, are willing to reconsider the "good and acceptable and perfect" (Rom. 12:2). The world is changed through men. On the basis of their renewed minds, men are called to responsibility for the world.

This renewal of men's minds can be seen, e.g., in our changing awareness of the very process of change. Slowly we are evolving the tools of understanding that will permit us to understand dynamically our dynamic world.

Missionary theology must consider two problems:

a) A Christian task is present in cases which involve the proper use of the mind.

b) The missionary task must lead us to a new way of thinking and talking about man as he lives in the world. In mission we are not to talk about religion but about the concrete questions and facts of life in this world, thus demonstrating our eschatological existence. Only by insisting on talking about this world can we break through traditions and taboos which have been determined by other-worldly criteria.

From this point of view the question of past and present history must be re-examined. The Bible does so from the point of view of the revelation of divine wrath (Rom. 1:18 ff.). The new human existence can be lost. This is something worse than the simple fact of sinful human deeds. For the rising of the sun cannot be reversed. Even the evil world is to be understood as a world *post Christum natum*. It is not untouched by the basic movement which has been set loose by the Christ event. The awakening to responsibility before God is irrefragable. Any refusal to accept this responsibility can only be understood as guilt, or in history, as the result of wrath. Human advance is made under God's wrath. The Humane, the new human existence, is set forth into history. It cannot be undone, although it can be perverted. Inhumane powers will indeed infiltrate human structures and the face of the world will be changed for the worse. In a very real sense, the world has also become more evil and more dangerous, since Christ, the new man, gave himself to the whole world and established the sacrifice of his body as the content of the mission of his Church.

We may, therefore, never underestimate the hold of evil. However preoccupied we become in the worldly tasks to which our commission leads, we must be alert to the possibility, indeed almost the inevitability of failure. Our assurance of final victory is no more than a promise towards which we can at times only submit in resigned but hopeful adoration. Our helpless "Thy will be done" is a permanent moment in all missionary activity.

7. Thus the task of Christians is the world—the concrete, historical world. Their task is determined and constantly renewed in a loving and serving dialogue with the world. In this world, be it light or dark, they are met by the Lord who redeems both of them, the church as well as the world, and who allows both of them to move (and be changed) under his promise.

Thus sent and directed into the future, the church cannot set itself over against the world. In so far as it allows itself to be changed first of all (through the renewal of its human existence, Rom. 12:2), it precedes humanity. It anticipates the meaning of human existence (this is its eschatological existence!). This head start is its distance from the world. With respect to human existence its lack is no less than that of its brethren in the world. Its task is even greater, because it involves a deeper concern for the Humane which is based upon eschatological love. Therefore the Church does not address the world from above or as an opponent but rather from ahead. It points out that the Lordship of Christ is not yet completed. His Lordship is dynamic and gives the Church courage to expect great things from Christ's power. Therewith it represents a dynamic element in human history. If we were to describe its situation in theological terms we would call it a "dynamic society"—in so far as its task is renewed by the power of the Holy Spirit within its concrete time and world.

But the church has a head start only in loving and serving. For only through love and service does it witness to the Lordship of Christ in the interim between "already" and "not yet." Love and service prepare us to enter into existing situations. Thus the *missio Dei* (Mission of

God) leads the congregation (Church) to be alive and present within good and not so good social structures. It will improve good structures and purify the not so good. It will incorporate all of them into the structure of the Humane by bringing the world to its true dimensions, by demythologizing and desacralizing it, by understanding it simply as a human world and by living in it as the "avant garde" of its contemporaries.

Thus Christian life in the changed world always takes place through the active transformation of what already exists. The congregation is called by its Lord to exist concretely and historically in the world. It bears witness to its "head start" through the courage by which it—lovingly and hopefully—enters the social structures of its time, renewing them boldly through its renewed (eschatological) life.

However, the Church can only be encouraged to such (daring) action if it assumes the form of a brotherhood and comes to know through brotherly encouragement those definite promises under which it must move (and change) in the changing world.

Western European Working Group
September, 1963

Sociological Comments on the Theme "World–History–Eschatology"

1.

In terms of contemporary thought the question indicated by the title "World-History-Eschatology" emerges primarily against the background of the experience of secularisation. When we raise the question of the "world"—perhaps even of the "adult world" (world come of age)—and when we ask about the place of this "world" in history and the continuity of God's action in history, our interest is immediately focussed on how we can experience God's action in history in a world which we presuppose to be "secularised."

We must take into account what we mean by this question of the "world." If we fail to do this, a specific (contemporary) situation will immediately run up against the biblical concept of the world; from the very beginning we will have eliminated that basic element concerning which we are seeking information: God's action in history. Abstract chronological classifications ("post-Christian age" and in social ethics "the personal age"), the phenomenon of "structural fundamentalism" and the misunderstanding that missionary activity takes place in a movement from "the" Church to "the" world—these attitudes are the result of a thinking which seeks to avoid (the perception of) God's action in history.

2.

A further misunderstanding must also be avoided: it is not so much a question whether the fact of secularisation is to be evaluated positively or negatively, whether it is to be seen as a movement away from Christianity or as its natural and legitimate consequence. As long as both attitudes are related to the same understanding of the problem (of secularisation), the clarification of secularisation will only be hindered. At best a positive judgment can aid in doing away with certain prejudices with regard to the understanding of the problem. (Herein lies the limited function of contemporary theological ethics.) But to understand this problem is precisely what we are seeking (and this is one of the foremost tasks in our study). In the terms of our study, we are limiting the problem to that dimension of the "world" which encounters us as "society." The phrasing of the problem then becomes: are we to understand the secularisation of "society" as an *emigration* of the church and of Christianity from society, i.e., as a process whose result is an opposition between a self-sufficient society and a church which has been forced out of this society? If we answer this question affirmatively, and place it in the context of the biblical attitude to the "world," we find a remarkable transformation of the tension contained in the New Testament understanding of "world." Out of the tension between "Church" and "world" which belongs to every age, we have created an epochal tension between two isolated entities, "Church" and "society" (as a dimension of the "world"). In the terms of this thinking, God's action in our present history is broken down into two sectors, the responsibility for which is then handed over to the missionary activity of the *institutional* church, i.e., to human activity. (How far is this way of thinking "heretical?")

3.

At first sight there are numerous concrete observations which seem to justify this thesis of the emigration of the Church from society. The "femininity" of congregational life and the disproportionate percentage of older people and of specific social classes in congregational life seem to prove that the Church lives its life outside the main stream of society. *Hans-Otto Wölber* (Religion ohne Entscheidung, Göttingen 1959) speaks of the church's "marriage with the disintegrated elements of society." *Reinhard Köster* (Die Kirchentreuen, Hamburg 1959) says that the church today has established a "confirmation of its own value" which is "independent of the norms of modern society." Such statements are not false. But if we take them as *general* theses and if we understand them simply as proof of the secularisation (Entkirchlichung) of society, we will then necessarily raise the question of the causes of this fact (of secularisation) and thereby descend rapidly into the realm of over-generalisation. *Mary-Ann Thung* (Sociologische opmerkingen bij het begrip 'functie van de kerk,' in: Sociologisch Bulletin, 1956, p. 2 ff.) indicates as a meaningless generality the thesis that industrialisation is the cause of this fact. *Norman Birnbaum* (Säkularisation, in: Monatsschrift für Pastoraltheologie, 1959, Vol. 3, p. 68 ff.) proves, on the basis of extensive material, that urbanisation is in no way the unique cause of secularisation (Entkirchlichung) and that the alternative—rural area equals churchly, urban area equals unchurchly—is false. The concrete observations, which seem to confirm the thesis of the social emigration of the Church, are only partially valid. In this sense they offer only a part of the missionary task; as such they say nothing about the epochal secularisation of society.

4.

These insights compel us to formulate a comprehensive revision of the thesis about secularisation and its related understanding of the polarity between church and society (as a dimension of the "world"). From the point of view of sociology, two further steps are needed:

a) the definition of secularisation must be seen in the context of the total process of social differentiation and emancipation;

b) we need a sociological criticism of that kind of theology (and that kind of church-awareness) which does not interpret this process (cf. a. above) as such but which relegates it to an epochal polarity between a secularised ("unchurched") society and an "unsecularised" (entgesellschaftete = de-socialized) church.

To a)

The recent process of comprehensive differentiation in social life has brought forth both the phenomenon of the independence of social forms, processes and relations as well as a highly complex inter-relation of these factors. In connection with this process, far-reaching functional changes have taken place which have concerned the church itself, as an historical-social constitution. A whole series of social functions which belonged to the church in pre-industrial society have been taken over by other institutions (cf. J. P. Kruijt, De onkerkelijkheid in Nederland, Groningen 1933). To describe this *change* of function as a *loss* of function, however, is to grasp only one side of the problem, even though it may be the side which strikes us most immediately. The other side of the problem is that this loss of function corresponds to a significant *increase* of functions, which has not yet been acknowledged sufficiently. (Here we might think of the role of the churches in the public and social life of many Westeuropean nations, or of the influence of the Roman Catholic church in world politics, or of the role of various Christian groups in the political life of the U.S.A.) In addition, numerous institutions and groupings have developed and are continually developing (new forms of church work such as academies, social work, etc.) which are transmitting the impulse of the Christian faith to the many sub-divisions of social life. All of this must be kept in mind when we speak of secularisation (Entkirchlichung = de-churchification); and it must be kept in mind that all of this is possible only because there is a "Christian core" in modern society from which all of these concerns can be derived. The complexity (and thus also the partiality and ambiguity) of this core merely corresponds to the incompleteness of the world and is no argument for the thesis of the social decay of the Church and Christianity.

To b)

The paradoxical structure of emancipation and dependency which is found in modern society and which emerges constantly as a problem in our action and consciousness, makes possible the development of an emancipated self-awareness whose own dependence on historical-social processes remains hidden. A sociological criticism of the polarity between Church and society in theology (and church consciousness) must begin with the fact that the "unsecularised" (entgesellschaftete = de-socialised) church possesses an unhistorical self-awareness. This self-awareness produces a fatal consequence for the starting-point of mission: A church which understands its change of social function as a *loss* or as its emigration from society, orients itself to its supposed "pure" structure and supposes that it can undertake its mission to a secularised (entkirchlichte) society on the basis of this structure. In so doing it necessarily overlooks the core which it possesses in society and thus undertakes its mission in a void.

5.

In a somewhat exaggerated form, the following statements can be made:

a) Secularisation is nothing other than an aspect of the historical-social processes of differentiation. This aspect assumes unrealistic proportions when an interpretation of it does not pay sufficient attention to the complexity of the differentiations. In this sense there is also a secularisation of atheistic ideologies.

b) The collapse of the *corpus Christianum* is—sociologically—the transition from a comprehensive system of political, cultural and social control within a relatively stable society to a differentiation of political, cultural and social functions (and controls) within a pluriform and constantly changing society.

c) Under the conditions of social differentiation, the continuity of of God's action in history is difficult to represent. However, this says nothing about a loss of such a continuity (which had to be compensated for by an even more urgent missionary activity!); it merely raises the question of the adequacy of supposing that the continuity of God's action in history can best be conceived in a system of social control which is dominated by the church. This presupposition has become questionable in our new situation. But it has undoubtedly been an historical possibility in the past.

6.

The question concerning "Church" and "society" (as a dimension of the "world") should not be prejudiced on the basis of their contemporary confrontation—as if this were a definition of the structural problem. The Church and Christianity—in an eschatological perspective—have always been in harmony with society as concerns God's action in history. This fact is true empirically, provided that the horizon of empirical observation is wide enough. All thought about the "confrontation" of Church and society can have no more than a hypothetical character and should not be accepted as a statement about the problem itself. The present crisis of the parish system has placed the church in solidarity with every form of social activity which sees its goals in either a local context or an overall social perspective. The limited functions which the parish still performs today (cf. *Wölber, Köster*) are as such not signs of secularisation (Entkirchlichung); they are concrete social functions of which we cannot simply say that they are not appropriate to the church. The fact that the parish performs different functions in a city and in a rural congregation (*Greinacher*) corresponds to the social differentiation of modern urban society. The fact the "Volkskirche" can perform only a limited number of functions (baptism, confirmation, weddings, Sunday morning worship services) corresponds to the differentiation of the society in which it lives. The fact that large church organizations can exert considerable influence in social development corresponds to the social need of an organizational unification of individual goals. The fact that the church again and again hands over elements of its social functions (welfare service) to society does not indicate secularisation but rather the shaping of society by a Christian core.

7.

Therefore the question of the missionary structure of the congregation should not be understood as an epochal question concerning the fate of a secularised society. It can only be understood and answered in terms of concrete contexts. This does *not* mean that larger perspectives are to be ignored: the thesis is precisely that an unprejudiced consideration of concrete social problems is possible only against the background of a comprehensive—and eschatologically determined—understanding of history. *Neither* does it mean that *concrete* contexts must always be identical with locally limited and surveyable contexts. (e.g., structures of a congregation, of a "Landeskirche" etc.) It is much more a question of quite concrete contexts which are extensive both in time and space (and thus perhaps are *unsurveyable,* although nonetheless concrete, e.g., the idea of a "Volkskirche," religious pluralism, etc.).

P.S.:

From my point of view, a decisive question concerning the participation of sociologists in our study is the extent to which the theologians demonstrate an understanding for empirical thinking. This empirical thinking is bound to concrete facts and does not use them simply as proofs for all-encompassing theses; in other words, its intention is to proceed to theory on the basis of empirical analysis. Is it not so that theology—on the basis of a pre-supposition of "polarity" (between church and society)—is inclined to accept empirical statements in the latter but not the original sense?

Joachim Matthes
Dortmund, September 1963

An Interpretation of Secularisation

Secularisation may be given three definitions:

1. The term secularisation usually refers to the historical process starting with the Enlightenment and developing in various stages up to the present. The term was first used at the political level to describe the change in the relations between State and Church. Today we understand secularisation sociologically as a continuing process of social *differentiation* by which also the problem of social *integration* is posed in a special way.

2. Secularisation may also be defined as secularism, meaning a psychological climate which can, perhaps, best be described in terms of a "pure" type. It must be acknowledged that this is an abstraction, in which many features are combined that in actuality are never found all together in one person. We therefore define "secularised" man, in contrast to "religious" man, as follows:

Man, who in *thinking* does not operate with the hypothesis of an Almighty God, who in *action* is certainly guided by humanitarian values, but makes choices on a utilitarian basis in an autonomous way;

who has no religious *feelings* (awe for the sacred, fear for supernatural powers, feelings of sin) or, if he has them, questions and distrusts them.

As far as this man's social conditioning and relationships are concerned (which touch all the three above-mentioned levels) he is not under the control or influence of any church body or religious group.

In reality this pure type is hardly ever fully realized. Consequently there are many non-secular phenomena in our present cultural climate; in *thinking* many people have question marks and while arriving sometimes at a kind of agnosticism, occasionally return to the hypothesis of an Almighty God; in *action* many inherited Christian values are effective; in *feeling* there are many moments of fear and sensations of sin.

It is especially in the marginal situations (in the face of suffering and death) or at the climaxes of life (birth, marriage, achievement of some goal, etc.) that such reactions reappear. They appear, however, mostly in the context of private life and have hardly any bearing on public life. There is a measure (retained or recovered) of social control by church bodies or religious groups (social service organisations, churches, confessional religious parties), the effect of which is the presence of some non-secular elements in public life also.

3. Secularisation may also be understood as sharing in society on an equal basis. In this sense the church is seen as refusing to contract out of the world. Thus understood, secularisation is best defined as identification. The secularisation of the Church is then its identification with the world, even as the son of God identified himself with man.

The different types of secularisation, distinguished in the preceding paragraphs, must not be seen as totally distinct. There is an interrelation and an interplay between them. Sometimes they are interrelated as cause and effect, e.g., the change or loss of function has affected the psychological climate; conversely the psychological climate has issued in a loss of function. A change of consciousness within secularism leading to an awareness of God would immediately have its effect in the realm of differentiation. Nevertheless, while the several types of secularisation are closely connected, it will simplify the task of interpretation if they are kept apart and the attempt is made to evaluate or rather to interpret each.

I. *Sociological Differentiation*

1. The sociological interpretation of secularisation (under the aspect of differentiation and interpretation) should be seen in close connection with the political-historical view. The new situation between Church and State in terms of law was but a first expression of the general process of social differentiation. This process should not only be seen under the aspects of division of labour, or of separation of work and habitation, though these aspects are, of course, constitutive for it. Differentiation means—in general—a continuing specialisation of social conduct, social groups, social institutions and social interests, and, at the same time, a highly complex interrelation of these factors *because of* their specialised character. This process of differentiation also affects the system of values and norms a society represents (pluralism of values) and the life of the individual (man playing various social roles). Thus, differentiation involves the problem of integration: the highly complex interrelation of all social actions and institutions and the pluralism of emancipated values and interests makes it difficult to keep society in a stage of balance, and to prevent its disintegration. Under these conditions integration can no longer be described as a stage that can be once reached and kept (e.g., by an assured and stable set of common values and common patterns of behavior), but it must be understood as a steady process that demands a *continuous* reorientation of social conduct and institutions. On the other hand, integration as a process also demands a certain centralisation and concentration of social organisations as elements of continuity in constant social change. A special aspect of the interplay between social differentiation and integration is the constant shifting of functions, which social groups and institutions fulfil: quite often certain *manifest* (declared and intended) functions of a group degenerate into a mode of self-understanding, the only real function of which is the self-preservation of the group. On the other hand, a social group or institution may fulfil *latent* functions which are not at all included in its self-understanding or intention.

2. In its general sense the term secularisation may sociologically also be applied to societies undergoing the process of social differentiation without standing in a Christian tradition but having once been dominated by a comprehensive system of values and beliefs of an ideological kind. (The recent developments in the USSR and the East-

ern bloc as a whole may within certain limits be taken as an example.) But it should be considered that the historical context, in which secularisation has its origin, is that of Western Christian culture without which even the recent developments in the Communist countries cannot be understood adequately. Leaving this historical aspect aside, the following aspects characterise the present situation in Western Europe:

3. In the course of secularisation (understood as differentiation) certain institutionalised forms of behavior have developed that are specialised as *churchly* functions among the pluralism of other social functions. Naturally those elements of church life proved to be most effective in a context that is general enough to reach potentially a maximum number of people regardless of the differences between them in respect of other dimensions of social life (status, class, etc.): baptism, confirmation, wedding, Sunday morning worship service, etc. The parochial system, formerly in correspondence with the social life of a more or less self-subsistent community as a whole, developed into an organisational frame-work of the patterns of social behaviour now specialised as churchly ones.

4. The churches went the way of becoming a social system among others, but related with other social systems and realms of social conduct merely by the scarce elements specified above. This experience resulted in the thesis of secularisation understood as a process of de-churching and—by interpreting the church (as a social system among others) as the nucleus of Christianity (Christendom)—as de-Christianisation.

Many new forms of church-life, especially those arising in the second half of the 19th century, but also those springing up after World War II, were soon integrated in this church-system: they were simply understood as adding new elements to the traditional set of patterns specialised as churchly among the pluralism of other social patterns.

5. This process has, under the conditions of social differentiation, a certain degree of inevitability. In respect to mission it means that missionary actions, started on the basis of the understanding of church as a social system among others, tend to lead to the establishment of new specialised church groups, possibly selecting various social categories of people, but soon finding themselves confronted with problems of interrelation to other groups and dimensions of social life. The demand for "open" church-groups easily leads into misunderstandings:

a group is defined by realising a certain distinctiveness and a certain degree of being "closed." The setting up of such new groups in reference to special functional categories (vocational, professional, etc.) may nevertheless be considered as a legitimate function of missionary action. But for the whole of the missionary structure of the congregation three further aspects should be considered:

a) the plurality of church groups cannot be pressed into an obligatory set of special forms of "churchly" behaviour without provoking a reduction of the missionary realm of the Church.
b) Certain far-reaching organisational structures of the Church are necessary to keep the continuity of church life. This includes the maintenance of certain standards of churchly conduct accessible to many people regardless of their social distinctions, though it is inevitable that always only a minority of Christians will participate in these standards regularly.
c) The correspondence between plurality and unity (problem of integration) can be established structurally only if theological thought is ready to open its mind to the complexity of social differentiation and to acknowledge a broad variety of churchly behaviour in terms of theology.

II. *Secularism*

1. The problem before the churches confronted by secularism is whether they are to revitalise an awareness of God exclusively on the basis of the non-secular elements in society and find structures in which they can bring them together, focus and strengthen them anew—or whether they are also to take account of the fact that this secularisation lies at the basis of the whole of Western society as it exists at present. In the first case, they will sometimes reach the point of trying to reverse in part the course of secular history—which may be a legitimate and valid conclusion of theological reflection. In the second case they may arrive at a point where they will have to discover a new awareness of God, that is not necessarily contradictory to the way of thinking, acting and feeling described above. The organisational problem will then be to find structures where this awareness can be awakened through close collaboration and discussion with those who are seeking truth and meaning within the context of this secular cultural climate. There might be more opportunities of encounter and more forms of

collaboration in service than in merely assembling so-called religious people.

2. The problems of reaching a new awareness of God, using the previously mentioned categories of secular thinking, or of practising obedience without acting on the basis of inherited Christian values are already being investigated. The problems of meeting God outside the sphere of the previously mentioned religious feelings has not been sufficiently clarified or examined, and in connection with this the whole question of worship needs to be considered.

III. *Identification*

In seeking to evaluate secularisation as identification, the attempt must be made to bear in mind the fact of social differentiation and, in terms of theology, to acknowledge a broad variety of behaviour. A survey of some of the main points raised, which is at the same time a definition of identification, may be given as follows:

1. Since the Church is "a segment of the world," so that one can say there is "a fundamental unity between the Church and the world" (Casalis), then, the Church must commit itself to the world as "God's own history with man and the world" (Schmidt). The Church must therefore accept "the form of the Messianic life (election—witness—service—self-identification—suffering)" (Hoekendijk). This means "that we recognize honestly and completely, without any ulterior motive, the existence of the world with all its own principles of movement, hopes and possibility . . . and identify ourselves fully with the things and the people of the world" (R. G. Smith quoted by Hoekendijk). In the words of the report of the Theological Commission on Christ and the Church (North American Section) page 24: "the Church is necessarily in, as well as with and for the world . . . the Church stands in and with the world by its mission, by its taking the world to itself as the object of its love and concern, by identifying itself with the world as Christ identified himself with sinful humanity . . . the Church's life before God is not a life for itself but for the world." This is what Bonhoeffer called "being there for others."

2. While this identification, in strict accord with the Christological analogy, will necessarily involve a *kenosis,* it has to be recognised that just as this self-emptying or self-limitation of Christ did not mean that he ceased to be what he was, while he was identified with man he was

still distinct from him, so the Church's *kenosis* does not mean that she ceases to be or that she is merely merged into the world. "There can be no distinctive witness where there is no distinctive life" (Theological Reflections on the Work of Evangelism, p. 18). It is not "the business of the Church to become a social welfare organisation" (R. H. Fuller, The Place of Bonhoeffer, p. 179). Rather the Church is to live within the world as the "avant-garde" of its contemporaries (Vogt). It is the first fruits of the whole creation. It should further be recognized that *kenosis* of itself may achieve nothing; *kenosis* must be directed to an end; in the context of Phil. 2 the *kenosis* was for the sake of unity; in the context of today the *kenosis* of the Church must also be directed towards unity, of world and Church that both may be at one in God.

3. Since the essential life of the Church lies in the area of awareness of God and of one's neighbour, this must overflow into the service of Christ in one's neighbour, into recognizing Christ in the world. In relation to her own faithful members the Church must help them to answer their questions "how is God calling us to be obedient within the world in which we live and from which we cannot, nor should not, seek to detach ourselves?". There is perhaps a lesson to be learned here from both the success and failure of the priest workers.

What then does this mean in terms of structures? It means

a) a reformation of those structures that fence off the Church from the world and make her an inward looking cultic community;
b) that while the Church must have structures open to the world she must also keep open her lines of communication with him who is both her Lord and Lord of the world;
c) "that we devise missionary structures inductively, close and relevant to the human situation and therefore in a contextual rather than an absolutistic fashion" (Hoekendijk).

These points pose two problems:

1) Is it possible to have structures that are at the same time both distinctive and open?
2) If the church is to seek to identify herself with and not to dominate the world, how can Christian belief express itself within the context of secularisation, in its first sense as social differentiation?

Western European Working Group, Villemétrie
September, 1963

Concerning the Mission of the Church in a Changing World

Introduction: The Contemporary Situation and its Problems.

Alfred Delp, a Jesuit who was arrested after the 20th of July, 1944, and executed on February 2, 1945, wrote during his arrest: "The historically developed structure of the churches seems to block their own way. I believe that current historical events will hit us like a judging and destroying lightening unless we do not divest ourselves from the way of life of the present church. This is true for the personal life of the individual church member as well as for the institutions and customs. In spite of all the correctness and orthodoxy we have arrived at dead center . . . Most people in the church and the official church itself are bound to realize that for most people in the present, the church is not only a misunderstood and unrecognizable reality, but it is, in many respects, a disquieting and even threatening fact."—What can be done? What is necessary?—"The hard and honest realization of how we got to this point, not reflecting on the guilt of the others. Furthermore, the old question, what would result for the structure of the church. A sober realization that today the church does not belong among the leading forces of humanity. The church has to understand itself much more as a way and an instrument, not as a goal and an end. Personal renewal is more important today than a comprehensive statement of theology." (*Im Angesicht des Todes,* Freiburg, 1958, p. 104 f.)

In the meantime the danger has not lessened that the church is being forced into an exodus from society as a result of the differentiation of society (see J. Matthes, *Die Emigration der Kirche aus der Gesellschaft,* Hamburg, 1954). Also, theology, driven by a false confessionalism and concealed self-centredness, does not take up the challenge and the struggle of the world as experienced today but creates its own independent world by renewing confessional statements and structures.

What are the realities from which the church and theology live and act? Have they not been worked out, first of all, within the context of the culture and the civilization of the late antiquity which, meanwhile, has become outdated? Are church and theology (including the tradition and the structures of thought) not in danger today of becoming a sign of a past social order and a relic of an outdated scientific view? Unless they are in a vital contact with the questions and tasks of our time they will lose the authority of their mission. They have to seek anew their tasks in the midst of change. A preservation of the continuing mission is possible only in an obedient acceptance of that which confronts us. The church together with the world, is placed in the midst of change. A reflection upon this continuing change of the world, however, produces a fundamental change of what thus far has been understood with reference to church and theology.

I. *The Changing World*

Ever since human memory existed, the world has been full of stories which are always our stories; and yet only for the last 250 years has "the world as history" become, slowly but surely, one of our greatest and most difficult problems. Until the 17th century, the world lived within the comfortable horizon of a closed, measured and ordered world view and a controllable understanding of history. But with the new discoveries came the breakdown. The structure of the world could no longer be thought of as a temporary reflection of an eternal original. Rather, it was experienced as transition within the continuous flow of events. Nothing could be anymore taken for granted. Everything was in change. The mythological clarity of comprehensive views of the essence of things had been deceptive. Their given structure could be destroyed by an analysis and new constructions could force their way. Knowledge became a matter of ability. Man discovered himself as the steward of an open world, which thereby became the concern of worldwide and world-moving conversations. The critique of the world no longer aimed for a metaphysical understanding of the world. The earth was no longer taken to be the valley in which human misery had to be submissively endured, but it was now recognized as the wide field on which man could and should satisfy his needs.

Already Francis Bacon (1561-1626) has deduced from this development the equation of knowledge and power. The systematic conquest of the world by a scientific-technological community is indicated. The divine geometry of the world of Pythagoraic-Platonic origin, became an independent science in the form of mathematical physics. Man's thought became an end in itself. The world no longer was understood in analogy to the divine *logos*, but according to human reasons. Ancient piety, once christianized, was replaced by a modern understanding of the world. The world was no longer an order of divine creation and preservation, final and everlasting. It became the field for the development of unheard-of possibilities. The *gubernatio mundi* was replaced by the *transformatio mundi.* Nature was to become the raw material for the achievement of daring human programs. The development of science and technology shook and transformed the social structures and led to political upheaval which caused the breakdown of the universal-synthetic systems of the Ancient Western tradition, its combines of thought, of its social structures and commitments.

The empire was being dissolved. The "last" day which was expected at its end did not arrive. Metternich, the leading figure of the Vienna Congress in 1814-15, noted in his papers "in my most secret thoughts I believe that the old Europe is at the beginning of its end. I have decided to fall with it—knowing that I have done my duty. But the new Europe is yet to come. Between the end and the beginning there will be chaos." The century of crisis had begun. The structure of the old world was being dissolved. Franz Baader warned in 1818 in a study about the concept of time that "the Divine Word is the principle of all true evolution, and it assists it everywhere; every revolution (that is, a revolution in which social power is gained by usurpation) is to be understood as a consequence of a lack of evolution or of opposition to evolution."

In any event, the world was in need of much more far-reaching conversations than those which took place in the context of the Vienna Congress and in connection with the Holy Alliance.

Men were dismissed from the sacred order which sustained and restrained them. They were sent into the open history of their tremendous world-freedom and world-responsibility. The translatio Imperii was replaced by a race for the domination of the world and a concomitant race of world views, in which we are still engaged today. And what about church and theology? They were in danger of remaining, in spite of the broken horizon, within the world of the Ancient Western order. The discrepancy between the structure of tradition, bound to its origin, and the situation of a scientific-technological community, threatens to develop into mutual alienation of church and society. More and more, church and theology block their own way through their forms and their structures. For the forms and formulations which represented its task earlier (the formation of the confessions, the ordering of the church, piety and customs) are in a crisis because of the changing world, a crisis whose extent is still underestimated today and necessitates a basic review of history. (Cf. Hans von Soden, *Die Krisis der Kirche,* in: Urchristentum und Geschichte I, p. 25 ff., Tübingen 1951).

II. *The Crisis of the Church*

We are today in the midst of a far-reaching crisis regarding our relation to the world which dates back in time, and which calls into question church and theology and its ancient Western roots. It is not accidental that the Marcionite temptation which threatened the church at the end of the apostolic age again becomes a threat at the end of the Constantinian age.

The problems raised by Gnosticism have still not been fully answered and the fundamental decisions of the church in the anti-gnostic battles of the 2nd-4th centuries have anew become questionable.

The controversy over the gnostic other-worldliness led to a fundamental combination of the Israelite-Christian expectation of salvation with the Greaeco-Roman interpretation of the world and its administration; a combination of apostolic mission and catholic constitution.

The culture and society of late Antiquity was sanctioned and endowed with authority by the church. Culture and society were defined by Stoicism and Stoic popular philosophy as *the* rational and *the* natural society. It was sanctioned as the order of the world built by God and as such it seemed almost unassailable.

The church's view of redemptive history was combined with the idea that the existing order of things was also the ultimate order, and therefore, historically the final order; that it represented the best realization of the original order of creation under the conditions of a fallen creation, be it as a punishment for the fall, be it as a redemptive and educational means for fallen, sinful man.

The eschatological tension, given with the presence of the coming (Christ), was solidified into a conservative sanction of the present which had no longer its center in the coming but in an other-worldly complementation.

The problem and tension inherent from the beginning in this cultural synthesis can be indicated in four ways:

1) The idea of an order of redemption did not correspond to an ongoing historical development. The sanctioning and sacralization of the secular was inevitably followed by the constantly widening secularization of culture and society. Even in the Middle Ages, it had already led to far-reaching de-Catholization of culture and a retreat of the church to the reserved area of the guiding of souls and the taxation of souls (H. von Soden).

   Duns Scotus (ca. 1270-1308), one of the sharpest critics, examined at the turning point of the ages all the intellectual models and solutions of his predecessors. On the basis of worldly knowledge, he rejected the Platonic-Augustinian doctrine of illumination insisting that knowledge of the natural order had to proceed solely from sense perception, while admitting that the order of salvation represented a trans-rational, although not an antirational truth. The tension in the combination of fear of God and natural law sharpened a dialectic between a natural view of the world and a supernatural expectation of salvation. The questionable double standard of a positivistic view of world and science on the one hand, and of theological positivism on the other hand was already in the making.

2) The equation of an apostolic world mission and catholic world church could never be fully drawn. It led the world mission of the church of Jesus Christ to come to rest prematurely in a world of the church. It posed a double threat—the church became world as an institution of salvation with absolute power, and the world became church in the sense of a general sacred order. The eschatological tension between man and world (church and society as an *event*) was replaced by a hierarchical-ontological differentiation of all things (church and society as two *realms*).

3) Theology took over the concept of eternity, which Plato had used for the ideas. He had defined eternity as timelessness, as the ever-being. The Platonic axiom of the absolute unchangeability came to dominate in theology and church. The idea of God *becoming* man had to retreat in favor of the doctrine of the *assumption* of human nature by the *logos* (which was now conceived along the line of *Philo*), for the *becoming* of man would indicate change and transformation. The eschatological Christ event was now understood as the epiphany of his eternal presence.

Within this structure of thought, how was it possible to think of the kingdom of God opened up in Christ which aimed at all areas of life, and which placed man and the world in a situation of change? Here emerges an objective dilemma of the ancient church of which only today we seem to have become fully conscious. (Compare W. Elert, *Der Ausgang der altkirchlichen Christologie*, Berlin, 1957, p. 26 ff: Das Problem des politischen Christus).

4) A split developed in christological thought of the Ancient Church beginning with Nicea or with Constantine, depending upon whether one looks at it from the point of view of the history of dogma, or of the political and church developments. And it is not accidental that those viewpoints coincide here.

"Following the controversy about the Nicean Homoousios (that is about the incarnate Christ) theological thought concentrated definitely on the incarnate, earthly Christ, in order to provide criteria for human nature but also for the divine nature. Simultaneously, however, there arises a political christology which, too, derives its criteria no longer from the pre-existent Christ, but neither from the earthly Christ of the Gospels, but from the post-incarnate, the exalted, the heavenly Christ in power and glory. When Eusebius maintains that the Son of God had helped Constantine in the victorious battle against Licinius, he was referring to this heavenly Christ. He is the same, the great God and redeemer, Jesus Christ, whose name later prefaces the novels of Justinian and in whose name again, a hundred years later, Heraklius defeats the Persians at Ninive." (Elert, p. 31).

J. A. Quenstedt, the leading spokesman of Lutheran orthodoxy, once more pursued a Western theology. Even at the end of the 17th century he affirmed this liaison of state and faith which had been effective since the time Constantini Magni primi Christiani Imperatoris down to the military ventures of his Saxonian princes against the Turks as they arrived before Vienna.

Later the imperial claim of this "political Christ" was rightly disputed. This led many simply to reject this questionable idea of the "political Christ," and retreat to the "dogmatic Christ." But what about the biblical Jesus Christ with reference to the Kingdom of God which he represents? (See the remarks by Markus Barth: Minutes North American Preparatory Group, Warwick, 1963, CONCEPT, July 1963, p. 6. Also E. Kaesemann, *Gottesgerechtigkeit bei Paulus*, ZThK

1961, p. 367 ff.) And what is the relationship between the world mission of the church and the responsibility for the world of society, between *regnum Christi* and *dominium terrae?* The experience of the world within the context of a scientific-technological community was bound to raise questions for church and theology which had found its decisive shape within the context of a world view and a world order of late Antiquity.

In view of this crisis, it is eminently significant to remind ourselves of the dramatic efforts which, from the beginning of Christianity, (compare Romans 12 f.) were designed to sustain a correct interpretation and an adequate affirmation of political and Christian existence. Augustine, with his differentiation and coordination of *civitas terrena* and *civitas celestis,* was concerned about the correct distinction and coordination of church and world.

At the height of the Investiture controversy, the young European science developed a conceptual distinction between spiritual and worldly which, however, could not be made in practice, although the Ancient world order was already outdated (identity of Empire and church, be it in the form of an imperial church, of an independent church, or of a church-state). Thus the Concordat of Worms of 1122 was an unsatisfactory compromise. In the 13th century, the century of Frederick II and of Thomas Aquinas, Ptoleme of Lucca affirmed that since the beginning of the world the praise of God, science, and the power of the state, had accompanied each other. But it is precisely this Western synthesis of state, science, and fear of God which remains a contradictory synthesis of culture. Its renewal and fulfillment through Thomas of Aquinas was only apparent and presaged its final collapse.

Finally, Luther with his doctrine of the two kingdoms sought to answer the problems of the right orientation of the Christian in the world, and with it the question of the right relationship of apostolic world mission on the one hand (the Christ person) and the responsibility for the world in work and vocation on the other hand. For him, the political office and the office of the proclamation of the gospel, the worldly and the spiritual office, were both rooted in the double lordship of the One God. God preserves and redeems through the force of justice (the law), and through the weak word (Gospel), both being forms of love. Luther's testimony of God's action in the world for the sake of its salvation represents a break with the ontological structure of the Ancient Western tradition in favor of a confessional theology whose terms are experimental rather than fundamental, and which therefore could speak of the living God in his encounter with man. But even Luther remained within the Christian Western view of history and its understanding of the world as an ultimate and eternally valid order of things. (See my remarks concerning 'morphological fundamentalism'). The "liberty of the Christian man" (Luther) was to be exercised in the midst of the relationships and commitments of everyday life, but evidently still within the given concepts of the medieval order of economic states. It was based on the expectation of "the Last Day" and remained, therefore, still within the horizon of a Christian metaphysics of history. The movement of the Reformation had not yet grasped the worldly freedom of man which came to the fore after the metaphysical bonds of the Ancient Western world view were overcome, and when the world was discovered as the field of open and competing forces.

Otherwise it would not have been possible already for Melanchthon (but not only for him) to ignore the Reformers' break with the old ontological order of thought and to undertake, once more, the attempt to renew the synthesis of Christian faith and the heritage of Antiquity. After (Philo-) Clemens of Alexandria—Origen and Albertus Magnus—Bonaventura—Thomas Aquinas, it was the third and last great effort to think in terms of Ancient Western thought and to order conditions accordingly. This third and last attempt of traditional Western thought finally came to its end and breakdown in the crisis, caused by the socio-economic and political revolutions, and reflected in the teachings of German idealism.

It is not accidental, again, that Hegel's historical position can be compared to that of the theologians of the German empire and of the thinkers of that time (Rupert von Deutz 1070-1129, Otto von Freising, 1111-1158, Hildegard von Bingen 1098-1179), who attempted to preserve the vital unity of the cosmos in the midst of a great Western European evolution (distinctions of Pope and Emperor, of clergy and laity, of spiritual and worldly). Hegel thought to preserve the unity of the world events in order to provide the necessary trust in the "good direction of history" for those who (against their will) had been dismissed into history and into worldly freedom. He sought to think the "justification of God in history" in order to preserve men against the absolute submergence in society ("atheism of the moral world"). Yet Ancient Western thought failed to meet problems and tasks of a time in which the *gubernatio mundi* could only be perceived as *transformatio mundi* (under the conditions of a scientific-technological community). The question of concretely and continually changing worldly conditions was a question which could not be answered on the basis of the traditional Christian consciousness and way of life; hence, nothing could be expected from church and theology. The "Constantinian" age of the Ancient Western synthesis of Christian world mission and Graeco-Roman world view and world order had come to its end. A "break with the status quo and the tradition" had taken place, and a "spiritual revolution" had begun which Heinrich Heine had characterized in his *Betrachtungen zur Geschichte der Religion und Philosophie in Deutschland* in 1834 with the following sober words: "The old Jehovah is preparing Himself for death . . . People offer the sacraments to a dying God . . . This sad news of death needs, perhaps, a few centuries before it spreads, but we have already put on mourning clothes. De Profundis!" And Nietzsche responded: "God is dead! God remains dead! What did we do when we unchained this earth from its sun? Where is it moving now? Where are we moving . . . Are we not continually plunging . . . Is there still an above and below . . . Are we not erring through infinite nothingness?"

Whose God's death is here proclaimed? It is the general Ancient Western idea of God. It had become dead, even though it bore the eternal qualities of being in the tradition of Parmenides and Plato. Man had moved beyond the stable but limited horizon of its eternal values and rules, its sacred order and its sacred institutions into the open process of a scientific, technological community. But at the same time, he had moved into Western atheism and nihilism as the final form of the Ancient Western consciousness. (Cf. G. Picht, *Die Erfahrung der Geschichte,* Frankfurt 1958). "Nihilism is the end of the logic inherent in our great values and ideas." (Nietzsche). "This is the end of the way which began with an idea of a metaphysical God, an ontological cosmos and a natural law, Providence and the love of fate and which thereby overshadowed the light of the God of Israel." (K. H. Miskotte, *Wenn die Götter schweigen,* Munich 1963, p. 311).

"If we want to follow the understanding of the world of the old Israel (the openness of the world towards God and its being embraced by God) we must first—sit venia!—de-mythologize and de-philosophize our whole thinking . . . In the general development of philosophy of history this contribution of Israel for the understanding of the world has thus far been considered as minimal or even as completely irrelevant. Here we have to revise something, because even with respect to the understanding of the world, something has taken place in Israel which had tremendous consequences, of which we have to become conscious again. And this development took place on a completely different level from that of the *arche*-thought of the pre-Socratic movement." (G. v. Rad, *Aspekte alttestamentlichen Weltverständnisses*, Ev. Th. 1964, p. 64 f). Today the conceptual framework of late Antiquity is broken within which church and theology found their decisive shape through the anti-gnostic controversy. But this involves a crisis not only for church and theology, but also for so-called secularism.

III. *The Crisis of Secularism*

The latent secularization which has always accompanied the Catholic synthesis of Ancient heritage and Christian tradition entered into its final phase in the middle of the 17th century.

Until the middle of the 19th century various realms of life and thought became emancipated from the original theological-ecclesiastical context. The law of systematic search of world and self dominated more and more and enlightened the conditions of possible experience and the rules of possible causes of action. Secularization led to the technocratic form of world discovery and world order. The "secret of the great number" reigned. Everything seemed to be subject to counting and manipulation. Dilthey wrote in his *Einleitung in die Geisteswissenschaften*: "The transformation of the world into a comprehending subject effected by these modern world systems is like the euthanasia of metaphysics." It is a sentence which, however, can deceive us, because even the objective signs of modern times and the conceptual structure of physics have very often remained within the context created by Parmenides and fully developed in the ontological thought of Plato and Aristotle. We still face the contemporary world problems with an understanding of the world which has been outdated, and this situation deserves our full attention, especially the following aspects:

1) The Ancient Western thought is generally dominated by the principle formulated by Parmenides that knowledge is identical with

being. This sentence presupposes the fundamental distinction between continual being (immortal, timeless) and temporary being (mortal, nothing).

2) The resulting concept of truth is nothing but a pure form of the negation of a temporary change. In the forms of experience which correspond to this notion, history can always be present as a hidden and implicit factor, but it can never become explicit and it cannot be experienced as such.
3) The *logos* of Parmenides and Plato reigns within a cosmos which is closed in itself—an eternal cosmos. It cannot provide the basis and the context for man's historical existence.
4) The direction of our thinking about, and our experience of, the world is dominated by the 'timeless' (Greek-Catholic) *logos* concept. It is "the way toward a negation of history which, in modern times, has led to the attempt to subject history to the total planning legislated by logical reason. This step from the absolute truth to total planning is the last possibility and yet, at the same time, the turning point of an epoch." (G. Picht, *Die Epiphanie der ewigen Gegenwart, in: Beiträge zu Philosophie und Wissenschaft,* W. Szilasi zum 70. Geburtstag, Munich 1960. p. 201).
5) The trust in reason in whose name secularization took place needs to be de-mythologized. But if reason proceeds to radically enlighten itself, it arrives at the knowledge of its own limits. This is the crisis of secularism. The world as an event cannot be rationally assured. The data of our analytical technological knowledge about man and world are not sufficient to make a responsible decision. We find ourselves caught in a dangerous discrepancy between human abilities directed towards means and instruments and human will directed towards goals. We live in a "time of perfect means and confused motives" (Einstein). "Thus far, humanity has survived because it did not have the knowledge to realize its goals, however unwise they may have been. Now, as we are in the process of acquiring this knowledge, we need more wisdom than ever, in view of the goal of life. But where, in our confused age, can we find such wisdom?" (B. Russell).

The effect and attraction of secularism is still very great. Many find here the promise of a "revolution of facts" in the midst of a contest between the systems for world domination, and they hope that this revolution of facts will overcome the ideological controversies in favor of a more rational order of the world. But is it possible to replace political decisions by technological considerations? Can an awesome responsibility for the world, to which man with his worldly freedom is exposed and with which he seems to be overwhelmed, be quieted down in a mathematically conceived system? Never! This cybernetic utopia remains a fiction. A view of the relationship between man and the world can show this. Since it is of fundamental importance for the evaluation of the process of secularization, we must briefly sketch it. (Cf. by the author, *Verheissung und Schrecken der Freiheit.* Von der Krise des antik-abendländischen Weltverständnisses, dargestellt im Blick auf Hegels Erfahrung der Geschichte. Stuttgart 1964. Part VII: "Die unerhörte Freiheit")

1) *The freedom of men vis-a-vis the world:*

Man's belonging to the world can be defined as "world-relation" and as "world-distance." Both definitions are complementary. Human world-relation can only emerge out of world-distance and world-distance remains inhuman if it does not lead to a new turning towards the world.

Already the attempt to escape the everyday world by retreating into one's own, into a more real or "better" world remains a maneuver in which we flee into self-made self-justified isolation. This equals the imprisonment into a make-believe world. The commuting between the world of work and the world of leisure, or even between the so-called world of the "world" and a separate world of "faith" leads into the blind alley of a hopeless world and a worldless hope, and to nothing else.

Under the pressure of the tremendous tension which man experiences, he succumbs too easily to the temptation to oppose a second world to the world in which he has to struggle: the actual world, the world of the gods, the world of ideas, the world of his desires and plans, the world of knowledge, the world of technology, the world of the church, an esoteric-liturgical realm, a world of a holy salvation history. All these duplications and splits of the world are an expression of the worldly anxiety which does not dare to deal with the one world, its resistance and its paradox trusting in hope and love the power of the Creator who upholds the world and who is the fulfiller of heaven and earth.

The more the world (external as well as internal) is experienced as an interplay of powers, the more man becomes conscious of his unheard-of world-freedom and thereby also of the dangers inherent in the self-endangering of freedom. For the world has become the topic of worldwide and world-moving conversation in which the *transformatio mundi* is at stake (this is true not only for large projects, but also for small talk: we change ourselves by walking with one another). Man as the steward of the world is the advocate of a concrete future world. "The world is the signature of the Word." (H. Heine). Man with the freedom granted him has become the advocate of the presence of the Coming. For this world-freedom man has to be liberated in order not to be condemned to this freedom once he is dismissed into it. Thus man lives by the word, which is able to open to him the context for his historical existence.

2) *The openness of the world for man:*

Once man becomes conscious for his freedom in its world-relatedness and world-transcendence, he not only finds that his attitude towards the world in an event which constitutes history, but sooner or later he will also find that the world itself has to be thought of as an event which enables history. In spite of all its resistance, the world is open for history of human world responsibility. The world has a quality of time in itself as a history-enabling condition. Therefore, we find ourselves in an open drama in which world and man contend with one another and in which man is instituted as the advocate of the Coming. The world is therefore not only the time-space condition for a drama which radically transcends time and space. It is the field where man has to perceive his task. It is open for man. Man could not involve himself in the given world with a view to a transcending possibility, if the world in itself were not constituted in terms of language. Yet only man has the potential for language. It is, of course, always an open question whether the world is legitimately claimed by man, for what may seem conclusive and correct in terms of empirical logic is not thereby right and wholesome. Not everything which can be constructed is thereby constructive. The world cannot be reduced to mathematical schemes in order to be manipulated without risk. It is itself a historical issue which today has become a tremendous problem for man's world-freedom in which he is responsible to history. Evidently, the "law" which permeates the world cannot be reduced to a world formula. And this raises the question concerning the relation between freedom and world order as *the* problem of *time.*

How can opportunity for life be increased without its actually being decreased or even destroyed in mutual competition? How can the time for life be perceived and mutually shared so that those who have to share with one another and have to live in the same time, can live in peace with one another? How can men adjust themselves in space and time? How should they open up space and fill the time? What do we say of the world if man as steward of the world has to make decisions which transcend the world?

3) *The Transcending correspondence of world and man:*

We have seen that the world has to be thought of as the condition and as the consequence of human freedom. Man is involved in the *transformatio mundi.* He is not only placed in the change of the world, he is also to carry a co-responsibility for the change of the world. In his word which assesses the world, he can contain more reality than in the sense perceptions of the world that meets him. The question is how man acquires this word which directs him into the future, which will free him for the right perception of world responsibility. Man and world live from the right word. Man has to understand it in order to perceive, in his historical existence, the presence of the Coming, which presence is to be attested in man's openness towards the world. He cannot derive this word from a rational interpretation of the world in terms of a general constitutive principle, because the world is event and cannot be made safe rationally. It is this historical character of the relationship between man and world which causes the crisis of secularism.

Secularization can put into question more-or-less sacred bonds and more-or-less dogmatic views; it can therefore expose man's questionable existence of an open-ended history of his world-freedom. (This is a very necessary and inevitable process.) However, secularism cannot free man from the repressed historical fatigue of his experience of world and self. Man has been removed from the sustaining and restraining authority of sacred orders, the archetypes, and the continuous repetition, into a process of individuation and into the woes of a changing and changeable world. Thus he finds it all too easy to swing back and forth between resigning himself to the resistance of the world and rebelling against the world. In this process of fatigue, the language has become sick. Once more we are at the end of our wisdom with regard to the plans of systematic world exploration, as well as with regard to the idealistic systems of world interpretation and the religious rites for overcoming the world. The word of which we are in need cannot be formalized either by a formalized doctrine of language by cybernetic logistics which would dismiss history by way of total assurance of the world, or by a timeless *logos* which transcends history for the sake of a total assurance of salvation. This is the crisis of secularism and it is at the same time the crisis of Western church Christianity and its dogmatic schemes. Church and theology have to overcome their own form and structure of a whole epoch.

The church, under the influence of the Platonic axiom of unchangeability, has run the danger of presenting itself as timeless. It has, therefore, underestimated, despised and denied the struggles and the fatigues of its contemporaries; it has tried religiously to out-play them and to push them away. Thereby, it has forcefully contributed "to the letting loose of an aggressive pessimism which also can be called nihilism." (Miskotte, op. cit. p. 256). The change of the world, however, has brought about its loss of relevance to the world in the ancient Western sense. It now has to revise its historically developed way of existence and form of thought in order to be able to resume her task of apostolic world mission. The church through its *presence* "should carry into the world the expectation for today and tomorrow. It should not think in special categories of above and below, but in time-categories of now and then. It has to deny to itself the transposition of the 'then' into an unthinkable future. It cannot afford now, having caused so much unrest in a closed world, to resign to this world simply as it is, out of fatigue, and to concern itself only with pastoral care as if the spectre of the transpersonal powers moving towards judgment and liberation and new service would simply vanish from its horizon.

There can be no pastoral care which does not seek man in his world, which more and more is one with the world in its historical movement, and which does not renew him, feed him with the daily meal of expectation." (Miskotte, op. cit. p. 288/89).

This poses once more the question concerning the *task* of the church *and* society, the task from which church and society can live in the face of the crisis of the forms and formulae in which this task has thus far been defined.

IV. *The question concerning the task from which church and society live:*

The Christian Western synthesis of state, science and faith broke down under the increasing pressure of the European revolution. It has lost its universal value in view of the new experience of the world. The dramatic combination of spirit and power has been replaced thus far only by a tragic equation of knowledge and power.

Being caught in the circle of knowledge and power, we run the danger of being condemned to freedom. The incontrovertible process of scientific-technological developments finds in humanity its social structure, not in individual interest or power clusters, much less in the individual state. But it is in need of a direction, and this poses anew the question of who directs whom.

An illustration: Alvin M. Weinberg has calculated that the budget of the U.S.A. for research and development, doubling within seven years, would reach $25 billion by 1970. In relation to the attested fact that a trained physicist cannot use up more than $150,000 per year, this means that by 1970 the United States would need about 175,000 Ph.Ds in natural sciences and engineering. This number represents about 30% of those who fulfill the intellectual requirements for obtaining such an academic degree. However, it would amount to a national disaster, if 30% of all qualified became physicists, engineers or chemists. For the country needs no less doctors, lawyers, industrial managers, officers, civil servants, teachers, ministers, etc. How does a technological-scientific community arrive at the correct decisions and measures with regard to the needs of funds and personnel for the various functions of its total household?

A second illustration: 27 scholars who met for the inauguration of a new conference center of the Ciba-Foundation discussed the topic

"Man and his Future." Hudson Hoaglands made the following remarks concerning the guidance of human behaviour: "We are continually guided either by education, by advertising, by propaganda, by religious or ethical images and prejudices. Thus far, we know very little about the mechanism of this guidance, which, if we would know it, we could probably use much more effectively. Behavioral science and hallucinatory drug research bring us constantly closer to the guided formation of personality." Can we any longer leave ourselves to the unreflective and unguided display of free powers and forces? Must not the levels be explored and reshaped, out of which thus far the historical eruptions and explosions have been fed? From here it follows that not only the external but also the internal human world is to be conceived as an arena of various forces which has to be explored and opened up with all scientific and technical means, and has to be changed in a desired direction.

But which direction is desirable? Who guides those who guide? How can planning and guidance serve freedom? Is man not being degraded to a mere human material if the so-called "true freedom" appears only as a product of a guidance process which has been achieved with the help of a guided formation of personality? Should the problem of human freedom be resolved with the help of a genetic Utopia, the last of all possible Utopias, and with a program of education of the order of a higher zoology? Can somebody be tricked, educated, "weaned" or even vaccinated into freedom? And yet there is no doubt that in the service of freedom we need today more differentiated plans and considerations.

In view of these problems and tasks of our times, we should have a new socio-ethical treatise on "the freedom of the Christian man," which would deal with the task of man in the changing world and would open up the context within which historical existence finds itself and to which it owes itself. Theology and church have to step out from the narrow circle of being concerned with themselves. They got into this circle because of the changing world, but it is a circle which had not been foreseen in the christianized world-view of late antiquity and its view of history. We need a new quest for the right understanding of God's power permeating the world. Luther's description of the cooperation of God and man (historical-personal cooperation) posed the question of man as co-worker with God in secular life. This question has to be taken up anew in the view of the *transformatio mundi.*

It is the christological question which is placed before the church and theology in a new way: How did Jesus as the Christ claim and proclaim the universal lordship of God? How does Christ reign in this world? In how far is He the image of God and therefore at the same time the "second Adam," the "first-born among many brothers"? What is the office of Christ in the changing world, and which office is thereby given and opened up to man?

The difficulties which are to be overcome in answer to these questions are mainly a consequence of that strange split and doubling of the christological thinking of the Ancient church. The church assured itself of its dogmatic Christ on the one hand, and claimed also, on the other hand, a political Christ, without realizing the distance between the two concepts. In the name of the first, one expected and administered eternal salvation. In the name of the other, one made politics. And in both cases, the access to an understanding of God's righteousness was blocked—righteousness which had been revealed in the Christ once and for all. These difficulties can only be overcome, if the explications of the faith and the institutional forms of the church are revised. These have been acquired at the time and in the context of the structures of ancient society; they have been developed under the influence of the Platonic axiom of the unchangeability of the truth, and have claimed a timeless validity. But truth is always happening. Therefore nobody can make an image either of God, or of man, or the world. God, man, and world are the three known unknowns. Man and the world are placed in the midst of change for the sake of God.

At stake is the proclamation of the past and present event of God's righteousness which comes into its own with man and the world. For its sake, man and the world are justified in their continuing change in spite of an apparent contradiction and meaninglessness of the world's course, and the obvious contradiction of human existence.

Man and the world need a word which justifies them because, once dismissed from the protective sacred orders and rules into the world freedom, they will fall into a self-made prison in a world of their own knowledge and desires (even religious desires), and they will fall prey to the orphic temptation, to be only organ and function of the then-existing conditions. ("Atheism of the ethical world," socialization of man, "the fourth man," utopia of the status quo).

Thus society needs a church which is free for its world mission in order to assume its responsibility for the continuing world events; and every individual needs the liberating word which places him in the service of righteousness away from hopeless concern for himself.

How can the church today accept this task from which she lives? How can she be in the midst of the open and plural society of a scientific-technological community in our time? How can she be the "light of the world" and the "salt of the earth," and how can theology serve this apostolic world mission of church and society?

V. *Conclusions concerning the question of the structures for a church which assumes its mission:*

We are concerned here about the task which is appropriate to each generation in its specific historical situation.

For the sake of this task, Christians have to ask themselves which are the realities of which they speak—whether, within their seeking and acting, they take seriously the changing world as God's work.

It is evident that church and theology must see much more clearly how people are claimed by world events for the sake of Jesus Christ.

The Church is the people of God, not some private cultic society or a general institution which mediates salvation.

If, according to the New Testament, the presence of the coming Lord becomes real in the life of the church, the church is thereby not the goal and end of God's ways. Rather, it is an instrument and a sacrament of God in his action with the world. This is not the kingdom of God on earth. The Church to whom the kingdom is promised, but which is not itself the kingdom, finds itself vis-à-vis the world events, for God's kingdom is the goal of the total creation.

We are heirs of the promises which aim towards God's completion of the world. As heirs of the promises for which we are liberated through Christ (Galatians 4 and 5) we are not to succumb to the power of our own Christian, Western heritage. This heritage, with its limitation of the Ancient Western consciousness and way of existence, has undergone a slow, yet continuing devaluation. It has become a mortgage which has to be liquidated if church and theology shall become flexible again for the world mission which is given them. Two consequences result from this critical situation in which we are involved due to the dissolution of the Ancient Western synthesis of state, science and faith. It is the universality and the incontrovertibility of this process which we need to realize. The universality of this development corresponds to the solidarity of those involved. The incontrovertibility corresponds to the necessity of a change of structure.

1) The solidarity of involvement:

Vis-à-vis the questions and tasks thrown at us through the scientific and technological exploration and conquest of the world, church and society are bound together in a solidarity of involvement.

The responsibility for peace, which represents a social event and not an ideal goal, can only be assumed in cooperation. The dispute of the viewpoints, which has become more acute since the dissolution of the forced unity of the old Western order, has to be relativized in the face of the common crisis. It can only become a competing of opinions. And this competition has to be carried out for the sake of a common threat and a common promise of our world-freedom, within the context of a worldwide, open dialogue. We have to think of the consequences which result from this, for the mutual relationship among the churches, and for the relation of church and society.

a) Concerning the solidarity of Christianity:

We will have to deal with "the assets and liabilities of history."

With the liabilities, because it seems almost "as if it would be our task to guard history so that nothing can come out of it except stories, but by no means an event"! (Neitzsche). With the assets because the historical-critical considerations can avoid the danger of absolutizing ourselves and can lead to an open encounter with events.

We can no longer put off the often neglected open dialogue about the problems of an existence and forms of thought which have historically developed, with which the churches block their own way today. The world for which God's promises are meant and which the Church of Jesus Christ has to proclaim, should be informed about the questions and problems with which the churches have to deal today, because these problems concern at the same time the origin and the contemporary problems of modern society. Consequently, the ecumenical movement of the churches has to be lived out in world-wide concretion. (Cf. O. Hammelsbeck, *Säkularisation-Wegbereiterin für die Einheit der Kirchen?* ZEE 1964, 1ff.).

b) Concerning the solidarity of church and society:

Both church and society have entered the same crisis of change which has come about due to the increasing perception of human world-freedom. They are dependent on each other in order to carry out their task, which is different but which is ultimately given to them by the same God.

Society is in need of the church for the sake of the word which opens up the context to which a historical existence belongs and out of which it emerges. Society lives from the prophetic word which opens the world, and the church lives from the perception of its world mission. If it does not want to deal with the world, it degenerates into an unreasonable service of God within an isolated ecclesiastical world, and fails in its mission, inadequately perceived. (See Romans 12:1 f.).

Church and society, therefore, live from an open dialogue about the existing problems of structure. It cannot be irrelevant for Christians how the society is structured to which they belong and for which they are responsible, and it cannot be irrelevant for the society how the present structural crisis of the church will be overcome.

2) The necessity for structural change:

The contemporary crisis of Western society reveals that two basic structures have to be overcome. The catholic, and the paternal principle.

Truth never reigns *kat'holou* (Plato, Menon 73D, Aristotle, Met. 98a, 12ff). It never is timeless from above, above everything, but is itself an event which comes upon us and which liberates for historical, personal communication among men. We become sensitive today to the contrast between the Greek quest for a timeless eternal truth, and the Israelite-Christian testimony of the time-bound truth. It is the same contrast between the Greek concept of the world as a measured cosmos enclosed in itself and an Israelite-Christian understanding of the world as a mandate in history. The God of Abraham, Isaac and Jacob is not a God of the fathers, but a God of the grandfather, the father and the son—A God of the generations, who calls his people in order to work with them. "One is our Father, who is in heaven . . . But we all are brethren." (Matthew 23:8. Also compare John 8:31 following.)

a) Concerning the crisis of the Greek-catholic principle:

There is no absolute truth in the name of which there is a claim for worldly relevance. The world lives from the testimony of the truth which comes about in time, the truth of God's testimonies of his mercy, which is to be proclaimed ever anew, "contextually" with world events.

The era of catholic movements has passed. They are no longer world-wide, but world-threatening. The era of a world-wide open conversation has to begin. This conversation struggles with the event of a common world responsibility.

b) Concerning the crisis of the paternal principle:

The world of the national fathers, of the school-father, of the church fathers, is a passing world. But the more the former hierarchy of offices loses its useful function because of social changes, the more urgent is the question concerning man's office in the change of the world. In today's world, nothing is real if it hasn't been discussed in time and nothing can be achieved solely by routine agreement or memos from a central office if the existing differentiations and future necessities are not properly taken into account. In such a world, which needs love of individuality and joy in imaginative cooperation, men live from the liberation to deal responsibly with the word which opens to them the world as the field of their mandate for promising communication. And thus it is the most noble task of the church to offer opportunity to men to receive the word which frees them to freedom and which enables them to take the word itself which then, in the common struggle of everyday life, will have to be attested.

In a world which is the signature of the word, all men are called to accede to the word and, as carriers of the word, to assume the highest office which is confided to men.

It is therefore the priesthood of all believers which is the foundation of all different offices. Dignity of office, however, which leads to the devaluation of other functions, is arrogance of office.

(Compare First Corinthians 12:4 ff.).

The church of "the word become flesh" can only live in the continual exercise of its encounter between apostolic world mission and general social world responsibility. It thereby does not need to become a place of never-ending discussions. But it has to be the place where the word can freely and "richly" be received. (Compare Colossians 3:16), and also where it can be received by everyone. Whether this is the case at every opportunity or at specific meetings is a second question. But it is important that the congregation itself be the forum where everything can be taken up and where the praise becomes heard in the face of the contemporary experience, so that men who partake of it are awakened and encouraged to reflect and discuss everything in this forum, the forum of him whose spirit proves to be living in the congregation.

In the midst of the change which has come about with the crisis of the catholic and the paternal principle in the ancient Western tradition, we will have to be prepared for the fact that change will remain with us, and that never again will there be stable conditions in the sense of the word. Church and theology have to deal with the questions and problems of the *transformatio mundi* in order to enjoy the presence of the coming Lord in mutual testimony of scriptural witness and worldly experience.

Hans Schmidt, Hamburg-Bramfeld
September, 1964.

Mission in Our Situation

1. We owe it to the grace of God that we do not live in a world which is in bondage to a sacred code, but that we can design our life according to its own laws which are made evident by science. However, the modern scientific view of the world tends to become an ideological and hence a sort of sacred power when it is tied to a specific philosophy of history, e.g., when "scientific socialism" is proclaimed as the normative basis for thought. Those who are subjected to this claim give easily way to the temptation uncritically to take over the prescribed philosophy or to be pushed into a more or less conscious intellectual hypocrisy. The contradiction between their experience and their talk burdens their conscience and leads to double standards and unreflected accommodation. The task of the church is to offer men the totality of life under Christ, to liberate them from constraint and hypocrisy, trusting Christ's lordship over the powers, and to assist those who are tempted by an easy accommodation.

2. Relations in a differentiated industrial society always only claim a part of man's life and make it difficult for him to have a comprehensive view of society. This difficulty creates the tendency to view man according to abstract principles, to subsume him under alien categories and to make him the object of personal power drives. The individual is tempted to avoid social responsibility and to fight for his own interests without regard to others. The Christian congregation is called to demonstrate the necessity of responsible action and to equip persons to contribute their share for a truly human life in their respective spheres of social involvement. Christians know that their struggle may be without success or be exploited by other interests, but they are called to action, nevertheless, in their responsibility under God. They trust God and his intention to realize his redemptive design at the point where earthly powers pursue their own designs.

3. Life and work in industrial society are by necessity highly organized. Where the organizational demands become absolute, there is no room left for man as a person. Increased organization in all areas of life leads to reliance upon principles of a bureaucratic planning mechanism to which the good of man is subordinated. Men suffer from a sense of unfreedom and a consciousness of their own lack of power.

The congregation can witness to the fact that these various forms of anxiety and resignation can be overcome under the promise of Christ (John 16:33). It is to be the place where such needs can be openly acknowledged. The brotherly community represents the small social group over against the anonymous organization; it offers security in the context of obedience and free, personal inter-relationships.

4. Our modern situation poses heightened conflicts for man. They result from the opposition of an absolutist ideology to their faith as well as from the contradiction between their personal convictions and interests and the justified or unjustified social necessities. Christians must be equipped to witness through their attitudes and decisions to the fact that they are bound by God's command. They fulfill their missionary calling by facing the conflicts rather than avoiding them (whether in society or in the church), and by their willingness to assist others in their conflicts. For this they are in need of brotherly support for which adequate forms must be found.

DDR—Working Group,
March, 1964.

The Challenge to Missionary Action

Not only does the challenge of missionary action lie in Christ but also in the world which is the arena and end of God's mission. The world challenges mission in two ways; Its urgent need and its great possibilities.

The world calls for reconciling mission when history has made community imperative. Without it the world cannot survive. Today the world is one. Science and technology belong to all. Industrial culture belongs to all. All live in a common expectation of hope. The whole technological development confirms the gospel that God is acting to bring about the unity and oneness of the human family. But the emergence of one world has created frightful conflicts of neighbourhood. These social eruptions are struggles to confront the new reality. The fury of this struggle is a futile contention with the new world community. So the church should take heart.

We are also in a moment in history when expectation for justice and equality is for all. The scuttling of empires, the rise of new nations has brought fresh demand for equity and justice. The nation of Ghana has the same vote in the United Nations as the Soviet Republic. The will of Congo, Laos or Cuba can threaten the great powers. And a people long at the mercy of reckless whims and degrading insults of nations has now like a giant awakened from its sleep and upsets the peace of the whole world. China may be hated and feared, but she will no longer be ignored and insulted. "Every valley shall be filled and every mountain brought low." "He hath put down the mighty from their seats and exalted them of low degree." What a moment for the church to see what God is doing in the midst of the world, acting in judgment and mercy with the weak and the strong which compels us to pray for the spirit of wisdom that the eyes of our understanding be illumined that we may discern the signs of our times.

The challenge of the world is for revolutionary missionary action. Whether it be wealth in the hands of the few in Latin America, the shattering impact of industrialization on the social systems of Africa or the powerful structures of segregation in the U.S., only an aggressive revolutionary mission can adequately meet the crisis of our age. If the church is to speak and act in the present situation it must do so in a revolutionary way. This is true not only in Africa or Asia, it is also true in the U.S.A.

Jitsuo Morikawa, Philadelphia
April, 1963

Third Part

THE CHURCH IN THE WORLD

The Presence of Christ and the Church

So far in the Ecumenical Movement we have dealt with the problem *from the inside*—speaking of the marks of the church. But here now we seem to be driven to look at the question *from the outside*—speaking of the marks of God's presence in the world; and of the calling of the church to be the missionary presence of Christ in such a way as to reveal to the world God's redeeming presence. If this is so—and I believe it is—it would appear that these two discussions must now come into full relation to each other. To ask, for example, about true preaching, due administration of the sacraments, and valid ministry today, without asking *at the same time* about witnessing to God's presence in history now (on the basis of the Word given once-for all); about Christ's purpose to unite us across all our divisions at his one table; and about our calling to be the ministering presence of Christ in the midst of the modern shapes of need—would be to fail to speak about the church of the Living Lord.

Colin W. Williams,
What in the World, New York, 1964, p. 21f.

The Church–A Segment of the World

I. *"The Church Reduced to its Simplest Expression"*

1. Let it be noted immediately that for the Bible the Church appears as a *secondary* reality and that it is not the focal point of the New Testament. Beginning with the Old Testament (Gen. 1-11) the decisive factor is the relation between the living Lord and humanity. Wherever the Word—that is the act by which God presents himself to the world—reaches the world, *it is possible* that the people of God or the Church may be born. I repeat: it is possible, for the Bible indicates throughout that God acts and is present in the world through persons who do not know him (and thus who cannot be called the Church): here one thinks of the line of *pagan witnesses*

to God, from Melchizedek to the rulers of Rom. 13, including Cyrus, the pagans of Mt. 25:31 ff. and Rom. 2:14—when the act of God is *acknowledged,* if only by two or three, there the Church is born. The fundamental basis is thus the confession of faith by which the Church seeks to "live up to" God's action of showing forth his glory by reconciling the world with himself. Because Christ is the perfect fulfillment of this action, the Church's confession of faith is necessarily *christological* and thus also *trinitarian.*

2. The Church is nothing other than *a segment of the world* which confesses the universal Lordship of Christ: thus it is the place where the world becomes aware of its true destination, its true face (configuration). In this sense, as a "pars pro toto" of recapitulated creation, it is the body of Christ, the fullness of him who is all in all. *The Word, the sacrament* and *brotherly love* manifest the new and true relationship which God has created between himself and man, between man and man.

But at the same time the Church is the *sign* or the *instrument* by which God reveals himself to the world which is still unaware of his reconciliation. It does not exist for itself, but for those who are not of it: it is *mission.*

3. What we have said so far implies that:

a) At no time may the Church separate itself from the world by placing itself in the impossible position of spiritual pride. It is the Church only as it knows itself to be a "piece" of this world which God loves and to which he has shown his grace. If solidarity ought to exist in the Church it is with atheists, who remind us constantly of what the Church is unless the love of God gathers and protects it unceasingly.

b) The Church which lives in order that the world may know its true being, has no more important task than to be present to the world, knowing that every loss of contact with any segment of the world betrays God's plan for the world and destroys the Church. The quest for the means of this presence must be the dominant concern of the Church at all times: this is true of its message as well as of its structures.

c) Because it knows that God's presence and action are not manifested in it alone, the Church must be extremely attentive to signs of them in the whole world: there is no true Church apart from humble dialogue with pagans or apart from confrontation and life with them, since in this dialogue and confrontation the Church is called to listen and receive as much as and more than to speak and give.

4. One might try to formulate the following theses:

a) Wherever the God of Jesus Christ *and* the world are taken seriously, there is the Church.

b) Like its Lord, the Church must accept the risks of *visibility* without being imprisoned by it. Every *institution* is at the same time indispensable, relative and constantly open to the commands of God and the needs of the world. Just as Christ learned obedience (Heb. 5:8), the Church too must learn constantly to adapt itself to the requirements of its calling. Flexibility and transitoriness of institution are signs that we have understood the mystery of the *incarnation.*

c) *The whole Church,* without distinction or privilege, is active in solidarity, presence and dialogue.

d) The being and action of the Church must primarily be of a personal character: God's presence to the world through the Church is not manifested by anonymous organisms or abstract declarations but by acts which imply the authentic involvement of the "actors" in the service of Christ among men. Wherever a man lives in a true relationship with others in the name of Christ, there is the Church.

e) Thus, the witness of the Church is inseparable from *serving presence.* Not by directing and gathering, but by risking and abandoning itself to men does the Church proclaim the Lordship of Christ. The true Church does not exist apart from poverty, sacrifice and death. Unseen humility and lowliness are inseparable from the being and the mission of the Church.

f) The Church takes seriously the continuing existence of the world and thus it also takes seriously material conditions, social and political life and the concern for man's fate on earth. It can live in hope only by recognizing the decisive importance of each moment.

g) The expectation of the Kingdom is expressed in the Church by a refusal of all barriers between men, by intercession and by a movement toward unity.

There is no definite sign, no absolute guarantee that the church(es) is or may become the Church. Here more than anywhere else we must guard against magic, religion, idolatry, and we must remember that the Temple of Jerusalem was the trap in which Israel's faith perished and that the Magi did not find Jesus in Herod's household but in the stable of Bethlehem. Thus the only temple is Christ himself; for the Church, Christ is never separable from the other, i.e., the atheist. That is why we can construct ecclesiologies or ecclesiological phenomenologies, enumerate signs and draw up theses; but the Church "reduced to its simplest expression" is Christ risen in glory, suffering in the world and guiding history toward the revealing of his cosmic victory. To reduce the Church to its simplest expression is to say: I believe the Church to be *one, holy, catholic* and *apostolic,* which means that, with the Bible which is the *apostolic* witness, we confess *one* Lord, Jesus Christ the *Holy* One of God and the Lord of the *World.*

We can neither guarantee nor possess his presence but we know that he is faithful—thus in the unceasingly renewed *event* of his epiphany we say: ubi Christus ibi ecclesia and with the prayer: "Veni Creator Spiritus," we add fearfully: ubi ecclesia, ibi sit Christus.

Georges Casalis, Paris
February, 1963

II. *Discussion*

1) (Restatement of the main thesis:)

There is a fundamental unity between the Church and the world: the Church is that part of the world which has discovered, and thus manifests, its true "face." If the Church is the manifestation by certain men of the universal recapitulation which has been effected in Christ, then Christians cannot separate themselves from other men: the new man is not less human but rather truly human, as he recognizes and accepts his solidarity with the whole of humanity.

—The Church is thus:—the presence of Christ, communion and new life,

—the sign and instrument of God's present action,

—the concrete brotherly presence and solidarity with men in space and time.

To the extent that it lives in the fulness of the charismatic life, the Church is at the same time mission. It is not a question of two different realms, one the being of the Church and the other its missionary action. The very being of the Church implies its missionary activity.

2) Theology is not a simple recitation of formulae but an effort to formulate the current problems of the message and missionary action in terms of specific situations. While this position does not assure a precise balance among the theological theses, it does enable a dialectical advance. The contemporary ecclesiological impasse is the result of a misguided theology which sees the world as the place of damnation and of danger to the Church. The "insular" view of Christianity means that the Church will alternate between an attitude of defense and attack, of strategic retreat and crusade. The order of theological reflection is: God, the Church and the world, seen as the object of joint action between God and the Church. The proper order of thinking and acting should be: God, the world, the Church.

3) For the Bible, the world has several meanings:

—as *creation* (as the place of the covenant with Noah and as a reality with our historical future) it is the theater of the glory of the artistic Creator who wishes to establish perfect communion between himself and his work;

—as the place of *rebellion*, it is the theater of the glory of the judge, who condemns and restores;

—as the object of divine *love*, it is the theater of the glory of the suffering servant who inaugurates the kingdom and who rules until its final manifestation.

Gathered by the Spirit, the Church is both the final witness of this work as well as the means of its communication.

4) We were agreed in our group that traditional ecclesiology has been too ecclesia-centered. That whereas investigation of the re-

lationship between the Church and Christ has gone on for centuries, and rightly so, the equally important aspect of the relationship of the Church and the world still requires a great deal of investigation. The question of the nature of the Church is not a closed question, not a question to which an absolute and definite answer can be given at any point of time or will ever be given at any point of time. We cannot settle this question and then go on and say: we need not bother about it any longer, now we shall discuss mission. For as we study mission, our understanding of the Church will expand and develop.

5) It is by the leading (anechthe—Mt. 4:11) of the Spirit that Jesus is thrown (ekballei—Mk 1:12) into the desert. It is by the leading of the Spirit that the Church is thrown into the world (cf. Heb. 13:12f).

Every religious innovator undergoes a desert experience: from this profound encounter with the self-imprisonment of this world he emerges to proclaim true salvation to the men of this world. The ancient religious innovators returned from the desert to proclaim that this world cannot be the true world; salvation lay in overcoming the world through pious hope and discipline. The ideological innovators of our time return from their desert experience to overhaul the present world by revolutionary forces. Both place their hope in an abstract future and are not prepared to commit themselves in hope and love to the world of the present.

Jesus, however, accepts this apparently merciless world as the arena, and even as the work, of the active mercy of his heavenly father. He commits himself to the world as the property of God: He neither withdraws from this world in order to mark off a special segment as a special "holy" world (cf. Lk 12:1), nor does he succumb to the temptation of achieving lordship over the world through the practices and methods of Satan.

In this way Christ overcame anxiety in the face of the world and committed himself to this world on the basis of trust in his heavenly father. In God's name, whose purposes for man and the world are always fulfilled, he freed men from their holy and unholy attempts at self-righteousness; he pronounced them righteous in terms of God's effective grace and love.

Jesus Christ returned from the desert and entered this world as one who exploded its social and ideological categories, broke through traditional barriers between the holy and the profane, revealing them as sanctimonious divisions of God's one world, and opened new life in the seemingly hopeless zones of this world.

The world is not simply the stage on which God's acts of salvation are played out; it awaits its own fulfillment which will come at God's own designated time. Thus God's people are called "to walk humbly with the Lord your God" (cf Micha 6:8—Luther translates: "*be* humble before your God"!)

6) A Church which considers itself to be the sacred order of this world—a world whose primary characteristic is historical—becomes a threat for the world. The Church must commit itself to this world as God's own history with man and the world; only in this way will it "walk humbly with the Lord its God" and thus continue in creative and obedient discipleship to its Lord.

Western European Working Group, Bossey
February, 1963.

Notae Ecclesiae and Mission

This attempt to describe the Church in dynamic terms drawn from its role as a servant of God's mission to the world, even to the point of seeing the lines which mark the boundary of the Church's relation to the world dissolve, is one which cuts beneath the unfortunate separations between the Church and the world and forces the Church to seek continually for forms of life which will enable it to maintain situations of dialogue in the world and lines of service within the institutions of the world.

Nevertheless, it is the view of many that we are required by the New Testament to give more definite recognition to the unique characteristics of the life of the Church than this view of Casalis (S. above, p. 122 ff.) They believe, moreover, that it is vital to give this more definite statement of the unique "marks" of the true life of the Church, precisely because the characteristics which distinguish it from the world are of vital importance to its mission. These "marks" are signs to the world that the miracles of God's grace already evident (in imperfect form) in the life of the Church, are a foretaste of God's final purpose for the whole of his world. So J. G. Davies claimed that Casalis' view makes "too little of the Church's discontinuity with the world," too little of its own peculiar "givenness" as a separate institutional organ set by God in the world as the sign of his saving purpose.

Clearly this aspect of the Church's life needs careful examination. If the Church is called to show in its life "given" or unique characteristics which mark the difference between its life and the life of the world (and which therefore are signs to the world of God's purpose for it) then this will make a big difference to the nature of the Church-world dialogue. The forms of the Church's witnessing life will then need to be such that these unique characteristics are clearly expressed.

When we ask, however, what these given "marks" are, the contemporary theological discussion soon pushes us back into deep water. We are forced to recognize that the marks are not "things" that we can control. They are living characteristics of the Church which God gives to her as she is obedient to him in his mission to the world.

When, for example, we speak of "the Word" as a mark of the Church, there is here a responsibility for "right doctrine." Yet, "the Spirit giveth life"; and no amount of care to control the Word can assure the Church of the presence of "the Word truly preached." Only as she risks her inheritance in twentieth century trade—in obedient mission—can she expect the Spirit to give life.

Similarly when we speak of "unity," in one sense this too is capable of control. The New Delhi Assembly was able to state the large measure of agreement among member churches as to the "nature of the unity we seek," and was able to see this as a goal toward which the churches should move with real determination. Nevertheless it is still true that beneath and beyond all external unity is "the unity of the Spirit . . ."

Here we see the inseparability of *mission* and *unity;* that God gives us the new unity in Christ in order that he may reveal to the world his mission to gather all things into the unity of his life. The ecumenical movement is an expression of the growing recognition in the Church that God is asking us to receive from him the gift of unity in order that we may be truer servants of his mission . . .

We need a redefinition of the traditional reformation "marks of the Church" by placing them firmly within the framework of the Church's mission. We have seen that in Act 2:42 ("they continued in the apostles' teaching and fellowship, in the breaking of bread and the prayers") these characteristics are given within the missionary context of the Pentecost story. As the apostles were driven out of the upper room and set on the road to the uttermost parts of the earth, the life of their fellowship was one in which there was a constant breaking down of the boundaries of the world—nation, race, language, class, culture. The Pentecost story witnesses to the way in which the gift of the Spirit carried the believers into a new unity of common life in Christ across the previously impenetrable barriers of language, religion, race and culture. The life of apostolic fellowship therefore, far from being the self-enclosed life of a new and separate institution in the world, is a life that reveals within the institutional structures of the world a new life that transcends the old walls of division. It is in this way that the Church reveals to the world the new unity of life in Christ.

We are thus brought to see that the "marks of the Church" must be understood as pointing to the missionary purpose of the Church. The pure Word that is to be preached witnesses to Jesus Christ whose mission it is to gather all men into the unity of his life. The pure Word summons the Church to reveal to the world that in the Church's life, the old structural hostilities of the world are being dissolved by the reconciling life of Christ. Similarly the sacraments duly administered are understood as signs of Christ's power to draw believers out of the separations of life in the world into the love and unity of his own redeeming life.

Colin Williams,
Where in the World, New York, 1963,
pp. 49-54 passim

On Theology and Sociology

I.

1) As we deal in this study with theology and sociology we are guided by the conviction that both are relevant to the matter at hand.

2) Theology and sociology cannot and do not want to do without each other. This is easily explained: sociology has undertaken important research in the field that interests us here. Obviously, the historian might also cooperate in our study since we are essentially concerned with the problem of the relationship between eschatology and history. The difficulty for the historian lies, however, in the description of the significance of present facts.

3) What, then, is the function of sociology in view of the theological work to be done? Sociology calls the attention of theology to the relativity of the structures of ecclesiastical life: it formulates the question of the historicity of the life of the church and marks the trends that might be relevant to the obedient responsibility of tomorrow's Christians.

4) History is opened up for man by God's promise. Trusting in these promises, man no longer needs to assure himself of history, i.e., of the future by means of institutions and revolutionary planning.

   Whatever the future may bring, we know that the believer of tomorrow will have to stand among his fellowmen trusting in God's unchanging faithfulness. A dynamic concept of the incarnation forces theology to reckon with sociological findings.

J. C. Hoekendijk, H. Schmidt, W. Simpfendörfer,
Bossey, June, 1962.

II.

1) How do we discern the calling of God in the dynamic of what is happening to the world? This, I take it, is the function of Winter's concept "metropolis." Dietrich von Oppen expresses it as the personal society. Should not both of these sociologists, how-

ever, recognize what they are doing with these concepts? They are confronting us with the vision of a non-communal structure, fluid and dynamic in its essence, as a sign of the promise of God to our common life. But this is the operation of a New Testament understanding of the oikoumene, the cosmopolitan world of Rome receiving the promise of the coming of the kingdom of God. This means that the revelation of the power of the risen Christ to that oikoumene must be rather carefully examined for the light which it might shed on our current metropolis. It also means, however, that metropolis will not stand up as a sociological concept per se arising out of sociological arguments. It is a theological insight which liberates sociology from fear of facing the world as it is, a fear which naturally arises from discovering the way in which old social structures are disintegrating. It gives hope and discipline to more empirical investigation.

2) Similarly with the sociology of the Church. It is a theological understanding of the secular, that is of the time and space and person-limited character of all forms of church life, which must liberate the sociologist to explore the misuse of the church with impunity. But sociological investigation cannot be neutral even in its discovery of secondary structures of existence. Both judgment and grace are operating on the Church. The sociologist who is aware of neither possibility will become a mere statistician. He, however, who is aware of both will need a constant dialogue with the theologian, or with the theologian in himself, about the character of judgment and grace as they are found in the life of the Christian institution. Too often the semi-Christian, or disillusioned Christian analyst has found the language of sociology a good instrument for expressing the inadequacy and hypocrisy of the Church, but has made the unspoken assumption that the operation of grace would be the expression of an absolute moral ideal.

3) We need combined sociological and theological insights to discover where human decisions are being made through and beneath the technical ones. Here it makes a tremendous difference whether the sociologist operates with a Christian or some philosophical understanding of freedom and determinism. The Marxian

dictum that "Freedom is the recognition of necessity" is not so un-Biblical, if one understands necessity to be the direction of God's purpose through and in spite of the determinants of human institutions, and freedom as the perception and acceptance of this purpose. At this point Winter's sociology needs theological explication though it points, it seems to me, in the right direction. Freedom from repeating our past comes from understanding it. But the understanding is a theological as well as a sociological comprehension. It is not simply emancipation from determinism as a man is freed by psycho-analysis from a neurosis. It consists in perceiving the themes of God's judgment and God's reconciliation in and around human successes and failures. Understanding of the consequences of our future action must happen on this level.

4) These are only tentative feelers toward answering the critical question: Just how do sociology and theology interact in understanding the details of the human social situation and in giving guidance to the Christian's witness therein? A theologian such as myself is always in danger of using words (like judgment and grace!) which are systematically and Biblically impeccable, but which are meaningless because they do not become channels of the interaction between the Biblical situation and our own. On the other hand the sociologist is continually tempted to translate the theological basis of his understanding into terms which will pass as currency among the generality of his scientific colleagues. Thereby however, he becomes a philosopher of society who cuts off his direct interaction with the word of God on the one side and with his scientific colleagues on the other. Such philosophers of society have been giants in their days and have contributed mightily to the Church's self-criticism. One need only mention Karl Marx's criticism of religion which still operates in Peter Berger. But the task of a Christian sociologist is, I take it, somewhat different, namely to eliminate as far as possible those ideological generalities which made Marx a destroyer as well as a purger of society, and to put in their place a constant interaction with the living word of God. As such he can be most helpful in

bringing the theologians and ordinary churchmen to surrender the false institutional alliances and social concepts in which they have embodied their faith, and to take part in the real human drama. This is why we need each other.

Charles C. West, Princeton, N. J.
October, 1964.

"Morphological Fundamentalism"

Introduction

In this early stage of our enquiry into the problem of a missionary structure of the congregation, we have used on several occasions a concept which we found in some recent literature on this main issue, i.e., "morphological fundamentalism."

In its broadest sense, the combination of the term "morphological" and "fundamentalism" indicates a rigid and inflexible attitude toward the *morphe* (structure, "Gestalt") of the congregation similar to the attitude prevalent in "biblical fundamentalism." Consciously or, more often, unconsciously, the existent *forms* of the life of the Christian community are taken to be fixed once and for all; their historical nature—and that means their changeability—are likely to be ignored. A case in point is, for instance, the parish system, designed at a particular period of Church history for the specific needs of those times, and henceforth very often misunderstood as *the* one *morphe* in which the congregation expresses its obedience in an authentic way.

It should be understood that we are dealing here with issues which —to use current terminology of the discussion on Faith and Order regarding the Old and the New—belong to "*organization*" rather than "order."

J. C. Hoekendijk, Utrecht
August, 1962.

1. The structure of the congregation is as much an *expression* of the activity of the Holy Spirit as are the biblical writings. The Holy

Spirit never becomes a timeless manifestation, neither through the letter of Scripture nor through the order of the church.

2. The Scripture always asks to be heard and to be proclaimed anew, and the orders of the church are signs of the response to this word. They are the expression of the church's obedience in faith in a particular time and place. Wherever these orders are taken to be holy law, the obedience is *formalized* and the Spirit of Christ is equated with the spirit of a given ecclesiastical tradition.

3. A congregation which is to walk "*kata pneuma*" must, therefore, take seriously the *historical nature* of its life in its attempt to understand the Scriptures and the church.

4. The Reformers re-opened the question of the historical nature of revelation. Their distinction between law and Gospel which is characteristic for this problem was applied to the question of justification and the interpretation of Scripture. However, it was not applied to the problem of history itself. Consequently, the result of the Protestant renewal in the empirical-historical realm, including the socio-political as well as the corresponding religious life, strangely enough was in many respects a restoration of the ancient European form of the medieval Corpus Christianum.

5. We are facing here a strange ambiguity of the Reformation. On the one hand, it radically calls into question the basis of the *sacred order* of Western Christendom, as supported by Roman Catholicism. On the other hand, the Reformation once more subjects for another 150-200 years the corresponding political order, already in the process of dissolution, to the norms of Western Christendom. In the end, these orders were overrun in a revolutionary breakthrough, rather than overcome by the dynamics of the Reformation.

6. Since that time society has radically changed. Only the ecclesiastical structures seem to have survived as a witness to a world of orders that has long since passed.

7. It is true that the churches of the Reformation were made aware of the problem of "*biblical fundamentalism,*" and in adherence to the Reformers' understanding of the historical nature of revelation

they advocated an interpretation of Scripture in terms of historical criticism and of the history of the biblical traditions. But the equally important problem of *"morphological fundamentalism"* was not discovered.

8. How this was possible can be seen from Luther's own attitude. He still adhered to the doctrine of the four realms (c.f. Weltchronik by Joh. Carion, newly edited by Melanchthon in 1532, which determined the general view of history until the 17th century). Consequently, Luther was expecting the *"beloved last day"* simultaneously with the end of the Holy Roman Empire. And as the signs of dissolution of the empire were already manifest everywhere, he himself lived in a state of immediate apocalyptic expectation. At any rate, he could not imagine that the breakdown of the existing orders of the empire would open up the possibility and necessity of new forms of society.

9. But when the empire collapsed the last day had not arrived. Rather, people became aware of the ongoing historical process. They learned to reflect on everything, and therefore to expect everything. They began to understand the world as the field of their destructions and their constructions, as a place where they could realize their analytical and synthetical potential. The world had become the history of their *own changes*, i.e., their *own responsibility*. Human activity was no longer regulated by a world order (order of creation or necessity). The world changed according to human rules. There arose the crisis of world expansion of modern times and along with it the crisis of world devaluation of historicism.

10. Early Christianity, faced with the great process of world devaluation initiated by *Gnosticism,* had assured itself of the world as the good and divine creation by borrowing the Greek-Stoic concept of a timeless and reasonable cosmos and its all-pervading teleology. This meant that the world had become re-naturalized and that the history of redemption had become supranaturalized as a supernatural order of salvation.

11. This Ancient Western sacred order has broken down. In obedience to the historical witness of the prophets, fulfilled in Jesus as the Christ we are called instead to acknowledge the world as God's

history with man and the nations. Obedient in faith we are called to make room and time for God's redemptive activity in the history of this world (c.f. Rom. 12:1ff.).

12. The form (*morphe*) of the ancient Western world view belongs to the past. The structures of Western Christendom are no longer capable of helping the congregation to fulfill its task. Even worse, in a time when the churches of Jesus Christ, for the sake of their calling, must once more involve themselves in this world, these structures support a "morphological fundamentalism" which not only renders difficult any acceptance of responsibility in the world, but also threatens to enclose the churches in an ecclesiastical world of make-believe.

Hans Schmidt, Hamburg
June, 1962.

Public and Private

One of the social consequences of the industrial revolution has been the segregation of work from the private sphere. In fact, it has been the creation of the private sphere, because the concept of "private" in our modern sense did not exist before the industrial revolution. The factory must be segregated from private life—from the family, etc. From the industrial area proper, the same segregation has spread to almost every type of occupation. It is quite interesting, by the way, that the ministry is one of the very, very few occupations where this is not yet quite true. The parsonage, from the point of view of he sociology of occupations, is an extremely interesting phenomenon. There are very few such occupations left. The farmer is another case, But in urban cultures there are very, very few.

Organized religion and the church are very much involved in this dichotomization of existence. They belong very clearly to the private sphere in terms of what is really meaningful to people's lives. And this raises obvious problems for the existence of religion in modern society. Of course, people don't say this very much. They say that religion is relevant to everything, politics, business, but I believe that it is mainly a rhetorical meaning which it has in public life. It is a rhetorical cover over what happens in public life, but the real meaning —what religion really means to people—I think is primarily in private life.

Peter Berger, New York
September, 1963.

The Church Serving the Lord of the World

The New World

1. In Jesus Christ, his death and resurrection, God reconciled the world with himself (II Cor. 5:19). The glorification of the Crucified Christ marks the beginning of a new age, in which everything that the living God designed for his whole creation shall be accomplished. God crowned Christ's voluntary self-abasement by making him Lord of a whole world in rebellion against its God—a world which had nevertheless been mercifully preserved from destruction and which was already moulded by his power.

2. After Christ's Ascension, the world entered the aeon of the Last Days. The history which Christ assumed by becoming man, and thus the Saviour and judge of all, is henceforward directed towards the manifestation of his Kingdom. The whole of history thus becomes the scene of a promise and a crisis. The power of evil is released, bringing with it terrible menaces and catastrophes; but the rule of Christ has been inaugurated in the world, which cannot escape from its Saviour. A radical transformation has taken place, completely changing the course of the world, and directing it towards the Kingdom.

3. The history of the world is therefore passing through a phase which is determined by something which has *already* happened but has *not yet* been consummated. The distance between them manifests what has already been accomplished, but is still hidden. The seed has been sown, the leaven has been introduced into the lump; soon it will become apparent that all things have been made new (II Cor. 5:17). Secretly, although the continuity of the process cannot be revealed, the world is involved in a history which is positive because Jesus Christ is present in it and at work in it.

The Eschatological People

4. The Church is simply that part of the world which, through the Holy Spirit, has realised the basic transformation that has taken place in the universe. Between the coming of Christ, by all that has been accomplished and the final manifestation of his victory, the Church is called to indicate the Kingdom and to foreshadow the things to come. The Church is the instrument used by God in order to reveal (through the Word, through obedience, through service, through freedom with regard to all the powers, through critical discernment . . .) its own future "raison d'être" and the motivating force of the whole of history: Christ's merciful reign and his judgment in the midst of the world. The Church is thus the mirror and the promise of the new creation, the sign and the manifestation that evil has been vanquished, and that grace is stronger than damnation.

5. It is therefore not possible to speak about the confrontation between the Church and the world except from the angle of the common denominator which unites them: the consummation in Christ of God's whole work. In a world which has already capitulated and been unmasked, the Church (gathered and illumined by the Holy Spirit) bears testimony that Christ is Lord and that the Kingdom is coming, amid the ambiguous events of a history which seems incomprehensible but which is already illumined and moulded by glory. The confession of faith (i.e. the existence of the Christian community worshipping, interceding, proclaiming the Gospel and serving) is the concrete affirmation of the Lordship of Christ over the world, in a certain time and place, amid the contradictory movements of history. This knowledge of the faith involves on the one hand the active service of the reconciliation brought about in Christ and consequently the rejection of everything that is opposed to it; on the other hand it involves the recognition of Christ's presence and of his power wherever the signs of his Lordship are perceptible in the world. The Church greets him with joy and thanksgiving amid those who do not know him and who are in his service and accomplish his will without knowing it.

Serving the glorified Servant

6. The Church is the mission that the Holy Spirit is carrying out now in the world. It believes that Jesus Christ is its Lord, because first of all he is Lord of the world. It makes the living God known by

recognising the signs of his victorious work in the world. For all these reasons, the end and the centre of the Church do not lie within itself. It is through solidarity with all men, through sharing in the destiny of its contemporaries, through humble dialogue with Jews, pagans and atheists, through meeting them and living with them as brothers, that the Church manifests the glorious Lordship of the Suffering Servant through whom God has reconciled the world with Himself.

7. Consequently the Church participates resolutely in history, not because it is competent to write a philosophy of history, nor because it holds an optimistic theory concerning progress or evolution. It does so because it knows that, owing to Jesus Christ, it shares fully in the destiny of the world; because it believes that the changes taking place in the world (however ambiguous) are tending towards the manifestation of what was inaugurated by Christ's Ascension; namely, the universal presence and the eternal reign of the Resurrected Christ. But just because of that, as a result of it and in expectation of it, the only form which the Church's presence in the world can take is that of selfless service freely given without any ulterior motive and without expecting any advantage for itself. The Church will always be at the crucial point on which everything hinges, wherever the world unconsciously reveals simultaneously its rejection of God and its submission to its Lord. Like its Lord, the Church (which is the Body of Christ and the eschatological people) will always be in a vulnerable, risky situation with no power, no wealth and no guarantee, manifesting, through its abasement the victory of him who, for love, suffered sacrifice and death. At all times and in all places the Church will follow Jesus Christ where he goes before it, in the flexibility and the diversity of its ministry.

Structures

8. Thus the Church does not endeavour to set up an institutional schema "for all times and places" (and arbitrarily selected, for there are many forms of Church in the New Testament). It works out the form of its message and of its presence in relation to the movements of the world in which it bears testimony of the incarnation of the Word (i.e. its humanisation, its "expression in history"). It is in response to a situation outside itself that the Church will define its own structures; it is therefore clear that these structures are constantly

in need of revision; the process can never be completed, because it is always having to be considered afresh. The greater a church's sense of mission is, the more diverse and flexible its structures will be. Consequently if it seems to us that people today can be met and re-grouped in small cells and in great assemblies, there is nothing final about this characteristic. Perception of the movements of history (facilitated by the work of sociology, of economics, of geography, of philosophy. . . .) will involve a constant process of change in missions. But in any case, the Church's task is not "to bring Christ to men," but rather to recognise him, to listen to him, to serve him, and thus to signify him in every sphere of human life.

9. The most elementary structure of the missionary congregation is the gathering of a few people to carry out a joint defined missionary task. In our opinion this structure ought, by definition, to be open and to enable a dialogue to take place between Christians and non-Christians; because the question at issue is not to extend the Church (by means of skillfully-modernised methods of proselytism), but solely the service of Jesus Christ in which Christians who know him, and pagans or atheists who do not know him, gather for a common task in the service of mankind and in expectation of the Kingdom. In saying this we affrm that the presence of the other, the non-Christian, is just as indispensable to the true life of the Church as the presence of the Church is essential to the health of the world.

10. We realise that two dangers are involved. On the one hand, an attitude of this kind is in danger of leading to the break-up and the disappearance of the Church, which would lose itself in the world and no longer have any significance there. On the other hand the recognition of the Lord's presence in other people is in danger of leading Christians into a fatal confusion between the world and Jesus Christ, so that the world's events or doctrines take the place of Holy Scripture. Realising also that the church-ghetto or Christian imperialism are the worst betrayals of the Gospel of the Suffering Servant, in our opinion missionary presence cannot be effected unless it constantly renews its strength in the Word received and meditated upon together and experienced in Holy Communion, the sacrament of the Body of Christ foreshadowing the unity of all men in him. Thus it is not of ourselves that we shall recognise Christ, and serve Christ, in every aspect of life. It is as a result of his specific presence in the Word which is heard

and interpreted in the community. This is not a chronological order, as if one could know Christ apart from history, community and service. It is through obedience to the missionary order, through dispersion and spreading the message, that the Church renews its life in the communion of saints.

11. This means that our search for structures which are sufficiently diverse and flexible goes hand in hand with the fact that no one can commit himself to this course by isolating himself from the body of the Church and creating (with a few other people) a small independent cell. On the contrary, it is clear that the renewal of the churches' structures in the light of the given mission must be accompanied by the re-discovery of a true ecclesial order. This order should be based on sharing, on interdependence, on mutual aid between Christians engaged in extremely varied forms of service, but all united in the communion of the same Church and sharing in its total ministry. Consequently the deeper we go in our search for the structures of the missionary congregation, the more we shall realise that progress towards visible Christian unity is the indispensable condition for it. It is within the full harmony of one, holy, catholic and apostolic Church that this mission-movement will find its true balance. This trend is already apparent, it is making progress in all the Christian confessions, leading us to discover brethren from other confessions who are committed like ourselves to the same Christian service among people who do not know him. The wealth of our different church-heritages and of our particular traditions often seems quite unimportant in comparison with the common obedience to which we are called today.

Liturgy

12. In this context it seems necessary to define what this involves for the worship service, in which we express our thanksgiving to the living God. According to the 12th chapter of Romans, the service of the Word (*logike latreia*), which is the expression of our Christian liberty, is an offering of our whole life to God (*thusia zosa*). It is in serving the Suffering Servant, who is now glorified, the brother and Lord of all men, that this worship is expressed. It is therefore both mission and "worship," serving presence and adoration. We have tended too much to regard mission as secondary in importance to worship; but we know

now that "worship" is unfaithful if it is not adoration and the renewal of the community scattered all over the world.

Therefore worship can and must be celebrated where mission is exercised, although this does not exclude larger gatherings. Worship is then the moment when the community explicitly relates its own existence to Jesus Christ, and when it relates to Jesus Christ the world in which it serves, and to which Christ sends it to meet men with renewed joy and strength. When we speak here of worship in basic cells we mean worship in the full sense, namely with the sacraments. And in particular: as in the Early Church Communion was celebrated in "houses," so today it can and should be celebrated in every cell of the missionary congregation, due account being taken of the consideration of order and fraternal communion mentioned above. Celebrated in this way, within the concrete setting of a committed community, Holy Communion is both the culminating-point and the starting-point of missions. It is the meeting-place of those whom Christ then sends out to meet men, and of all who, by their presence, will have been led to recognise the Lord whom they served without yet knowing him.

Western European Working Group
Villemétrie, October, 1963.

Fourth Part

MISSIONARY PRESENCE

Gathering at the Point of Mission

I.

It has been said at the beginning of our study that "there is no such thing as *the* structure." We were reminded of this by a sociologist. In this connection our attention was called to historicity, differentiation and flexibility . . . and the term "morphological fundamentalism" was introduced . . .

On this basis it is necessary at all costs to avoid the temptation to look for a perfect structure. It is an extremely powerful temptation as long as the attempt is made, perhaps with best intentions, to replace the present generally valid structure by one new *generally* valid structure. Our aim, however, is not one single structure but structures (plural). Our concern is not a new order in a "post-Christian world" which could take the place of the old order of a "Christian world." We are looking for the possibility of multiple organization. We are not concerned about a new system, but about a . . . movement.

In the light of these remarks the title of our study is not correct. The title speaks of "structure" and yet should speak of *structures*. It speaks of "congregation" which in the singular always immediately comes to mean the local church or parish, and yet it should speak of congregations in the sense of any kind of community of Jesus Christ.

February, 1963.

II.

When we first discussed the theme in August 1960 in St. Andrews, Scotland, while working on proposals for the Assembly in New Delhi we understood it to mean "the missionary structure of the *local* congregation." As far as I was concerned the study should inquire into the question of how a local congregation should be structured in order to be a missionary congregation, and what steps would be required. In this way the theme was understood in New Delhi and afterwards. With this understanding we started. Only very few knew from the beginning, that the local congregation was in fact to be only one of the objects of study.

But these few had very sharp eyes. And what they saw can be read in the report about the study to the Central Committee of the World Council (See below, part V). The local parish is mentioned only at the end. This may be cause for regret and reproach, but it is very revealing with regard to the subject matter. As far as its treatment in our working groups is concerned, the first question was that concerning mission itself, God's relation to church and world, to world and church. The reason for this was not the theological habit always to start out with "fundamental questions." The reason was that obviously here was the sharpest dilemma. Secondly, in regard to the church's structures needed for the mission given to it, it turned out in spite of much uneasiness that the focus was less on the structure of the local parish than on *forms of missionary presence* (as we tried to express it) which are usually referred to as "experiments."

Several if not many participants in the discussion observed this development with some anxiety. For them it represented a deviation from the theme and a shirking of the immediate responsibility given by the churches. But it stands to reason that the difficult topic of the local parish might resist any approach which attempts to start out with this topic or to put it into the center. Answers to the question of the local parish may emerge only when the attempt is first made no longer to absolutize the local parish.[1]

---

[1]Dr. Jitsuo Morikawa, chairman of the North American Working Group, summarized the issue in the following way during the second meeting of the Working Group (Warwick, April, 1963):

> That the existing structures be renewed is the hope of all of us. But some prior questions face us, in the light of which we suggest the following procedure:
>
> 1) That we not by-pass the question of the renewability of the existing congregations, but that we return to it *after* we deal with some prior questions.
> 2) That we assume that existing congregations even as they are serve a useful purpose. They provide, though in a limited sense, corporate worship, preaching of the Word and Sacraments, some measure of fellowship, Christian education for children and young people. Surely to have crowds on Sunday morning is nothing to despise even if only on rare occasions deep encounters with God and neighbour take place. The fact of their being well attended may indicate to some degree their meeting a felt need. A limited evangelism is taking place there, an individualistic kind in relation to one's private needs and life, as so well stated by Gibson Winter.
> 3) That for the present we delimit our work to that phase of the subject which is prior to the renewal of existing congregations, namely the nature of missionary action. This will of course raise the question of the "Mission of God." But to focus this phase of the subject more concretely we suggest, "Shapes of the Church in Missionary Action in the Social Structures of the Modern World." Only as we discern what the church looks like when acting in mission in the frontiers of the modern industrial world, can we deal with the missionary structure of our existing congregations.

This does not mean the denial of its actual existence, its historical value and its renewability. It only means that the church of Jesus Christ does not need to be conceived in all and every circumstances as a local parish. To put it differently: perhaps the problem of the local parish, the problem which is experienced by many pastors and members can best be brought toward a solution by a close examination of new forms of missionary groupings with which the recent past has provided us, considering these groupings not as the norm but perhaps as examples.

September, 1964.

III

There is one particular problem of which we need to be aware at this point. In emphasizing "gathering" we must not be led to defend and protect the inherited forms of gathering. Rather we must first focus on the "mission" of today and tomorrow as it is facing us, and it is in the midst of our participation in this mission that we discern where and how there ought to be a gathering. In offering this as a thesis I am fully conscious of the difficulties involved. The main difficulty is perhaps the fact that gathered congregations do exist and that we are, therefore, not entirely free to move toward new forms. But in this discussion we are not only, and perhaps not even primarily, concerned about immediate possibilities. The God-given possibilities involve larger periods of time. With respect to these we need to ask toward what other possible forms we can already now point the congregations as we enter into conversation with them about their call to participate in God's work, the missio Dei.

Hans Jochen Margull, Geneva
November, 1964.

The Local Christian Community in the New Testament

It was in connection with the question of what the New Testament teaches about the congregation and its structure that I was asked to prepare an annotated bibliography of recent studies of the life of the congregation in the New Testament. To my surprise I discovered that there existed very few studies of this type and that treatments of biblical theology give only marginal consideration to the question. The article on *ekklesia* in Kittel's *Theologisches Wörterbuch zum Neuen Testament,* for instance, talks about the general concept of the Church but never specifically about the different forms of this *ekklesia* in varying historical situations.

To my mind, the one significant effort to look in this direction has been made by Eduard Schweizer in his articles "Unity and Diversity in the New Testament Teaching Regarding the Church" (*Theology Today* 13, 1956/57, 471-483), and "The Local Church and the Universal Church" (Ecumenical Review, 1956, 254-263), and in his book, *Church Order in the New Testament* (SCM Press, London, 1961). For our purposes, Schweizer's work is of special interest because he has undertaken to demonstrate the great variety of forms of the church in the New Testament, while at the same time pointing to a deeply rooted unity.

In seeking to evaluate the obvious variety of ecclesiological forms in the New Testament, Schweizer formulates the historical problem as follows: "The purely historical question, therefore, about the form of the Church at different times and places, while admittedly necessary, needs to be asked only insofar as the actual shaping of the Church is always evidence of the concept of its own nature to which it testifies" (Church Order, 7). In other words, the variety of church forms itself is of significance in that *no* contemporary congregational or church structure may claim exclusive justification on the basis of the New Testament and that *every* such church structure can, to a greater or lesser degree, claim justification on the basis of the various traditions within the New Testament.

As has been affirmed in the course of the current ecumenical study on "The Missionary Structure of the Congregation," the forms of congregational life (or of church order) are a part of the church's response to the Gospel. This response, and hence the forms of congregational life, vary considerably according to different historical, sociological and theological orientations. Thus we do not (any more) insist that forms of congregational life developed in the West are necessarily appropriate for churches in Africa or Asia, although we are still hesitant to admit that forms of church life which arose in Western rural society are no longer valid for Western industrial and urban society.

In these terms we must affirm that the Bible offers no normative pattern of congregational life which can be transplanted into our own time. As regards the historical question as such, the principle of variety and diversity is the only conclusion which can be applied in our situation. The attempt to claim exclusive justification for other elements of church life ignores the fundamental theological and historical basis of the diversity of congregational life as it is reflected in the New Testament. Schweizer writes: ". . . A mere repetition of New Testament formulae or regulations no more guarantees the Church's authenticity than does the continuance of the same line of development within a given tradition" (Church Order, Ie).

What, then, is the underlying theological basis which can be seen through this surprising variety of church offices, liturgical forms and sacramental interpretations? Is it possible to reconcile Luke's and the Pastorals' emphasis on tradition and continuity with Israel on the one hand with John's emphasis on the radical freedom of the new—communal as well as individual—life under the Risen Lord on the other hand? This much at least must be affirmed. If there exists a common basis between these two extreme—but scriptural—forms of congregational life, it will not be found in specific organizational, sacramental or ministerial principles as such. To focus attention on the tradition of presbyters and bishops, for example, is to overlook the unique historical circumstances which provoked, and in a sense necessitated the emergence of these special forms of church order. Furthermore, the strongly Jewish-apocalyptic background of certain New Testament writings and the later threat from gnosticizing "heretics"—against which both Paul and John were struggling—present conditions which are far too polemical and problematic to serve as a solid foundation for establishing a pattern for church order or congregational life in other situations, be they Paul's, John's or our own.

The implication of these statements, coupled with the great variety of congregational life in the New Testament, is that the variety exists not merely at the level of congregational structures but also at the deeper level of the ecclesiological basis itself. In his book *Images of the Church in the New Testament,* (Westminster Press, Philadelphia 1960) P. S. Minear indicates 96 different images of the Church in the New Testament. Among them are "the salt of the earth," "a letter from Christ," "unleavened bread," "exiles," "ambassadors," "the people of God," "twelve tribes," "Abraham's sons,' "the Holy City," "priesthood." To the extent that we cannot simply separate the notions of form and content, we must recognize the diversity of (ecclesiological) content behind the variety of (congregational) forms.

As examples of this fundamental diversity, we may accept the following summaries of Schweizer as representing a broad range of agreement among biblical scholars. ". . . It is not accidental that the churches we met in Acts and in the Pastorals, and to a certain extent in Matthew and the Synoptics, see the decisive turn in the times in terms of the *future,* in the Parousia of the Son of Man" (Unity, 478).

"John stressed more strongly than Paul that everything has now taken place, the Aeon has broken in . . . John saw the newness of the Church even more sharply than Paul. Church "offices" existed only on the side of the enemies of God . . ." (Unity, 481). "The Pauline Churches stood in the middle. They knew that the event marking the beginning of a new epoch had already come to pass . . . At the same time, however, they knew that they were living inside a community that was not identical with the Kingdom of God" (Unity, 483).

The problem of locating a principle of unity within this great diversity of church life is nothing other than the problem of the unity of the New Testament itself. We have already seen that this unity cannot be grounded in specific theological or organizational principles as such. With respect to the canon, the cherished principle of apostolic authorship can no longer guarantee even this minimal basis of unity. In like manner, with respect to church order and congregational life, the equally cherished principle of apostolic succession, in whatever form, is no longer valid as the unique, or even primary guarantee of authentic communal existence in Christ.

Rather, the principle of unity and authenticity is to be found in Schweizer's affirmation in connection with the Pauline congregations.

"For that reason the man from outside, the fringe member or the Gentile, is for Paul the proper yardstick by which the whole proclamation must be measured (I Cor. 14:16f, 23-25) . . . For the same reason Paul will in the last resort allow no distinction between prophetic preaching to church members and to those from outside" (Church Order, 28). It is in terms of the "outsider," the hearer of the Gospel, that the life and proclamation of the local Christian community is to be judged and conceived. The basic truth of this affirmation is that even the most solid of church members is himself an "outsider" and that every element of church order is but a provisional and limited response to specific situations. Every attempt to codify and institutionalize this response denies both historical change as well as social and institutional variety. By separating itself from the social and historical processes of the world, the Christian community unfailingly demonstrates its profoundest worldliness. On the other hand, when the Christian community recognizes that its authenticity depends not on given forms of order, worship or service, but on God's own action of calling, sustaining and forgiving, then it will be free to reshape its life and worship in terms of the particular historical and social reality in which it must bear its witness.

Consequently, what is needed is a thoroughly sociological study of congregational life within the New Testament, which would indicate precisely how the life of the "outsider" (by this term I imply the general cultural and social milieu) did—and often did not—dictate the forms of congregational life in different areas of the New Testament world. Such studies have already been carried out with respect to the specifically theological traditions of the New Testament. But we must recognize that theological reflection does not exhaust the life of early Christianity. This reflection was but one element among others in the life of the community. The shape of the community, as well as the shape of its theology, was created by a concern for authentic existence in a given—undoubtedly unique—historical situation. Once we have recognized this fundamental principle, we will be set free *from* slavery to the specific forms of the church in early Christianity and set free *to* discover their more fundamental theological and historical significance for our own Christian communities.

John G. Gager, at Tübingen
October, 1963.

A Reminder from Church History

The Latin church in Switzerland of the 6th and 7th centuries can be considered as an example showing the failure of old structures of thinking and organisation. The Roman Empire had collapsed, a new and young people, the Alemanni moved in and celebrated their heathen rites. They planted lime trees and oak groves on many hills and gathered for their moon festival. They despised the cities and lived on isolated farms around Zurich (names of city quarters like Hirslanden, Fluntern, Hottingen, etc., still indicate their Alemannic origin). In the city the Latin-speaking pastors lamented the fall of Christianity within the Roman culture. The thought of christianizing the barbarous Alemanni whose language they did not understand did not even occur to them. At this moment missionaries from Irish missionary monasteries arrived with a new structure of proclamation and mission.

The indignation of the Latin-speaking Christians who were well established in the region and who resented this intrusion was no hindrance to the efficiency of these new evangelists who did not heed the parochial system. The Irish missionaries built up small centers in Switzerland, in Alsace and in Southern Germany. These centres (one of which is St. Gallen which played an important rôle in the history of the church and culture of Central Europe) guaranteed the continuity of the church and the proclamation of the Gospel among the Alemannic tribes.

Walter Hollenweger, Zurich
September, 1964

The Experiment in the Church

Thus far we lack a theological interpretation of the experiment in the church, although the term is more and more used in the discussion about forms of work and life. Indications of a theological clarification are found in Hans Schmidt's *Vita Experimentalis* (Munich 1959). There is need to continue this work.

Unfortunately, the discussion usually equates the experiment with "new forms" or "new ways," which are immediately set up over against the old. Hans Schmidt clearly points to the fundamental issue by saying that "The courage for the experiment lies in the obedience of faith. Experimenting without presuppositions, on the other hand, is merely a guessing of emerging possibilities in order to capture them. The possibilities are played through for their own sake. Such an experiment is no longer guidance and station on the way to a goal, but an end in itself. Why not do it differently for once? Is it not thinkable, is it not possible?—In contrast to this fascination with the possible the vita experimentalis of the Christian and the Christian congregation remains under the force of the necessary" (p. 7). If this is correct, our aim must be to remove the distrust in the churches with regard to the notion of experiment.

I. SOME THESES

Based on the thesis by Hans Schmidt we assume that *the experiment is essential for a missionary congregation.*

1. In the context of the experiment the congregation offers itself up. The Lord of the experiment is Christ Himself. At first, the congregation is the initiator of the experiment, but then mainly the object and thereby part of the experiment. It takes the risk to be changed in the course of the experiment.

2. The experiment of the congregation aims to uncover new territory. It wants God "to show the land." This is its promise at all times and in all directions. The experiment seeks the breakthrough to this new land. It "sends out explorers" and seeks "the crossing over the Jordan."

3. Every experiment in the congregation is "for keeps." For each interaction of the world with the congregation as the bearer of witness to Christ amounts to a *test* of the Gospel, a *test* of the Christian, a call to faith, the possibility of obedience. Experiment does not mean to play in the sense of not being serious, but it means partiality in terms of the area of involvement. The multiformity of church structures which is called for today is unthinkable without the experiment.

4. The experiment must always be conscious of its limited scope and can only be aimed at one sector. Therefore, every generalization

or even ideologization of specific observations and results must be avoided. However, the experiment yields guidelines and pointers for comparable situations.

5. No experiment can ignore what is already known. Also, it works with prior assumptions and uses proven means. In most cases the result is not totally new either. Nevertheless, there must be openness for the possibility that an experiment might break through into completely new territory.

6. This also means openness for continual revision. The possibility of failure must be built in from the beginning in the sense that the questions with which the experiment started out may find a negative answer.

7. On the other hand, the experiment might possibly lead not only to a change of the "system within the system," but open up the access to new systems (structures). But this presupposes *responsible experimenting.*

8. Responsible experimenting in the church demands the art of seeing what is going on and to understand what is seen as an *issue.* It means above all to hear and recognize the *critique* which is implied in the results.

There is too much and to quick talk about the invisibility and unmeasurability of spiritual developments—but: "You shall know them by their fruits!"

II. COMMON TRENDS IN EXPERIMENTS

The group discussing "experiments" during the first meeting of the Western European Working Group at Bossey, February 1963, observed the following "trends" common to "experiments":

1) Discovery of the laity and its significance.
2) Discovery of team work, fellowship (brotherhoods) and cooperation.
3) Rediscovery of the charismata.
4) Discovery of the fact that without confrontation and engagement in the world (theology of incarnation!) faith withers.
5) The conviction: God speaks to Christians not only in worship serv-

ice, but also in encounter with contemporaries and with present events.

6) Experiments arise where Christians discover the diaspora in a secularized world.
7) Many experiments arise where the rapid change of our times is recognized. Consequence: mobility which abandons (traditional) structures.
8) The rediscovery of the laity leads to a rediscovery of the nature of ministry.
9) Across dogmatic traditions a new and direct access to the New Testament message is found.
10) The personal relations developing among members of an "experiment" team are more effective than traditional orders. The experiment transcends the limitations of race, class, nation and education.
11) Practically all those who partake in experiments are of a "realistic brand" and they are "optimists." In almost every case, however, they know of their limitations.
12) In many experiments people have embarked on an exodus from the traditional institutions (independence from the taboo).
13) Teams working on experiments tend to follow a discipline appropriate to their experiments. At the same time, however, they are prone to ideologies.

Werner Simpfendoerfer, Bad Boll
November, 1963

Presence in Pluralism

In the following statement on new forms of missionary presence, it is assumed that these forms emerge from the interplay of the Gospel and the new social situation as Christians seek to be obedient to the Christ who is both the content of the Gospel and the Lord of the world.

It is in a multiplicity of powers and situations that even the New Testament confesses one Lord, one faith, one baptism, one hope. A multiplicity of situations is therefore nothing new, and pluralism has always been not only a numerical but a dynamic system, which did not allow for a single mould into which the Christian message and its form should be poured. The commission of the Church has always been marked by Paul's call to "serve the Lord," which also appears in another version in the New Testament's critical apparatus as "serve the time": "Be at the disposal of the *kyrios* and as such of the *kairos*."

The obedience of the Church demands that we obtain a clear picture of each particular *kairos* so that the Gospel may reach the poor and the service of the Church may be performed where the hungry and thirsty, the naked and the imprisoned are. The commission of the Church in itself is pluralistic in character—that is, it is always concrete. The message and shape of the Church can only be formulated in view of the concrete multiple reality.

I. *Diversified Society in Search of Unity*

1. Industrial society is constituted by division of labor and separation of work and habitation. The consequent social and economic specialization has produced a multiplicity of centers decisive for social action, constituting "a multiplicity of worlds" in which man lives simultaneously. This multiplicity of centers (differentiation) involving at the same time the problem of integration, is understood as pluralism in industrial society. As the degree of industrialization differs throughout the world, the problems of pluralism appear in different urgency.

2. Thus pluralism diversifies all spheres of modern life. This is exemplified in four major structural spheres:

(a) Pluralism in basic elements of culture (e.g., interpenetration of culture, breaking up of traditional cultural, ethical, social patterns, appearance of conflicting Weltanschauungen).

(b) Pluralism as a result of the technological and material processes (e.g., mobility set in opposition to local roots).

(c) Pluralism in roles of the individual (e.g., problems of identity and integrity).

(d) Pluralism in organizational patterns. In this structure the most pervasive strains occur for the society at large (e.g., interests of producers set against consumers; technological elite isolated from the masses; values of a planned society violating free small communities).

3. This diversifying effect of pluralism makes man experience life as being broken. But against this fracturing experience forces are at work towards a sense of unity. Ideologies try to establish coherence by common ideals. There is a widespread search for a way of life which imparts unity within diversity by one sphere of life becoming central and others peripheral (e.g., family, occupation, leisure). In some places nationalism becomes an ideological unity. In others we see the rise of ancient religions to negate pluralism. Notions of "Christendom in Western Europe" and "religion in general" in America attempt a similar service. Finally, mechanical procedures for efficient coordination convey the impression that pluralism may be overcome in terms of outward unity and order.

4. While these forces attempt in a mostly reactionary way to rule out divisive effects of pluralism, the same dynamics which work towards pluralism have certain universal consequences both positive and negative.

Man's drive to master nature (science);
Man's adoption of the method of the *rational* organization of means to ends (technology);
Man's thirst for knowledge to accomplish 1 and 2, with the result of mass education (democratization of education);
The rising expectation of masses to participate in social and economic progress;
Mobility as freedom to move in geographical and social areas;
High degree of specialization, with man depersonalized as a function;
Increasing differentiation threatening atomization, creating fear and despair, forcing search for new ways of coherence;
Emancipation of women through education and occupation;
Mass communication uniting the world;
The common pressure on all nations to maintain peace being confronted with the nuclear threat (apocalyptic umbrella).

II. *Resulting Challenges for the Mission of the Church*

The social process defined by pluralism might leave the church untouched if it conceived itself as the goal of history and end of God's purpose. Then simply to survive and strengthen its position would be the only need. But ministry rather than survival being the commission to the Church it is challenged by those factors in history of opportunities and threats and called by Christ to freedom shaping the future of the world.

1. Pluralism of roles enables man to reach out into the fullness of reality and try out his powers in all spheres of life. This imposes upon man a variety of claims often conflicting. On the one hand he may lose his identity aind integrity in this role-play. On the other hand he is caught up in the ongoing process of choice between different roles. The danger is to give up changing the roles, to settle down with only one aspect of his existence and losing his full destination.

2. Pluralism of values is another opportunity for man realizing his freedom and shaping the future. A pluralistic world horizon confronts man with a multitude of cultural and ethical values. Yet there is danger in the relativism of values, which discourages man from shaping his own history. So pluralism of values is but another still deeper threat to man's sense of wholeness and direction.

3. Pluralism of centers of decision bears the chance of balance and even of democratization of power while on the other hand these centers show a concentration of anonymous decision making. This poses the problems of loyalty and integrity. Man must submit to different centers of decision and yet not bind himself to one of them. Man needs to move and yet is threatened by the quest of each of these centers to keep his full loyalty and to take away his freedom. The challenge to the church appears in this respect not only as ministering to man under the power of decision-making centers but also as ministering to these centers of decision—working out a serving presence *for* a pluralistic society.

4. Pluralism being a neutral structure of social process offers the opportunity for both good and evil. Yet there is the danger of relying upon this pluralism as a well-operating system while this pluralism poses new kinds of threats: the process of constant role-shifting and change of groupings makes it utterly difficult to identify "my neighbour." The poor and sick, the naked and the imprisoned somehow disappear within a system which outwardly seems to operate perfectly. Those who do not know the rules of this game are lost. In face of this the churches in the power of the Gospel need to identify and serve those who need the ministry of Christian fellowship.

III.

IV. *Types of Missionary Presence*

Christians are already engaged in new shapes of missionary presence that are successfully penetrating the social structures now isolated from the traditional congregation. What have been called "little congregations" are beginning to be formed in very diverse shapes in order for Christians to be present in places from which traditional congregations are excluded. Some of these may roughly be classified as follows:

a) approaches to man at the points of his secular strength, such as industrial missions, evangelical academies, coffee houses for discussion with artists and intellectuals, conferences for scientists;

b) forms for penetration into the diverse "worlds" of modern man, such as cell groups in factories, offices and hospitals, house churches, student and faculty groups in schools and universities, truck-stop ministries (e.g., Kobe/Japan road);

c) planned approach of the churches to the interrelated patterns of modern metropolis, wherein diverse groups are brought together for consideration of their common problems;

d) those taking form to meet man in his crisis situations, such as alcoholics, narcotic addicts, threatened suicides, couples facing divorce, juvenile delinquents, deserted old people, refugees, and migrant workers;

e) participation in and identification with social revolutions of our day, such as the race revolution in the United States and the popular movements for radical social changes in Brazil;

f) temporary ad hoc groups of various congregations and Christian groups for the promotion of a program or for the attack upon a specific problem of a city or regional area;

g) comprehensive missionary outreach to the total neighbourhood by the total congregation, such as the East Harlem Protestant Parish and rural projects in India;

h) experiments in community life, such as Taizé, the Ashrams of India, the Agape Community, the Iona Community or Koinonia Farms in Georgia.

These types or examples of missionary presence may be called paradigmatic forms that inspire other Christians to see the possibilities for creative response to the calling of Christ in our day. In any case they must be acknowledged as authentic fellowships of Christians in missionary service. This multiplicity of forms that the Church must take and actually is taking poses the problem of Christian unity with new force and in quite new terms.

V. *Ecclesiological Implications*

We must call attention to the fact that the acceptance of these new forms of missionary presence carries with it far-reaching ecclesiological implications, including the following:

1. According to the traditional ecclesiological understanding, the residential local congregations alone are recognized as valid units of the Church, i.e., having the right to administer sacraments. If the multiple forms, indicated above, are accepted as authentic expressions of the Church's life and mission, then it would imply that they also need to be considered as valid units of the Church, just as or in place of the present forms of local congregations. This would call into question the normative position of the traditional congregation in relation to the ecclesiological status of these new forms.

2. If the diversification of ministries as advocated above, is recognized as valid, then it will lead to a renewed understanding of the Church as "one Body with many gifts and diverse functions." However, if this is the case, will it not call into question the traditional bifurcation of the people of God into clergy and laity? Will such diversified ministries require special commissioning and if so what are the implications for our understanding of ordination? Furthermore does not such a step require reexamination of both the content and method of catechetical instructions, lay training, and training of clergy and church workers?

3. It is conceivable that acceptance and encouragement of multiple forms of church life might result in such proliferation that will create disorder and threaten the unity of the Church. Therefore, it is necessary to keep the order of the churches and the multiple forms of mission in integral relationship. However, is it not in such situations, when the order of the churches and the multiple forms of mission are kept

in healthy tension that the churches realize their dynamic character and organic nature? Is it also possible that the "ad hoc" nature of the new forms will tend to lead to an underestimation of certain permanent features which form part of the heritage of the tradition of the churches? There again, will not a healthy tension between them help the churches to understand themselves better as a "pilgrim" people who live out here and now the glorious liberty of the children of God, in living communion with the saints of the past and in the living hope of the Kingdom?

Many of the emerging new forms are already and will be ecumenical. Will not such a situation help the churches to realize the necessity for unity in mission and consequently recovery of unity in their very being?

It is our convictionthat the new situation gives new tasks which require new structures. It is also our conviction that such new structures should be accepted not as additional or secondary forms of Church life, but as its authentic expressions. But in order to be so, these forms should be rooted in a genuine self-understanding of the Church itself. Yet such self-understanding may follow rather than precede the establishment of new structures and the actual working out of such missionary obedience. The Church grows in its self-understanding, as it grows in missionary experience.

Enlarged Working Committee of the Department on
Studies in Evangelism
Bossey, April 1964.

Beginnings of New Forms of Life

1. In several congregations of the DDR some initial, if only small, steps can be seen which lead to a new recognition of responsibility towards those who until now were not to be found in the congregation. In wrestling with the heritage of the past and with manifold attempts of restoration, some beginnings of new forms of life are discernible, even if only in a sporadic way at present.

2. *From separation to brotherhood*

While in the inherited and still-existing Territorial Churches (Landeskirchen)—in contrast to the small Free Churches (Freikirchen)—the members of the congregation existed in greater distance from each other and still so exist, here and there in the DDR they have begun to come closer to each other and to live with one another in forms of brotherhood.

3. *From care-structure to cooperation*

While the two inherited forms of life (characteristics: being cared for and being managed) still largely determine the picture today, in some places the activities (Veranstaltungen) by and by become gatherings of Christians who have come of age, and who carry themselves the responsibility for all life in the Church and who understand themselves as cooperating communities. Likewise, in some congregations, the abundance of a variety of gifts is discovered and the respective charismatic person is formally confirmed in his service by the congregation. With this the functions of a pastor are partly changed.

4. *From Private Christianity to Witness*

The individual Christian participating in Church life and trying, in his private life, to live according to God's commandments will in a special surrounding (see 3) be torn out of this private sphere by God. Through this he becomes a gathering point in non-Christian or anti-Church surrounding, even—or especially then—when he has to suffer as a witness.

5. *From rites to gathering of fellow-travellers*

The so-called ministrations (weddings, confirmations and funerals), are largely a mixture of indispensable magic rites and solemn family festivity—this goes especially for Christenings. Misunderstood, and in former times generally demanded, they are noticeably decreasing in number and gain more and more a new character. They are becoming gatherings of the people of God which, on its way, collectively hears the Gospel in its relationship to specific situations of life, and where the members of this people are brotherly companions of each other. The missionary character of these gatherings is especially clear through the presence of non-Christians.

6. *From the parochial to supra-parochial structures*

More and more Christians—through the challenge of society—are led to be active in their existence as members of the local congregation as well as to cooperate in supra-parochial structures, if they do not want to be guilty of omitting a series of acknowledged tasks and necessary services in church and society. (Evangelical academies, evangelical student congregations; working groups for sociology, social sciences, natural sciences, technical sciences, psychology and others; furthermore, youth conventions, lay seminars, training centers of church elders, groups of members of the same crafts or similar interests.)

DDR Working Group
March, 1964.

Missionary Presence in the Racial Revolution

I. *The Freedom Movement in the South of the U.S.A., 1960-1963*

The problem of race is a world problem. Men in every nation have been guilty of making distinctions which are contrary to the Christian doctrine of the unity of mankind in Christ. The United States is one of the places where this problem has loomed as one of major importance and where God's activity reconciling his children in and through the events of history seems most apparent today. For this reason we have selected the Freedom Movement in the United States of America as a parable of new forms of missionary activity in the world.

1) *Ad Hoc Activity,* which seemingly grows out of unplanned incidents, is characteristic of the Movement. Persons of concern, both Christian and non-Christian gather in response to needs, crises, or incidents and rapidly organize their response.

2) *Direct, Non-violent Action* is the method which is usually employed in response. Here the concerned persons seek to call attention to the particular injustice dramatically by exposing themselves to it openly and deliberately.

3) *Demonstrative Commitment,* which involves the bodily participa-

tion of the concerned in large numbers, seems to have a catalyctic effect upon other persons of good will who observe the action and results in a spread or continuation of the action.

4) These *actions* are consciously *ecumenical,* seeking to involve as large a segment of the population as possible. Those which meet with most success seem to bind the classes and the masses, youth and adults, clergy and laity, and blend traditionally sacred and secular elements into one movement centered around a single issue.

5) The *leadership* which emerges from these actions is of a highly *charismatic* nature; someone who can grasp the emotional impact of the situation and express it either verbally or through his actions to the masses of people involved.

6) *Voluntary Suffering,* accepted on one's own behalf or in the behalf of others, seems to be the source of the group's power. This is to be distinguished from situations in which people cannot avoid suffering. Here the group deliberately exposes itself to risks in order that the injustice might be made public and "raised before the court of world opinion" where they might receive favorable judgment against injustice.

7) Public Meetings, held at least weekly, and often on Monday nights feature a *contemporary liturgy* which includes songs about the events of the past week based on traditional spirituals or secular groups, prayer for the Movement and the enemies of the Movement, preaching around the issues of the Movement, recruiting for action in the coming events of the Movement, and an offering to cover any expenses incurred by the Movement. Usually these meetings are held in a church building, but there is very little if any distinction made between clergy and lay leadership.

8) *Training and Nurture* are carried on in the context of action. You are trained for immediate action and nurtured in the Movement by those who have had more experience as you participate together in the task at hand. When the action involves jail, training and discipline are continued in jail by the leader of that particular demonstration. Periodic worship is also scheduled as a part of the *jail discipline.*

9) The Movement usually grows out of the particular incident which

initiated it, but gradually expands to include the *whole list of grievances* of the oppressed community. The right to eat at lunch counters, the right to employment without discrimination based on race, and the right to vote and obtain an equal education are some of the key issues.

10) The *motives* of the Movement are often quite mixed. The stated goals might also be complicated by personal hostilities, ambitions and interests, but so long as these do not interfere with the progress of the Movement, they are tolerated.

11) These demonstrations result in a *mass education* of the entire nation and world as to what the issues and problems are for the Negro community. Persons in other areas find themselves confronted daily by the news of injustice in their midst and whether they want to or not, they are gradually forced by public opinion to come to some decision for themselves. Mass media are a key factor in this type of mass education.

12) The Movement involves a *non-ecclesiastical approach to mission.* The care of the sick, poor and needy become issues of public concern and rather than meet them with traditional charity from individuals or groups, the Movement demands that society change the structures which cause these conditions. Hence you have fulfillment of mission through political action.

13) There is always present in the Movement a sense of *largesse:* results accruing beyond those which were intended. This is evident to all involved. The Christian takes this as an indication that this is God's activity in the course of history. This might be illustrated by the demonstrations in Birmingham, Alabama, which initially intended only to desegregate lunch counters and employment opportunities in local department stores, but which resulted in proposed Federal legislation which could drastically change the whole of American life in behalf of racial justice, North and South.

14) Much of the leadership in the civil rights movement is Christian. The large majority of the followers are committed Christians also. These persons are *God's People in the midst of the world.* They are gathered around the immediate concern or urgent issue and God gives them the form which their obedience should take. (Experience has shown that while there are some common factors in the Movements of different localities, each local community must discern the form

which its protest must take, and seldom can patterns be duplicated unimaginatively.)

15) These Christians are called from active participation in their congregations, or from inactivity, to work as *partners with God* in the Reconciliation of the world to himself and the races of mankind to each other. In the Movement they may or may not develop a life together as Christians, but when this is possible they become a powerful evangelical force witnessing to the world and to their brothers in the Movement as to the mighty acts of God.

II. *Congregation*

1) A clarification is needed here with respect to the term "congregation" before we seek to evaluate what is involved in the Freedom Movement.

2) A congregation cannot be but a community of pro-existence. It exists for God and for the world; worship and effective service to man belong inseparately together. A congregation cannot exist for itself. We, therefore, call congregation in this context any group brought together by Jesus Christ around his word and sacrament, responding in service to men, especially men in crisis, and thus experiencing his living fellowship.

3) On the basis of this definition, the conclusion should be drawn that *little congregations*, as the over-all term used to designate "witness and service groups," "ad hoc congregations," "special issue/problem-centered groups," "cells," and so on, the common characteristic of which is that they reflect on specific problems and situational challenges in the light of the Bible, and feel obliged to act upon the results of this reflection, as much as *existing churches* in the sense of (national) denominations, and *existing congregations*, in the sense of (local) parish churches, are to be considered as (legitimate) expressions of the church universal, and therefore can lay equal claim to the "right" of proclaiming and receiving the word and the sacraments, i.e., of being congregations in the ecclesiological sense.

Enlarged Working Committee of the
Department on Studies in Evangelism,
Bossey, April, 1964.

The Witness of Laymen in the Secular World

A summary of Ecumenical Thought on the Laity in Relation to its Mission in the Secular World.

1. The rediscovery of the "laity" has been hailed as an event equal in magnitude and momentum to that of 16th century Reformation. If this is true then we are only mid-stream in a mighty movement which it is not yet possible to survey, even less to summarize.

I. *Historical Perspectives*

2. In retrospect we can clearly see that the lay movement in its modern form originated as a part of the renewal of the churches in the last century. The emergence of the Young Men's Christian Association, the Student Volunteer Movement and the Student Christian Movement as the first great lay organizations is as closely interrelated with that of the Ecumenical Movement as it is with the revival of world mission at that time. They all express the rediscovered ecumenical character of the Church. They all share the same slogans like "evangelization of the world in this generation" and the same leadership of which names like John Mott and J. H. Oldham are imperishable symbols. Their commonness lies, however, above all in the renewed awareness of the mission of the Church in the world which was one of the basic driving forces of the whole revival. Later on the formation of, for instance, the British Frontier Council or of the Kirchentag Movement and the Evangelical Academies follows the same pattern in that they sprung from a new encounter with the modern world. Also, one could point to the prominent role which the laity is often playing in a minority church situation be it in Asia or Eastern Europe. The dissolution of Christendom and the emergence of secularized nations challenged the churches to rediscover their laymen as the true witness in the world.

3. Here we find something like a red thread which runs through church history. The Church's awareness of its responsibility to the world and the active participation of the laity in the life and mission of the Church always go together. Of the Ancient Church, a time of vast missionary outreach, it can be said that it grew spontaneously through the informal and unorganized witness of "ordinary" Christians

"who carried the gospel into the recesses of society"[1] The "Sitz im Leben" of the theology of the laity and the witness of laymen is in historical perspective this point of meeting between Church and world.

II. *Biblical Foundations*

4. Soon, however, the active participation of laymen, which characterized the Ancient Church, was doomed to a more and more passive role. The notion of the term "laymen" became predominantly negative: "non-cleric," "non-ordained," culminating in that legalistic distinction of the medieval Roman Church: "duo sunt genera Christianorum." No wonder that the revival of lay consciousness had to take the form of almost a revolution of the "laity" against the "clergy" and of the "people" against their "pastors," demanding equal rights before God and in the Church. Until this day the "rediscovery of the laity" is often chiefly interpreted as a restoration of the proper balance between layman and cleric. But in fact its main significance lies in a breakthrough to the original biblical understanding of the Church.

5. The experience of the Ancient Church pointed back to the New Testament concept of the Body of Christ. It became clear that the biblical foundations had to be restored and used as the only basis. Foremost in this rediscovery is the re-evaluation of the meaning of *baptism* as the basic event in the Christian's life and as the fact constituting the people of God. "Baptism is the ordination into the apostolic, charismatic and sacrificial ministry of the Church . . . It is therefore wrong to define the laity over against especially ordained ministers and vice versa" (from a statement to the Montreal Faith and Order Conference).

6. Resulting from this understanding of baptism, the words "kleros" and "laos" are used for essentially the same group of people in the New Testament. To quote a summary of the exegetical findings: " 'Laity' as a word goes back to the Greek *laos* which denotes the totality of a country's population . . . In the Old Testament it is used in relation to God and usually means the people of God par excellence, i.e., Israel . . . It is in this sense that the word is used in the New Testament where, however, it takes on the meaning of the 'new people

[1] G. H. Williams: "The Layman in Christian History," ed. by Neill and Weber, 1963, p. 52.

of God,' composed of Jews and Gentiles"[2] In other words, the basic assumption is the fundamental unity and equality of all members of the Church who form together the body of Christ. What is at stake is not a mere readjustment between different ministries (clerical and lay), but a renewed understanding of the Church itself as the people of God sent into the world.

III. *Theological Implications*

7. At this point there is an exciting ecumenical consensus among theologians. Both, the Roman Catholic scholar Congar and the Reformed professor Kraemer, for instance, unite in their classical treatises of the lay question in the conviction that nothing less than a *redefined ecclesiology* must be aimed at. In Orthodox theology there has remained throughout the centuries a greater awareness of the essential oneness of the Church rooted in a sacramental unity of love which binds together both clergy and laity. Some present Orthodox theologians have taken up and expanded this theme and so come to parallel conclusions.

8. The theological implications of this ecumenical consensus are reflected in the opening sentence of the Statement of the Central Committee of the World Council meeting at Galyatetö: "We have come to see that the *whole* Church shares Christ's ministry in the world." The operating terms in this context are "whole church" and "in the world." The "ecclesiology" which is taking shape is dynamic and world-directed. It interprets the Church in terms of "mission" and "apostolate." In the statement to the Montreal Conference this is spelled out further under the heading: "The apostolic ministry of the Church" on the grounds that all members by virtue of baptism partake in the apostolic succession and the charismatic status which is conferred through it (see Appendix).

9. Such theological thinking leads mainly to two general criteria for a redefinition of ecclesiology.

a) It must express the missionary character of the Church in bringing together worship and fellowship with witness and service. The boundaries of the Church must be extended to include its

[2]H. H. Walz in: "Ecumenical Review," Vol. VI, 4, July 1954, p. 470.

life in the world in the persons of its laymen. The total existence of the Church must be understood in accordance with its calling to be the firstfruit of all humanity, the part for the whole.

b) It must express the essential oneness of the ministry of Christ in the continuation of which every member of the Church shares. It is only against the background of essential equality that a differentiation of ministries is perceptible. The traditional separation of "clergy" and "laity" has to be redefined as a difference of the "manner" of service (Congar) or as a secondary, merely "functional" distinction or as a "pars pro toto" relationship by which some are set apart to serve the whole "laos."

IV. *Structural Conclusions*

10. Within the framework of such a wider world-oriented "ecclesiology" it became possible to conceive of the church structures in a new dynamic way. Instead of describing it basically in terms of a hierarchical order or an institutional organization the Church could now be seen as a "*wandering people*" constantly on the move into the world as it follows the footsteps of its Lord. The Galyatetö Statement uses in this context two biblical modes of description.

a) One is the metaphor of "*salt*" employed to characterize the Christian's interrelation with the world. In the same way as salt cannot fulfil its salting function, and is therefore not really salt as long as it is undissolved, the Christian cannot be a witness and therefore a true Christian until he involves himself in the life of the world.

b) The second description pictures the congregation as a "*gathered and dispersed*" community. Its life oscillates between these two poles of gathering and scattering in the world. Its realm is as much the "secular" sphere as the place of worship. The rhythm of receiving and giving, of listening and proclaiming, of adoration and action is the Church's heart beat. If only one of the strokes fail, her heart-beat stops.

11. The revival of the present death-causing structures is a problem yet to be solved. The aim is clear, namely, to re-form structures so that they will not fence off the Church from the life processes of the modern world, but rather support the Church's dynamic outward-

bound movement like piers of a bridge. This implies in particular two structural changes:

a) To redefine (structurally as well as theologically) the place and function of the especially ordained "priestly" ministry as part of a pluriform pattern of ministries. The problem is mainly to find the right interrelation between the world-centered calling of laymen and the church-centered function of set apart "clergy." The job of the latter is the strengthening (sterizein) and building up (oikodomein) of the Church for its mission, the job of the former to be the witnessing Church in the "diaspora." Neither of these functions, however, must be seen in static isolation. On the contrary, it should be the very objective of the structural framework to safeguard vital cross-communications which ensure that the "set apart ministers" participate in the pioneering apostolate as much as that the "laity" is involved in the formulation of theology, or in the pastoral and liturgical ministry.

b) The second structural change must provide for new forms of congregational life and common mission in the secular spheres of modern society to express the reality of the Church outside the Sunday gathering and to serve as living cells of witness within factories, offices, or laboratories (cf. Report of the Section on Witness, New Delhi).

12. At all these points the "laity concern" meets with that of the study on "The Missionary Structure of the Congregation." The advance of both will depend on each other. The experience with structural reform which the lay movement has gained over many decades, is, for instance, encouraging for the "missionary structure" discussion as it is a warning. On the one hand progress has obviously been made. The need of lay-training, to use one illustration, has been largely accepted by churches and resulting structural changes become progressively effective in the field of training and education. This shows that change can come about through and within the old structures though only slowly. On the other hand there are warning signs of premature institutionalization. They demonstrate that a piecemeal reform of one aspect of the Church's life cannot survive without a total revival of the whole body.

V. *The Content of Lay Witness*

13. The more decisive line of advance on which a final breakthrough may depend is now that of clarifying the content of lay witness. The Galyatetö Statement indicates the prevailing agony when it says: "None of us fully understands, in our complex modern world, what the ministry of the laity really is." Undoubtedly the discussion has firmly advanced beyond the personal sphere to a consideration of the Christian responsibility towards society as a whole. But what is the substance of Christian witness in society?

14. Exploration so far concentrated on answering the question for particular professions, e.g. what is the witness of Christian lawyers, teachers, etc., as for groups of laymen sharing one particular situation, e.g. what is the witness of Christians in industry, of laymen abroad? The result has been a clear understanding of the guide lines for an experimental Christian living in each of these situations. A new style of Christian life is taking shape. "Holy worldliness" is no longer just an empty word for many Christian laymen who practice it in their work day by day. "House groups," "factory cells" are a new reality even if they are still pioneering ventures. But this kind of exploration is naturally limited to the modes of behaviour either of an individual person or a group. The governing question is largely: how to be a good Christian at the conveyor belt, etc.?

15. Here the "laity discussion" has to move on. The "*witness of the layman abroad*" may serve as one example. His prime responsibility as a Christian in a foreign country does not lie in the sphere of personal or social behaviour, important as these may be. The main significance of his witness is based on his participation in an historic process. As technician who goes to a developing country, or as a teacher who comes to the West for training, as a roving businessman or volunteer in a local service project, he has become one of the chief agents of secularization in today's world, who carries the processes of industrialization and urbanization further into rural societies, into cultures with a "primal" concept of religion and a cyclical understanding of time. Such laymen cross national, racial, cultural, sociological and religious boundaries, and their task can, therefore, not merely be understood from a perso-social perspective nor indeed from the point of view of the churches' needs. The question is rather what

is a layman's role in this historic process through which God deals with humanity?

16. The indications of the present discussion are thus that the full content of Christian lay witness in the secular world can ultimately only be discovered if it is related to the whole of that world. The points of decision and the points of contact of Christian witness cannot be introduced from outside but are given as the total Gospel meets the total reality of the respective world. Such approach involves vast theological issues. For the "laity discussion" a new understanding of creation as part of the cosmic Lordship of Christ in a truly trinitarian setting is perhaps the most important issue.

VI. *Concluding Questions*

17. This summary of the ecumenical discussion on the "laity" has drawn attention to many parallel strands of thinking and cross-references to the discussion about structures of missionary congregations. Common to both are theological insights like the centrality of baptism, the missionary nature of the Church, the calling of the whole congregation to witness and service in the world. Common to both are also a wide range of problems like how to implement these insights in structural reform of the church, how to express them in new dynamic forms of worship, church life and mission. Common advance in the future seems, therefore, to depend also on answering an equal set of questions:

a) How can we develop a theological framework and new theological categories which will be wide enough to express the mission of the Church in relation to God's whole dealing with the total world in history, the mission of God?

b) How can we develop a relationship of dialogue with sociologists, technologists, economists, etc., which will give us an understanding of the interrelated complex pattern of each respective "world" so that the Christian witness can become a part of it?

18. The modern lay movement has begun as a part of the new meeting between Church and world. Ever since then the danger has been to seek a short cut and to produce a semi-renewed "ecclesiology." Any such attempt reduces the lay mission in the "secular world" to a

mere application of traditional witness to new spheres of life rather than seeing it as a dynamic event which will only take place in the proper context of understanding God in His meeting the world in the living processes of history.

Paul Löffler, London
April, 1964.

New Gifts

In order for the congregation to understand itself again as a charismatic community, the following must take place:

1.

The pastor is charged with the public proclamation of the Gospel and the administration of the sacraments on the basis of an existing charisma, recognized and confirmed by the congregation or expected in prayer and the laying on of hands. So charged he must learn to understand himself as being surrounded by a diversity of gifts, which, together with his own, are to become effective in the congregation. The monopolistic misunderstanding of ministry must resolutely be abandoned. The pastor is a member of the body of Christ like everyone else. In exercising his functions, the proclamation of the word and the administration of the sacraments, he, like others charged with proclamation, stands vis-à-vis the members of the congregation in the authority of the head (in the name of the Lord Jesus Christ) but the congregation is thereby not to be kept under tutelage. Rather, it is called critically to listen; it has to discern the spirits and to reject false teaching. The members of the congregation are "his" co-workers insofar as they, together with him and like him are co-workers of the Kingdom of God. The pastor does not delegate services which he actually should perform himself as belonging to his "all-inclusive" office, but which unfortunately he cannot perform due to his great work load. Rather, he understands the other services as the unfolding of the one office, given to the Church, which in no way is identical with the "ministry" as commonly understood. Never is he only giving but is in need of intercession and of the admonition on the part of the brethren, and he lets the congregation know how much he is dependent and in need. In this way the pastor is liberated for his task. Complaint about too much work often is rooted in disobedience to God's spirit which provides the necessary gifts for the congregation. Here radical re-thinking is needed for many pastors.

2.

Such re-thinking will change not only the relationship between the pastor and "his" co-workers in the congregation but also the relation among the brethren in the leading posts and the "office bearers" (pastors, superintendents, etc.) in the congregations under their supervision. This relationship will become free from all hierarchic or organizational categories of superiority. In the Church there is room for subordination but not for subservience.

3.

The congregation must begin its understanding as a charismatic community by intensive work on such biblical text as Rom. 12; 1 Cor. 12-14; Eph. 4. Such work will have to extend over a long period of time.

4.

The congregation must learn to discover which gifts are given to its members. Gifts need to be recognized, for the charisma does not necessarily and irresistibly express itself, rather it dries up when it is not used. Gifts not only need freedom for expression, they also must be put into service, charged with the carrying out of specific tasks, and for this purpose they must be encouraged and trained, for a charisma is not always from the beginning fully developed. In this regard it would be desirable if ordination were not limited to pastors but if corresponding ordination existed for the service of instruction, of liturgy, of pastoral care, etc. This would gradually overcome the disastrous idea that the "fullness of the office" is located in the pastor. When the congregation learns to discover and to put into service the gifts, it will find a new answer to the question of recruitment for service in the Church. It will no longer be a matter of individual decision whether someone will go to seminary; rather, the congregation will seek to discover among its younger members those who have to assume the necessary services and will approach and ask them to acquire a certain training.

5.

The congregation may count on, and pray for, new gifts to cope with new tasks which emerge. We had this experience in the DDR when suddenly we were responsible for the entire Christian instruction within the Church. But the congregation should look not only for charismata for the building up of the body of Christ but also for gifts for service of members of the body in the structures of the world. We must not only count on church-related but also with world-related gifts. Therefore: "Courage for new gifts!" (K. Rahner). For the new tasks in the service of society especially the need is not merely for competence but also for spiritual-theological judgment, the ability theologically to deal with economic developments, etc.

Werner Krusche, Lueckendorf/DDR
October 1963

Ministry and Ministries

I. ON THE METHODS OF THE TRAINING OF ADULT LAYMEN

Speaking out of the Swiss situation it seems to be impossible to report on more than initial experiences in the field of methods for lay training. The model which was started in the Heimstätte/Evangelische Akademie (Boldern-Zürich) and is now being developed rather extensively by a German-Swiss "Working Group for Church Training" ("Arbeitsgemeinschaft für kirchliche Schulung") in nine cantons of Switzerland is doubtlessly still in its preliminary stages. But I would like to describe its work as a contribution toward our discussion.

1) *The theological starting point* is the observation that in the New Testament dogmatic and ethical principles are always developed out of concrete situations. A catechism as such does not exist. But the resurrection from the dead is confessed before the background of a gnostic refusal to acknowledge the corporeality (1 Cor. 15). Or, the sacramental words of Holy Communion are formulated and understood out of an impending community crisis among Christians (1 Cor. 11). Or, the service of the Church is stressed in view of its responsibility and

witness in the Roman world (Rom. 12-13) etc. Instruction in the faith takes place in the context of worldly experience. The question of faith is raised side by side with the question of life in the world. It is well known that for this reason the congregation of the New Testament knows of no fixed dogmatics. It is just as well known that in our day the words of confession are unhappily isolated, and separate Christian life and faith from each other. The purpose of all lay training is to bring these separated parts together again.

2) *The theme must have its "Sitz im Leben."* It is necessary to take the layman's concern into consideration when subjects for instruction in the faith are chosen. In our search for and formulation of topics we must be guided by the questions and problems which laymen raise out of their own experience. Therefore, instead of speaking about "creation" we might ask: "What is the origin of man?" so as to be able to cover the whole scope of modern man's interest in the paleontological origin of man. Or, instead of speaking about the "Kingdom of God" we might say, "the reign of God in a world which is ruled by man," etc. Experience has proved that the topics have to be formulated with great care. One might even—rather boldly—expect thorough lay training here and there to shift the accents in theological dogmatics and ethics.

3) *We must not claim to be dogmatically perfect.* The first experiments already show a twofold result. Any subject that is taken up together with a layman who takes a keen interest, leads to boundless possibilities for discussion. The layman is concerned not only with the theological background or with the dialogical exegesis of a biblical text, but also with the manifold experiences of his secular life. This ample field must not be limited too hastily, or else relevance to life is lost. (We shall see later that this relevance is of vital importance.) But for still another reason we must reject any kind of dogmatic perfectionism: Any lay training should focus on essential theological issues and not lose itself in a discussion of narrowly specified questions; its task would be rather to open up an important theological issue from a clearly specified, concrete perspective. Just as the view through the "magic eye" on an entrance door opens up a view on the whole apartment, the whole Gospel must be revealed through the peephole of a concrete human experience, need or joy. The theological topics which

lay training takes up, must—each for itself—contain the whole Gospel. For in each concrete situation the layman—the member of the Church who lives a secular life—cannot but witness to the *whole* of the Gospel.

4) *The relation between the Gospel and the human experience* must be made the main point in any dialogue on questions of faith; the Gospel must shine through human experience in our world. Of course this is at root the work of the Holy Spirit. But if we talk about methods at all, we must say that this should be one of their focal points. No matter whether a biblical text is dealt with, or some phenomenon of individual life, or of the social world, the main thing is that whatever is said catches fire, that something flashes up, involves the personality and engages the mind. It goes without saying that any leadership in dialogue or training methods should stimulate this process in the best possible way.

5) *Confrontation as a prior condition.* We have so far had good results in deliberately confronting biblical texts with practical experiences from our secular-human life. A subject for lay training must have a thorough documentary foundation. This documentation can be obtained by different means (films, visits of factories, tape recorder, etc.); a possibility near at hand—though time consuming—is that of compiling a documentary file. We have had the experience that on the basis of such a file we can, at every point in the conversation, obtain a true confrontation of points of view which helps merge faith and life. The church-oriented individual is thus forced to take seriously the practical issues of our world and the hardworking lay partner, to listen intently to the word of the Bible.

6) *Information and dialogue.* The question is justified whether an emphasis on discussion does not deprive us of the possibility of imparting the necessary information. It is part and parcel of our information that we present biblical-theological facts in the context within which they are set. We have had the experience that discussion leads up to such information, even requires it. Once the interaction between the Gospel and our worldly experience has been recognized, a real hunger for knowledge breaks forth (especially for a knowledge of the Bible). Such information will then no longer be isolated, but set within

the context of the dialogue which has already taken place. As such it is "truth in encounter."

7) *Elements and phases of the dialogue.* It is not necessary to dwell any longer on the fact that the essential instrument of lay training is dialogue and discussion. It is vital that much thought be given to the way in which this dialogue is guided and that its art is mastered. Any experience of discussion on secular issues can, of course, be of great help. However, the main purpose being lay training, only secondary importance is to be attached to mastering this art. The following important steps would then ensue:

a) *Interaction:* The discussion leader must see that the spark flashes across, that it ignites, that an active interest is aroused and the partner is committed where he stands in life. Any details—however important and interesting they may be—must, at this stage, recede into the background. The criterion must be whether at some point or other the partner is met, whether a contract is established. This requires experience and ability, patience, but above all love for the partner.

b) *Exegetical work:* This is the most difficult stage as far as method is concerned. At this point confrontation means careful listening to the text, to questions concerning the subject under consideration, to experience—and at the same time having an openness for the word, for insight and toward the partner in dialogue. The most important thing at this point is exegesis which centers on the matter yet does not become mere catechizing: exegesis of biblical texts but also of the texts of our life and our thinking. The decisive question in our lay training is how to arrive at teaching with authority.

c) *Appropriation:* Appropriation is a joint process of thought and action, of a penetration into the matter and of personal venture. What does this mean for us, for every day life and for the faith which we confess? We have already said that the knowledge of the laymen is not an encyclopedic knowledge, just as its practical application is only partial. It is partial knowledge, practical application in a concrete sector of our historical life. The lay member of the church is right in claiming that his church authorizes him for and equips him for, speech and action in this sector.

Any church work will be effected in *three steps: going* (visitation of homes p.e.), *observation/reflection* (we must find the right word for differing situations), *service* (the offering of a helping hand). Lay training is not a method of instruction, not a programme for instruction in addition to and apart from the church. It is itself consummated as thinking and as acting: as thinking which is incarnate, as acting which is contained in the word and guided by it.

8) *Forms of practice.* There are, especially for congregation-oriented lay training, some working methods which have proved their validity and which enable the layman to practice what he has experienced and learned.

Discussion of special cases in which we try to see clearly the starting point of the lay partner have proven helpful. We have worked on questions concerning visitation service and pastoral care using detailed written reports of particular cases. It is surprising how much can be learned about the way in which we should proceed; obvious mistakes can be eliminated from the outset. We have also observed that participants take a lively interest in this working method and that many points important from the theological point of view can be made in passing.

Still another important thing is required: practical exercises in special situations. In some types of lay training we are trying to make exercises an integral part of the training. The participants have to carry out special tasks, to report on them and to receive criticism. (The purpose of such training might be to prepare people to exercise some sort of oversight in the church.)

Learning and training through practical examples and in special situations often stimulates work on smaller, more clearly defined experiments (a sociological group, a city district, a certain professional group might be chosen and thoroughly studied.) This has proved to be particularly fruitful. So far this has only been tried out in a congregationally-oriented lay work; we would, however, propose similar experiments in open courses and with partners who are less church-oriented.

The final goal of this undertaking is the development and study of *models* of behaviour. We have learned (and are still learning) a lot in this respect from the methods and experiences in the field of social work. At all times Christian witness has given rise to models of behaviour. Today we consider mainly their negative aspect (pietist piety, revivalistic methods of conversion, etc.). But it is of vital importance that we find our own models of behaviour. Which are the specific forms that Christian witness can assume in the world of our day? How do we as those who are bearers of the Gospel, and who live from its promise and for its hope, meet the man of our technical-industrial age? We pray that we may finally discover these new models. Of course (I would like to repeat this again) the spirit blows where it wills. One can never make the witness for Jesus Christ available by mere methods. But one cannot do the reverse either, namely point out that the spirit is not available and draw the conclusion that therefore our Christian existence cannot be incarnate in this our world (this would call forth the opposition of biblical pneumatology).

Theophil Vogt, Männedorf/Switzerland
September, 1964

II. THE EQUIPPING OF THE MISSIONARY PEOPLE OF GOD

1. The phrase "lay training" inevitably sounds condescending. We shall later stress that what is vital is what members of the missionary people do in their own right; what some do for others is at best a minor aspect. Moreover, those engaged in this find again and again that Christ has given far more gifts to his people than their leaders usually recognize. The word *equipping* is perhaps a step towards a more adequate title.

2. Equipping is an affair of the whole church. The traditional distinction between ministry and laity has increasingly broken down. We can only talk of the many ministries within one body, and seek appropriately varied patterns for their acceptance, equipping and recognition.

3. We can no longer talk of *a* task of the ministry and another task of the laity. We seek to equip a whole people for their missionary task.

4. On account of the complexity of our Western European societies and the multiplicity of differing social contexts, in which each of us is involved, each particular instance of mission (and of equipping for mission) cannot but happen as one fragment within a large number of other fragmentary missionary events, and will have its effect largely

conditioned by the degree to which it fits in with those others. Equipping must aim at some kind of common pointers for use in the variety and flexibility of a diaspora situation.

5. Equipping is not a particular limited process, at the end of which people go on to something else. It is a permanent process, within which those in the midst of equipping themselves will be sharing their equipment with others in a spreading network of effect.

6. The theology involved is not so much handed down by theologians outside the process, as discovered and pursued within their actual situations by those equipping themselves, to the theological enrichment of the whole church.

7. One chief result of the equipping of the missionary people is a clear demand for an appropriate equipping or re-equipping of the pastors among them!

8. Equipping is not an isolated process. It stands in a continuum with the normal, secular processes of education, in which the members of the missionary people have been involved. Its precise content and methods cannot but be elaborated with reference to that normal education.

9. It stands in a continuum with the regular life of the church and with all the varied activities of the Christian community, and must both draw from and share in shaping them.

10. There will be three main elements in any process of equipping,
—a certain degree of theological competence (e.g., in Bible study and in the capacity for seeing one's own situation in biblical perspective);
—a certain degree of information and awareness concerning the world and the worldly situations in which people are involved;
—a certain degree of self-knowledge, probably best acquired and fulfilled within a community of full mutual exposure, trust and forgiveness, such as a house church (itself then very likely a missionary institution, in that it will influence others by being what it is).

But these cannot be pursued separately; each involves the other.

11. In the case of each element, what matters are the questions men raise themselves and the answers they discover for themselves in their own situations and in their mutual relationships: answers from outside

will normally be useless, even false, though help from outside can be useful in setting people on the path of asking their own questions.

12 . . .

13 . . .

14. The process of equipping to a large extent replaces the traditional function of the sermon. Biblical exegesis, training in discernment, discussion of contemporary situations—all these can take place in the equipping of the people.

15. Those equipped very quickly object to a sermon which takes no account of their capacities or needs. If proclamation is both to arise from within particular worldly situations and be a word to them, then at least it must involve preparatory teamwork by those who live in these situations.

16. This opens a field requiring much more *investigation*. We suggest provisionally that as a structure of a missionary congregation, proclamation, strictly speaking, will take place rather seldom: on the one hand, the tasks of understanding, interpreting and judging worldly situations of the complexity and delicacy we know these days in Western Europe demand long preparation; on the other hand, theologically speaking, the one completely adequate proclamation took place once and for all in Christ, and the gift of prophecy is found but rarely in the church. What can regularly take place in the missionary congregation is perhaps a celebration of what has been proclaimed.

17. To what end is this equipping of the people? The earlier discussions all lead to this central question, in which we find again the whole theological debate about the nature of Christian faith in a secular age. But the question must be faced, as several current answers clearly will not do.

18. Are the people to equip themselves for faithful fulfilment of their daily work, being occasionally able within the strict limits of that social role to introduce an idea or perspective arising from Christian faith; or for a living out of Christian faith in all the relationships of life that will constitute a "wordless proclamation"; or for being ready to give answer about the faith one holds in reply to a direct question? (—recognizing the enormous difficulty in these days of talking of Christ in secular terms, in terms of shared realities, and that no per-

son can tell another from outside the confrontation how to talk, though perhaps the process of equipping can assure each man that his stammering answer in such a situation will be similar to that of others, and will share in the stammering of the whole missionary people).

Up to now we have largely given theological answers to the question of this paragraph. Can we move to giving more empirically expressed answers, that will among other things relate to one another inside some total picture such different aspects of the total missionary task as are mentioned above?

Western European Working Group,
Esslingen, September, 1964.

Worship and Mission

I.

THE UNITY OF WORSHIP AND MISSION

In the New Testament the life and work of Christ are spoken of in terms both of mission and worship. In John 12:49 we read: "The Father who *sent* me has himself given me commandment what to say and what to speak," while in John 6:51 cultic language is employed: "I am the living bread which came down from heaven . . . and the bread which I shall give for the life of the world is my flesh." In the same chapter at verse 57 both mission and cult appear together: "As the living Father sent me, and I live because of the Father, so he who eats me will live because of me."

So mission and worship refer to a single totality. This same unity is to be observed in the Pauline epistles. Paul can describe mission by using cultic terms and can equally describe cultic acts in terms of mission. So in Rom. 15:16 he speaks of himself as "a minister of Christ Jesus to the Gentiles in the priestly service of the Gospel of God, so that the offering of the Gentiles may be acceptable, sanctified by the Holy Spirit." In Phil. 2:17 he says: "Even if I am to be poured as a libation upon the sacrificial offering of your faith I am glad and rejoice with you all." Paul is also able to employ cultic terms of daily life and of ethical conduct, e.g., Rom. 12:1: "I appeal to you therefore, brethren, by the mercies of God, to present your bodies as a living sacrifice, holy and acceptable to God, which is your spiritual worship." This approach is not peculiarly Pauline, we find the reverse i.e., the cult spoken of in ethical terms, in James: "Religion that is pure and undefiled before God and the Father is this: to visit orphans and widows in their affliction and to keep oneself unstained from the world" (1:27). As an example of missionary terminology being used of the cult, we may cite 1 Cor. 11:26 where Paul says of the eucharist: "As often as you eat this bread and drink the cup, you proclaim the Lord's death until he comes."

Worship, therefore, is a term which is to be applied to the whole of life and is not to be restricted to specific cultic acts. Conversely, mission embraces not only daily life but also worship services. It is, therefore, possible to define worship and mission in identical terms. So, to take various phrases from 1 Peter 2, we may say that worship is to "declare the wonderful deeds of Him who called you"—but so is mission. Christians are called to be "a royal priesthood to offer spiritual sacrifices acceptable to God through Jesus Christ." This dedication to God, this self-oblation, is both a characteristic of true worship, in cult and daily life, and a mission, in cult and daily life. The whole life of the Christian is thus worship and mission.

Because of this virtual identity of worship and mission we are bound to say that only that is authentic worship which combines both the vertical and horizontal dimension, i.e., both communion with the transcendent God and mission in the world. In making this affirmation we are not condemning many acts of worship out of hand; we are not sitting in judgment upon others; we are simply saying that *for us*, who have now appreciated the dimension of mission, worship can henceforth only be authentic if it embraces both the vertical and the horizontal. Such a view seems to be involved in Matthew 5:23 ff. "If," says Jesus, "you are offering your gift at the altar, and there remember that your brother has something against you, leave your gift there before the altar, and go; first be reconciled to your brother, and then come and offer your gift." Here the two dimensions are inextricably linked and the horizontal is represented as necessary to the vertical. Just to enter into the vertical dimension of worship, to offer thy gift, i.e., to commune with God, is not sufficient; brotherly love is an essential part of the whole act.

Nor are cultic acts to be regarded as an escape from the world and so from mission. Worship is not something that happens between the church and God, but between the world and God, the church being no more than an instrument. The church worships, in Christ, on behalf of the world, and indeed as the world (pro-existence, firstfruits, etc.). For we both share and understand the joys, aspirations, failings and uncertainties of the whole world and are to offer them within the adoration, confession, thanksgiving, etc., which the mighty acts of Christ call forth from us.

The worship of God, according to some members of our group, is not to be confined to the church. Insofar as the activities of non-Christians declare the wonderful deeds of God, insofar as their lives bear the marks of self-oblation, some of us wish to recognize there the signs of incipient worship, which becomes fully articulate only through the exercise of the church's royal priesthood. Other members, however, hesitate to use "worship" for anything other than a conscious response in Christ.

This totality, this unity of worship and mission, of which we have been speaking, has through the centuries become disrupted. Worship ceases to describe the whole of life and is restricted to cultic acts; mission is regarded as an extra activity independent of worship. So the theological investigation of the meaning of worship has gone on apart from a consideration of mission and the modern study of the meaning of mission has largely disregarded worship. Thus arises the problem of the relationship of worship and mission—a problem of our own making which is the consequence of rending the original unity found in the New Testament. We have to rediscover and reaffirm that totality and at the same time enrich our understanding of it by the theological interpretation of worship and mission arrived at independently of each other. Hence our understanding of worship must be given a missionary dimension and equally our understanding of mission must once again be anchored in worship.

II.

ELEMENTS IN WORSHIP

Cultic acts may be investigated not only from the point of view of sacramental theology, i.e., of the specific meaning of baptism and the eucharist, but also from an examination of the separate elements or ingredients that are to be found within them. These elements, too, demand a missionary interpretation. We would advance the following suggestions, while emphasizing that not all these elements are necessarily to be found in every worship service.

1.

Confession of Sin—Instead of being merely individual, it should be collective. The private sins of each worshipper as well as his social, economic, national, etc. sins should be presented to God.

Absolution—This should not be static but dynamic and outgoing, in the sense that it is only as we forgive others that we ourselves are forgiven. Thus in the absolution is involved the ministry of reconciliation.

2.

Bible Reading—This is not only reading but proclamation. It is both the record of the divine mission and a summons to participate in that mission, hence it is further, as proclamation, a means of mission. It must therefore be intelligible to the hearers and the use of modern translation is important.

Sermons—This is an attempt to announce the Gospel message in the thought forms of its hearers. It should contain elements of dialogue, either explicitly or implicitly. It can be prepared by teamwork, taking into account the concrete situations of the contemporary world. It should lead to decisions on precisely defined problems and should issue in a clear message to be passed on to others.

Psalms—The Psalter contains material so diverse that no single statement can cover its content. There are, however, Psalms that declare the universality of God, the suffering of his servants, the hope of divine activity, the importance of secular life, etc. All these have relations with the concept of mission.

3.

Concerns—This giving out of notices or the making of announcements is an opportunity to bring before the congregation the news from the world, the needs of mankind and of members of the community. It is on these that the intercessions can be based and it is by these that the context and scope of the church's commission can be defined.

4.

Prayers—

(a) Intercession—When both prepared and expressed by a group this will hold the real world before Him who is its origin and end.

(b) Praise and thanksgiving—Praise, which is vocal adoration, acclaims the acts of God in his mission to the world through Christ and the Spirit. Praise declares the wonderful acts of Him who called us, and for those acts we also express thanks. This praise is to be expressed not only by our lips but in our lives, i.e., in mission.

(c) Silence—This may allow for reflection, for voiceless wonder and love or for intercession with a missionary intent.

5.

Benediction or Blessing—This will not be a cosy rounding-off of the worship service but the sending out of God's servants in mission.

6.

Music—What is sung will not be the archaic and individualistic hymns found in most of our collections but the expression of a community which out of a living relationship with today's world worships its Lord in contemporary forms and phrases.

The whole service should have the character of a joyful festival celebrated by the community which worships the risen Lord and Saviour of the world.

III

THE REFORMATION OF WORSHIP FOR MISSION

Hitherto we have been discussing the meaning of worship in terms of mission and the missionary dimension of certain ingredients in worship services. Acceptance of all this need not affect the actual forms of worship currently in use. Nevertheless we are bound to raise the question: Are there not forms of worship services which are archaic, lacking in vitality and are impediments to a realization of the unity of worship and mission? We suspect that there are, and would wish to suggest certain guidelines for producing new models of worship and for its practice.

We would affirm that Christian worship services in the 20th century should be:

1\. *Corporate*—They must therefore allow for the active participation of all present, they must not be clericalized, they must contain elements of dialogue, they must include actions and not just words—this last involves gestures of adoration familiar to contemporary man as well as sacramental actions as in baptism and eucharist.

2\. *Flexible*—They should contain both fixed and free elements. Each has its dangers and advantages. Fixed forms can become vain repetitions uttered by rote. Free forms can become clerically dominated and restricted in their scope to the individual taste and capacity of the leader. Fixed forms can provide balance and breadth and continuity and bring something to the worshippers in addition to what they bring themselves. Free prayer can be spontaneous, relevant and congregational. Either may exert a tyranny; a judicious use of both can help to revitalize worship.

3\. *Relevant*—Reformation of worship is not primarily a question of liturgiology although the history of one's tradition is not lightly to be disregarded. The worship service must comprise the whole life of the congregation in its missionary outreach and the entire context of that life, if worship in the widest sense is to be maintained. To confine oneself to liturgiology is to be shut up in one part of the life of the church, whereas cultic acts as parts of the whole of life should be open-ended and all embracing.

4\. *Intelligible*—All we would need here is to quote I Cor. 14:9, 16, 25: "If you in a tongue utter speech that is not intelligible, how will anyone know what is said? For you will be speaking into the air . . . how can anyone in the position of an outsider say the 'Amen' to your thanksgiving when he does not know what you are saying? . . . and so, falling on his face, he will worship God and declare that God is really among you." In effect, Paul is saying that when worship is intelligible, it is also missionary. But these verses also raise the whole question of the part the "outsider" is to play in the critique of existing forms of worship and in the creation of new ones. If worship and mission belong together and if the "outsider" is the one who must judge whether worship is intelligible or not, then it is the church's duty to ask those "outsiders" to criticize all the elements of worship (confession of sin, sermon, etc.). It may be that the "outsider" will speak on behalf of many Christians who do not know or who do not have the courage to say that they do not understand. So, if worship and mission belong together, if the liturgical and the profane are interwoven in the New Testament, if we are ready to accept I Cor. 14 as a sign-post for our reflection on worship, we must ask: how can we enable these concepts to take visible and audible concrete form in our patterns of worship? We are indeed faced with a number of questions to which we cannot pretend to have immediate answers: what is the role of "profane" makers of liturgy (journalists, dramatists, radio artists, etc.) who may help us to discover worldly forms for our worship? How can we assume that the outsider (before, during and after worship) may express his critique and say that he does not understand? What structures in the preparation of worship, of worship itself, in the designation of money, in the building of worship-centres, must be changed in order that the requirements we have specified might be fulfilled?

5.

Ecumenical—Patterns of worship which reproduce only the liturgical inheritance of a single church may be parochial and impoverished We must learn from each other.

6.

Timely—Services should be held at times when people are ready to come together. Social habits must be known and allowed for. No particular day or time should be accepted as sacrosanct; only that hour and day is to be approved when most people can and will come together.

7.

Not necessarily confined to church-buildings—Worship is now in Christ; it is no longer shut up in the Jerusalem temple. Christian worship is therefore independent of bricks and mortar. Nevertheless the gathering in churches is a right and proper means of bringing the community together, but this should not preclude meetings for worship in other places such as the home, factory, etc.

IV.
THE CULTIC DIMENSION OF MISSION

The emphasis in this report has been upon the recovery of the missionary dimension of cultic acts; we must in conclusion say something about the cultic dimension of mission. If we are to reintegrate worship and mission, we must acknowledge that the latter is open to correction through the theological understanding of the former. Just as Paul interpreted mission in terms of cult, so must we. Indeed we can say that mission without cult is not possible. Cult prevents a one-sided involvement in the world for the world's sake instead of for God's sake. It can be easy for an individual or a group to be so completely taken up with their involvement in the world that he or they lose the central recognition that what they do, they do within and because of the work of Christ. To participate in cultic acts and so to concentrate attention upon God in Christ and to see this as a *dimension of the whole of life* recalls us to the sovereignty, the freedom and the accomplishment of Christ which is at the heart of the assurance that we need in mission.

Conversely our cultic acts are saved from introversion and a fallacious rationale by perceiving their unity with mission. Worship is not a means to mission, *it is mission.* We must not prepare for mission through worship but be missionary in worship. The cultus is not an isolated act but part of something bigger—even the expression of something bigger—and is part of the whole movement that can be called both worship and mission.

Western European Working Group
Driebergen, March, 1965.

A Missionary Structured Congregation in a Metropolitan Setting —Some Sociological Pre-Conditions*

Facing a few facts

A church that wants to be a missionary church is challenged to be a "going" church. For, as Hans Jochen Margull has pointed out while reflecting *On the Meaning of Missionary":*

> "Going is essential in mission. (. . .) Going out in mission means to cross frontiers. Our fathers generally had to cross geographical frontiers. We also have to cross sociological frontiers. The missionary task has to be fulfilled on all six continents. It is a task to the ends of the earth and to the ends of society."[1]

A missionary church, in a word, goes out to where people *are*. It is committed to all places and all situations where human beings live their lives, in sorrow and in joy, in indifferentism and in concern, in bafflement and in perspicacity, in ungodliness and in godliness. And this, sure enough, means crossing frontiers, in particular today.

The first, and perhaps most formidable, frontier to be crossed is that of the empirical churches' apparently ineradicable self-centredness and consequently *un*missionary disposition to stand aloof from the full of modern life. These unhappy traits, which testify to what in brief might be called the ill-digested transition from Constantinianism to post-Constantinianism, can amply be illustrated. So, some of the findings and experiences written down in the foregoing papers are highly illuminating; the more so, because they relate to activities undertaken in an entirely new setting and/or launched by people of a downright unconventional bent. Even in these cases, it proves to be exceedingly difficult, if not impossible, to get rid of the inveterate churchmen's (be

---

*The evidence upon which the conclusions in this article are based is drawn from parishes in continental Europe. Therefore, they run the risk of being dismissed since church membership in the U. S. is largely based on voluntary association. However, it should be noted that the article adduces a considerable amount of evidence which has its parallels everywhere. We hope that both the difference and the parallels will be helpful. Ed.

[1]H. J. Margull, On the Meaning of "Missionary," *CONCEPT*, special issue 2, February 1963.

they clerics, or laymen) habit of self-preoccupation and keeping-the-profane-and-the-sacred-apart.

> ". . . it turned out that even those who attended the church of the newly formed parish appear to segmentalize their church affiliation as a separate world of interests." Thus reads one of the conclusions formulated by Vrijhof and Eichholtz, *Ways in Which the Churches Have Reacted to Changes in Urban Structure.*
>
> And in the first one of her *Two Illustrative Notes on the Need of Taking Secular Structures Seriously,* Miss Thung says of a recent conference on the laity problem, in which a considerable number of lay people participated: "Whatever attempts were made to concentrate on the worldly tasks and positions of the laymen, the discussion invariably landed in questions about the order of the Sunday service, the layman's contribution to church work, the role of the pastor, the founding of spiritual communities and other matters of church life."

In addition, mention should be made of what several authors bring to the fore with regard to some average church congregations investigated by them. Osmund Schreuder, a Roman Catholic priest and sociologist, analyzed a parish in a "Grossstadtbezirk" (metropolitan district) predominantly inhabited by labour class people, and the final chapter of this analysis is entitled "Die missionarischen Chancen der Pfarrgemeinde" (The Missionary Chances of the Parish). Obviously this title is an euphemism, for it heads a simply appalling collection of proofs to the contrary. To cite just one single set of figures referring to the attitudes of the parochial in-group towards the out-group:

> "15% . . . express themselves variously about the N(oncommunicant) group. These persons through their comments give to understand that they reject in general passivity with regard to the church but refrain from accusing individuals of lack of respect or understanding.
>
> "3% express themselves positively. It is understandable that noncommunicants avoid the church: 'They may not even be so far off.' For there are many things to be criticized in the church. . .
>
> "26% give no answer or—in most cases—are entirely disinterested. They have no relations with unchurched people, have never thought

about it, have never discussed the problem of religion, since it does not lead anywhere. (. . .)

"Most of the communicants, 56%, express an explicit and unqualified negative judgment. For them non-communicants are 'badly educated,' due to unstable family conditions. They refuse to relate to them and seek associations with like-minded groups. Others may have had religious education, but have forgotten it and bring shame upon their families. 'But some day they will find out; just wait until they get into trouble.'"[2]

Reinhard Köster studied the characteristics of such parochial in-groups, that is on the Protestant side of the fence.[3] One of his main conclusions is that the parish faithful belong, in the great majority, to categories of people who find themselves more or less on the outskirts of normal societal life, and it is intimated that many of those most active in the affairs of the church are (thus) compensating for their being out of touch with the affairs of the world. These findings are strongly corroborated by the outcome of Trutz Rendtorff's inquiry into the membership and regular church attendance patterns of a number of rural and urban congregations which are located in a region of Northern Germany with a heavy influx of post-war refugees. The following quotations may tell their own story:[4]

"Attendance at Church Services in the Church of Schleswig-Holstein:

(100 = total official membership)

	Schleswig	Holstein	Church
1903	6%	1.8%	4%
1953	5%	2.5%	3.8%

"The survey gives an unmistakable picture. . . . Only a small part of the church members participates in the central event of the local parish . . . It seems to be a situation which has already lasted for decades . . .

[2]Osmund Schreuder, *Kirche im Vorort* (Freiburg im Breisgau: Verlag Herder, 1962), p. 462-463.

[3]Reinhard Köster, *Die Kirchentreuen* (Stuttgart: Ferdinand Enke Verlag, 1959), p. 107f.

[4]Trutz Rendtorff, *Die soziale Struktur der Gemeinde* (Hamburg: Im Furche Verlag, 1959, 2. Auflage), p. 57f. (Italics mine.)

"In the rural parishes the majority of those attending are from among the refugees from the east . . . This surprising fact means that there has been a further development with regard to the situation fifty years ago. The indigeneous members of the parish, which make up the traditional membership are very rarely to be found in church on Sunday . . .

"A closer examination of the refugees which form the majority of attendants shows the following characteristics recurring in almost every parish: . . . They are people who have not been re-integrated into society, single women and recipients of pensions, the socially weaker who were not able to adjust to the new environment . . .

"In the urban parishes the refugees, too, represent a substantial part of the attendants at services, roughly two-thirds. They are primarily from the group described above. This is especially surprising since in the cities . . . we can find a considerable number of 'integrated' younger and active refugees. However, they are rarely among those attending church. Integration into the professional and social environment has been effected: *It seems to be part of this integration no longer to belong to the church. This is in conformity with a general attitude.*"

These illustrations may suffice to bring one thing home: on the road to a missionary church, as defined above, there is—very, very likely—no greater obstacle than the church itself, in its present day empirical manifestation of an almost entirely inward-bound outlook and an all but total alienation from the world. Bearing this basic fact in mind, one really needs a faith that will remove mountains to go by the assumption which is fundamental in busying oneself with the actual subject of this paper. This assumption is that, in one way or another, the churches *will* be ready to go out into the 20th century world, instead of recoiling from it by seemingly inbred reflex, and that they *will* be prepared for crossing the frontiers beyond which lie the places and and situations where the inhabitants of this very same world are allotted their everyday portion of happiness and toil, of action and leisure.

In order to trace—however tentatively—those places and situations, their location and nature, their relative importance and existential meaning, it is worthwhile to make an attempt at identifying—however roughly—some essential features of contemporary Western society, and a few principal forces determining its make-up.

With good reason, contemporary Western society has been labelled the Great Society. Horizons have widened, distances have shrunk, possibilities have been opened up, partitioning barriers have been torn down. It is a society in which almost everything acquires an aspect of hugeness, and simultaneously, of perplexing complexity. Boundaries are not only expanding, but also diffusing: contents are not only enlarged, but also lumped together and thoroughly reshuffled—with the result that levelling tendencies go together with diversifying ones, that uniformity competes with pluriformity. The Great Society is one big melting pot of ideas and goods, of values and forms, of interests and loyalties that continuously change and often clash. And of this melting pot the exponent is the Metropolis. The Metropolis is the dynamic pace-setter of the industrial-urban way of life, the spheres of influence of which are reaching out farther and farther. It is the complex power centre of modern civilization, the pull of which is drawing ever growing proportions of territory and population in its orbit.

In short, today's Western society is preponderantly a Metropolitan society, and, consequently, the lives of the bulk of us Westerners are decisively conditioned and structured by the paramount processes of which the Metropolis is both the product and the generator. These processes might be brought under the following threefold heading: concentration, differentiation, and mobility.

Metropolitan society consists of a whole series of, highly interdependent, urban concentrations, or what I would like to designate Metropolitan Areas.[5] In their turn, these Metropolitan Areas are composed of several so-called Agglomerations, which constitute intricately intertwined clusters of central cities, "fringe towns," and suburban villages. And between all these many component parts of different size and function there is a constant moving to and fro.

The (high) rate of this mobility may be illustrated with the help of

---

[5]In the present context, in other words, the Metropolitan Area is not understood in the sense of its technical definition, which includes a central city of 50,000 people or more that is socially and economically integrated with its contiguous communities. The latter phenomenon is termed here—on the analogy of a study of the (Netherlands) National Physical Planning Service: *De ontwikkeling van het Westen des lands* (1958)—an Agglomeration; whereas the Metropolitan Area, as I call it, comprises two or more of such agglomerations.

some statistics on two current population trends, as they present themselves in the Netherlands, but which are characteristic of any Metropolitan setting. The first one of these trends, which are brought about by a great variety of social and psychological, economic and technological factors inherent in an industrialized and affluent society, relates to the frequent change of residence and of community. As yet, it is not likely that the turnover of residents in Holland is as enormous as in the United States, where it is estimated that one person in five is changing his residence every year.[6] However, from the data mentioned later it is quite clear that also in Western Europe the number of people involved in residential mobility is far from negligible:

(a) in the 3-year period 1957-1959, the largest cities in the most heavily urbanized western part of the Netherlands showed a migratory deficit of 60.000, over against an "in-migration" surplus of 51.000 for their immediately surrounding municipalities;[7]

(b) between 1951 and 1959, the older residential sections of the city of The Hague lost 54.000 people, whereas the newer neighbourhoods gained 88.000;[8]

(c) in the first half of the 1950's, it was found in a study on internal, or intra-municipal, migration that every year an average of about 10 per cent of the total population of large cities as Amsterdam and The Hague is moving—without crossing the municipal boundaries:[9]

	Internal Migrants (one-year average: 1951-1955)	% of Total Municipal Population
Amsterdam	81.794	9.5
The Hague	60.983	10.4

The second population trend is the one which might be termed the daily (or also at somewhat longer intervals) recurring trek-back-and-forth of the workers between their residential communities and the

[6]Peter Rossi, *Why Families Move* (Glencoe, Ill.: The Free Press, 1955), p. 1.

[7]Rijksdienst voor het Nationale Plan, *Jaarverslag 1960*, p. 29.

[8]R. Kok, Verhuizen als maatschappelijke keuze, in *Tijdschrift 's Gravenhage*, December 1960.

[9]J. den Draak, *Rapport betreffende de interne migratie binnen de agglomeratie 's Gravenhage* (unpublished report, 1956), Table 10.

place where they have their jobs. A significant impression of the rapidly growing importance of this phenomenon can be derived from the following, comparative census figures on inter-municipal commuting in the Netherlands:[10]

Census	Inter-municipal Commuters Daily	Otherwise	In toto	All Commuters in % of Total Employed Population
1947	444.641	139.192	583.833	15.1
1960	746.372	362.126	1.108.498	27.2

An additional illustration is provided, if a glance is taken at one city in particular. So, for the city of Utrecht—having a total population of circa 255.000, of whom about 95.000 are economically active—the census of 1960 produced these results:

(a) commuters *from* Utrecht to other municipalities — 16.160
commuters *to* Utrecht from other municipalities — 15.898
out-going and in-coming *in toto* — 32.058

(b) daily *out-going* commuters from Utrecht
(= 100%) to directly adjacent municipalities — 46%
areas at a distance of ± 10 to 40 kilometers — 30%
areas at longer distances — 24%

daily *in-coming* commuters to Utrecht (= 100%)
from directly adjacent municipalities — 46%
areas at a distance of ± 10 to 40 kilometers — 42%
areas at longer distances — 12%

The obvious conclusion to be drawn from all these data is that, in a Metropolitan society, geographical mobility may well be considered the accepted order of the day for very large proportions of the population. What is more, however, this geographical mobility represents but one of the various kinds of mobility that are having a far from merely physical impact on the modern city dweller's life. In the 20th century Metropolis, people are continually on the move, both bodily and mentally, simply because there is a great differentiation in the fields of action, spheres of interest, and webs of relationships in which they are involved. In the course of one single day, for example, the

[10]Central Bureau voor de Statistiek (CBS), *Mededelingen Volkstelling 1960*, Nr. 15, March 1963.

ordinary urbanite is repeatedly changing from one locality to another —from his family home to his working site, from his residential neighbourhood to the down-town gathering points for discussing professional problems, debating political issues, or joining in club activities, and from there to the private parlour of an intimate friend to enjoy the stimulus of congeniality, or a place of public resort to spend a few pleasant hours of relaxation. In doing this, he is not only present at a good many scenes, but also participating in quite a number of separate social, cultural and psychological worlds, all having their distinct structure and membership, their specific goals and patterns of behaviour. In each of these worlds, the said urbanite is engaged in a different manner, placed in a different position, playing a different role, and subjected to a different norm system; but in all of them he finds himself at home, in one way or another, for they are *his* worlds, to him they constitute the meaningful segments of *his* existence.

In fine, the life of Metropolitan man is enacted in a diversity of milieus and situations that are more often than not spread over a wide geographic, as well as social, territory. It is a composite whole of many part-lives, not seldom being of more or less divergent nature. It revolves around a series of concentration points, or, to use a technical term, so-called frames of reference,[11] which one by one claim to being significant contexts of human self-realization.

Venturing upon some conclusions

Considering the facts examined above, one point stands out most clearly. If ever the concept of a missionary, or "going," church is to become concrete reality, nothing short of a total transformation is needed. A total transformation, that is, of organizational patterns, as much as of mental attitudes.

1. For centuries the churches (whether actually established, or not) have regarded the inclusion of the entire population in the fold of Christendom as right and proper. Consequently, their prevalent outlook became an inward one: tending the flock for whom they could not

[11]A frame of reference is, as one definition reads, a "universe of discourse, a connected set of 'facts' and 'axioms' in reference to which members of a group do their thinking, their defining of situations, their conceiving of personal and group roles in such situations, and their communicating of such thoughts and attitudes." *Dictionary of Sociology*, ed. by H. P. Fairchild (Ames, Iowa: Littlefield, Adams & Co., 1955), p. 123.

possibly imagine any other place to be than inside the well-defined corrals of institutional religion. However understandable this Constantinian turn of mind may be in the perspective of past conditions, in our contemporary situation of a thoroughly secularized social order it is just obsolete. Yet, up to the very present, the overwhelming majority of church people (of leading and of rank and file status alike; and including ourselves!) appears to persist in it. Consciously or unconsciously, we are always haunted by the spectre of unchurchliness and dechristianization, by the loss of influence of institutional Christianity manifest in declining membership rates and ebbing interest in religious activities of all sorts. Instinctively we react, therefore, by frantically searching for effective means to stem this unhappy tide. Means which vary from making ordinary parish life more attractive in its manifestations and more appealing in its approaches, on the one hand, to establishing special task forces geared to specific needs, on the other.

As goes without saying, all such attempts at devising more or less drastic adaptations in order to make the churches more up to date and better equipped are, in themselves, most praiseworthy—for they are in great request, indeed. At the same time, however, it is utterly imperative not to fool ourselves as to the true nature of these adaptations. This true nature is that they are, at best, nothing but poor palliatives . . . as long as they are having their common ground in the longing to preserve, or regain, the prominence of organized Christendom. And, to be quite candid with ourselves, this longing *is* —as a very general rule—the main motive underlying our reformist endeavours, whether or not we care to admit it. (This seems to apply even to the most radical ones of these endeavours, the formation of special missions and experimental outposts; if not by those who man them, then at least by those who do not oppose them: their function is believed to be a transit-station for channelling back lost sheep to the normal parish pews.) There is a deep-rooted tendency among us to take the line that, after all, the Kingdom of God is best served, if we succeed in making as many people as possible faithful churchgoers and loyal joiners in religious activities and organizations.

It is precisely this tendency from which we should most determinedly break away. The call is for a complete mental somersault—out of our ingrained habit of inclusive, church-centered thinking, towards an audacious preparedness for the dispersion of the body of Christians in two's and three's committed to an "Abrahamitic" venture into the *terrae incognitae* of 20th century secular structures. The real challenge we are up against is not how to counter the more or less apparent estrangement of modern man from institutional Christianity, but how to bring home to representatives of the latter that it is they who have lost contact with the actual areas of human responsibility. The crucial issue to be faced today is to acknowledge the naked truth that the churches as they stand exist in a situation of segregation from the decisive contexts where individuals and groups must act and make decisions for better or worse, that the churches are summoned to give relevant answers. These answers they *do not know,* in spite of all pretensions to the contrary. These answers can only be touched upon by entering into a sincere dialogue with the determining forces of present day urban-industrial society. That is, they can only be ascertained by the trial and error of experimenting, stumbling bands of Christian pilgrims who shoulder their task of making the redemptive ministry of Christ manifest through their prophetic and creative participation in the political, economic, and social complexities of what constitute their particular spheres of responsible worldmanship.

3. If all this is true, the implications with regard to the question of "morphology" will not be hard to guess. These implications can be summarized in the following twofold way.

In the first place, it is beyond any doubt that the empirical churches are in for a most painful reappraisal of their existing organizational patterns and the principles on which these are based. Or, putting it somewhat differently, they are confronted with the necessity of an as good as total restructuring process. Let me just mention a few pivotal points which are badly in need of revision. One has already been hinted at: the fact of the churches' segregation from the determining societal contexts of our time as a result of their predominant identification with what may be called the utter fringe-sector of the residential community.

Illustrative of this predominance of the "normal" residential parish approach is the following table on the proportional distribution of all Neth. Reformed ministers in the 4 Metropolitan Areas of the Conurbation Holland over territorial parishes and special assignment ministries of a "functional" or "categorical" nature.

Metropolitan Areas	% of Neth. Reformed Ministers Serving on: Residential Parishes	Special Assignments
Amsterdam	84.4	15.6
Utrecht	84.5	15.5
The Hague	86.5	13.5
Rotterdam	92.1	7.9
TOTAL	87.3	12.7

Another point is the all too clear cleavage between the main body of church members whose prime interest is "inner-directed," and the usually very small group of those who are, professionally or voluntarily, engaged in "ventures in mission." And, then, there is the subject of the ministry of the laity and its relation to the ministry of the clergy; a subject which, once we stop merely paying lip service to it and really start acting upon, is sure to cause a radical shift of focus.

"The shift of focus," Gibson Winter says in a recent article on what he terms the New Christendom, "could be dramatized thus: the past image conceived ministry as the work of clergymen with auxiliary aids among the laity; ministry in the New Christendom is the work of laity with auxiliary help from theological specialists."[12]

The second implication is that there is only one valid line of procedure to be followed, if and when the empirical churches seriously embark in morphological self-criticism. This line of procedure is: to weigh all church structures, old and new and still to be devised ones alike, in the balance of their being instrumental in enabling, supporting, and evoking Christian men and women to be true to their ministry of serving witness within each of the numerous spheres of public and private responsibility that can be discerned in the complex whole of modern Metropolitan society. It is a line of procedure, in other words, which urges us to take our point of departure, not in an attempt to preserve traditional forms as much as possible for reasons of their time-honouredness and the like, but in a consistent search for structures of Christian presence to be grafted upon and incorporated in the great variety of contemporary secular structures.

---

[12]Gibson Winter, The New Christendom in the Metropolis, *Christianity and Crisis*, November 16, 1962, p. 210. See also G. Winter, *The New Creation As Metropolis* (New York: The MacMillan Company, 1963), esp. ch. III.

In other words:

Human life in present day Western Society is decisively structured and conditioned by three interdependent forces: concentration, differentiation, and mobility. These three forces determine, therefore, what might be termed the *Zones humaines* of today.

In pre-urban, pre-industrial society, the integration of the comparatively limited number of different contexts of everyday life took place within the boundaries of one small territorial unit, such as a village, or a town of modest size. Nowadays, however, because of the working of the three forces just mentioned, the number of separate life contexts in which men participate and bear responsibility has greatly increased, and at the same time the territorial unit in which the integration of these contexts occurs has been greatly widened. Geographically and socially speaking, the daily life of modern man revolves around a series of concentration points. So, we understand by "zones humaines" the territorial scopes within which clusterings of such concentration points are situated. These scopes are, in other words, to be found in today's Agglomerations, made up of a central city and its encircling suburban fringe-towns.

It is on these "zones humaines," which are the basic socio-territorial units of our time, that the *churches* have to base themselves in their organizational structures and in their methods. And it is within these "zones humaines" that the churches have to decentralize according to the variety of life contexts that are found therein (residence, work, leisure, politics, etc.), and each one of which constitutes, in principle, the context for the formation of *congregations*. By doing this, one of the results will no doubt be that we can get rid of the perennial antithesis between territorial and functional/categorical structuring principles, between "congregation" and "Para-congregation." For, in this conception, the residential sphere is but one of the many contexts of human life that have to be taken into account, if we want to take into account the total life of modern man, *all* the spheres of responsibility in which modern man is living his life.

In sum: the basic organizational unit for structuring a central *church* is the extended "zone humaine," exemplified in the Agglomeration. And if the line is taken that the church is to serve in and to the actual contexts of residence, work, leisure, politics, and so on, then the principle for developing serving, i.e. missionary congregations is to create in these different contexts committed fellowships of mature Christians, or structures of Christian presence.

Paul E. Kraemer, Utrecht,
September, 1963.

On the Meaning and Use of the Self-Survey

In thinking about the position of the church in a rapidly changing modern society, we have come to realize our ignorance as to the extent to which the church is participating in the mission of God. A way to discover more of this participation is for the church to try to come to a better knowledge and understanding of itself in the light of a fuller appreciation of the way in which man's life and thought is being shaped by the changing patterns of the social life of our day.

In the course of this self-analysis it has been found helpful for church members to organize and participate in investigations into the position of the church in their own area. This instrument has come to be called the self-survey. It serves a double purpose. First it provides knowledge about the actual situation outside and inside the church. Secondly it ensures that this information is discussed and understood by the people who are most concerned and who will have to take any action that the results of the investigation show to be necessary. Two types of survey will be distinguished—the parish self-survey and the zonal survey.

I. The Parish Self-Survey

1. This type of survey may be undertaken by members of a local congregation. In general terms its purpose is

— to increase their knowledge of their own congregation, its composition, its method of organization, its activities and its effectiveness in the performance of functions for its members;

— to increase their knowledge of the community of which it is a part, its composition, its pre-occupations, its difficulties, the changes it is undergoing, the way it regards the congregation in its midst;

— to make possible some evaluation of the effectiveness of the congregation in witness and service within that community.

2. It is immediately evident that the fulfillment of these aims involves asking questions and providing answers of different degrees of complexity. It is by no means necessary that all surveys should be designed to achieve all the aims set out above. The collection of information of this kind, though it can be carried out by ordinary church members, is not a simple task. It is desirable therefore that the congregation should seek the advice of someone with experience in social survey work. If this is not possible the survey should be confined to the collection of very simple factual material. Even information of this elementary kind can be useful and may raise large numbers of questions.

3. The three questions given below illustrate the type of issues which the self-survey can be used to clarify.

— Is the preaching and instruction given by the local church relevant to the needs and problems of the local community?

— To what extent do members of the congregation participate in community life and what hinders their participation?

— To what extent does the life of prayer and worship in the church (praxis pietatis) cover the life of the local community?

4. It seems likely that surveys of this kind will not only raise problems which the local congregation can solve itself. It may also raise others which are not capable of solutions by the local church. The definition of a human zone (zone humaine) and the setting up of supra-parochial bodies based upon it, discussed in the following paper, is an attempt to deal with problems of this kind.

II. *The Zonal Survey*

1. The problems thrown up by a parochial self-survey which cannot be dealt with at that level may be of two kinds:

— problems confronting the church in its attempt to minister to the people of its locality.

— personal problems confronting the people of that locality which arise from their life outside it and with which the local church is unable to deal realistically.

There is, therefore, a need for an understanding of the wider social context in which the local community is set and thus a need for a survey or investigation wider than that of the parish survey. The purpose of the zonal survey is, therefore, to obtain an understanding of the position of the church in this wider society, its changing structures and the problems facing those people who compose it.

2. Generally, it is not possible for ordinary church members to participate in the collection of information in a survey of this kind. It requires rather the cooperation of the different churches and leaders of the local congregations within the area. Such cooperation would make possible

— the collation of existing information concerning the church,

— the use of expert knowledge available in university departments, government agencies and published sources which have a bearing on the social and economic life and development of the area,

— the assistance of experts in the social sciences in relating the different findings concerning the church and concerning society.

3. The result of such a survey can be used to facilitate the missionary task of the church by informing it of its current social position, making it possible for it to interpret the social understanding thus gained in Christian terms. It will also enable it to identify *both*, new needs which it is called upon to supply, *and* new means to supply needs whether those needs be new or old. It may then become possible to define a territorial area larger than the parish within which ministries may be gathered. This area can in general be characterized as a social and economic region whose boundaries will depend on local circumstances and social and economic developments.

4. At the same time the results of the survey should be discussed by local congregations, thus enabling them to widen their understanding of the situation of the local community. It can help them also to identify those needs which they can best supply and those which are better dealt with by new types of congregations concerned with particular problems within a certain area.

5. It has now become clear that ideally the two types of survey should not be regarded as separate but as complementary. *The parish survey* will raise problems that can only be answered by the zonal survey, and *the zonal survey* will be more effective if it has available the results of parish surveys. It is not, however, necessary that zonal

surveys should be carried out in each area where parochial surveys are being undertaken. The results of the zonal survey in one area may be in many respects applicable to another area in which similar socio-economic conditions exist.

6. We believe that the parochial survey should be more widely adopted than the zonal survey. It is a means whereby the church may be brought to a clear realization and understanding, both of the problems of the world and of the depth of her involvement with the living issues which affect the life of modern man.

Western European Working Group
Esslingen, September 1964

Zonal Structures for the Church

The origins of this paper lie in the discussions and reports of the Western European Working Group meeting at Esslingen in September 1964 and Driebergen in March 1965. At these meetings the concept of zonal structures was expressed by the term "zone humaine."* This term has now been discarded for two reasons. There was an ambiguity about the sense of "humaine"; and there was a danger that by emphasizing one particular term in the singular, attention would be distracted from the fundamental principle of a wide range of plural structures.

1. *Argument*

If the churches are to become effective instruments of mission in the world, then radical changes are necessary in their existing structures. These changes should spring out of a perspective of society which requires the churches to face areas larger and more complex than in former times. As the churches come to grips with these broader areas or *zones,* so zonal structures become highly significant for planting, co-ordination and integration.

---

*See CONCEPT VIII, November 19644: "Church Structures in the Zone Humaine."

2. *The whole of life*

Community life does not respect civil or ecclesiastical boundaries. The individual has various foci in his life (e.g. work, leisure, shopping, education) which may be geographically dispersed throughout a wide zone regardless of existing boundaries. Other aspects of his life are more local and based on a neighbourhood.

In the past the churches expressed their proper concern with the whole of life through parish and congregational structures. By these means the influence of the local churches spread out naturally in all directions. But in today's extremely complex society these traditional structures can only deal with a limited number of human activities. They can no longer express the original intention of concern with the whole of life. This function can now be fulfilled only if the churches base their action on zonal or regional levels.

3. *Caution*

In the process of restructuring the churches there is a real danger of absolutizing those concepts which prove most useful. It would be fatal to regard zonal structures *per se* as having some absolute value. A further fallacy would be to think that the churches become a missionary church, responding to the needs of the world, merely by adapting their existing structures to fit a zonal basis. It cannot be overstressed that detailed plans for new church structures can only evolve within a given concrete situation.

4. *Does the argument apply to the smaller churches?*

At first sight the case for zonal structures may appear to be relevant only in those areas where churches are in a traditionally majority situation. It is probably true that where the parish tradition has been strong it should not be difficult to appreciate the need for a broader framework in which missionary structures may develop. But it is not the majority position of a church that calls for larger territorial areas; it is the actual structure of society. It is likely, therefore, that minority churches in economically highly developed areas may also feel the need for regional planning, although the practical response may well be quite different from that of a majority church in similar areas. The principle of zonal structures providing workable levels of coordination is of equal importance in all church situations.

5. *Definition of a zone*

In the present discussion the term is used to describe a territorial area within which by and large the population lives out the complex network of movement and relationship which is its life. A zone thus comprehends and integrates most of the various contexts around which the population is concentrated for the basic activities of local life. The replacement of the parish by the zone is a clear result of three interdependent forces at work in Western society—concentration, differentiation and mobility. The first is characterized by the growth of vast urban areas. In these areas there is a high degree of differentiation between the various parts of an individual's life, his different and distinct worlds. This leads to the mobility aspect and the constant movement of the individual between his different world.

The traditional parish is useless as a basis for comprehensive action in a society determined by such forces as these. Zonal structures, however, can come to grips with them. A typical zone would be a city with its surrounding fringe towns—an area produced by, and caught up in, the forces of concentration, differentiation and mobility. Summing up, the zone may be said to have replaced the parish as the geographical area which comes near to integrating the different contexts of everyday living.

6. *Determination of a zone*

Zones can be of different kinds and covering greatly different areas. The basis of the zone in a particular area must first be decided in the light of the definition of a zone suggested above. The geographical boundaries can then be defined by those who have professional knowledge, such as regional planners and sociologists. All the essential information about the social and economic life of the area has to be collected and evaluated before the map can be drawn. In view of the constantly changing patterns of life today, it is essential that the boundaries of the zone are kept under constant review.

7. *The missionary perspective*

The missionary church is committed to a concern for the particular contexts or worlds in which people live, and also for the integration of those worlds into a meaningful pattern. A zonal structure provides the vantage point for the right perspective. On the one hand it is a constant reminder of the different worlds in which people live and which have to be engaged in appropriate missionary action. On the other hand a zonal structure is itself a symbolic expression of the wholeness of life.

The essential differences between zonal and parochial structures are rooted in this matter of perspective. As the churches become re-structured on the basis of a zone, they are able to engage in profitable and meaningful action at a level which brings into focus the rich diversity of modern life. If the churches were organized in smaller units than the zone, they would fail to face up to the vast diversifications of human life; if they were organized in larger basic units, then the immediate task of mission, arising from confrontation with the world, might well become unmanageable. In other words a zonal structure covers the smallest geographical area compatible with the right perspective and with good management.

8. *Levels of coordination*

Zonal structures may be based on smaller or larger areas, according to the particular area and its characteristics. An example of a smaller zonal structure would be a particular district like East Harlem in the middle of the great metropolitan area of New York. Larger zonal structures would be needed for other purposes e.g. in regard to regional planning. An increasing number of functional spheres, such as broadcasting, higher education and large-scale industry, require national or international levels of coordination.

9. *New direction for traditional structures*

It is the responsibility of leadership in the area to discover how far the traditional structures of the parish or local congregation can become sufficiently relevant to share in the new zonal pattern of missionary action. Mere adaptation is far from being sufficient. What is needed is that these traditional structures shall be caught up in the new movement and given a new sense of direction which restores their original concern with the reality and the wholeness of life. If this is not possible, then such structures should be discarded with the least delay, providing that there is general understanding of the whole principle.

10. *Differing responses*

The great variety of spheres of interest and problems of the modern world calls for a variety of responses on the part of the churches. Each context and function of life requires an appropriate structure which ministers to its particular needs. Although the whole church has a ministry in the world, the variety of situations requires in practice that this ministry be exercised by a variety of particular ministries and groups. Some of these will be large, others small; some will be permanent, others temporary; some will be functional in the spheres of interest, others functional in residential areas; some will be service groups, others will be servicing groups. All of these should be considered equally as being parts of the whole church, though because of the interdependence of each on the others, it would be wrong for an individual group to be understood as "the" church in isolation from the complex totality.

Group structures can be identified according to types, for example:

—groups associated with social, political and economic areas of concern, some of which may arise spontaneously to meet an immediate need;

—activities associated with the naturally given events of the family e.g. young married's groups, the pastoral care of the bereaved;

—"permanent availability" structures which demand the minimum of involvement from people seeking help in coping with particular problems, e.g. the telephone service, some aspects of industrial chaplaincy, the retreat house, counselling.

The church in the zone should work out its own list of priorities according to the needs of the zone and the resources available.

11. *Authentic characteristics*

The sensitivity of all these forms of ministry to the needs of the mission should be expressed by the following characteristics

—lively self-criticism and regular evaluation;

—flexibility and absence of rigidity in thought and action;

openness towards people and towards the problems of the world;

—a sense amongst the members of belonging to each other and of mutual acceptance;

—readiness to change and to disband at the right time;

—awareness of partnership with the whole church and with the whole world;
—continuing dialogue between practical involvement and theological thinking.

12. *Expressions of coherence*

The complexity and diversity of the emerging church groupings in the zone underlines the need for signs and guarantees of unity which express and safeguard the organizational and structural coherence of the church in the zone. Three such signs and guarantees are:
—The Word and Sacraments which bring into focus the wholeness of the church;
—the ministry, whether ordained or not;
—the *episcope,* in the form of a team, responsible for the oversight of the church in the zone. This team or panel will be thoroughly representative of the different parts of the zonal structure and will set the pattern of good communication between all the particular activities.

13. *Levels of decision*

Churches have traditionally made use of larger units for major policy decisions and for administration. Examples include presbyteries, dioceses, conferences, synods, etc. The logic of the zone as the basis for local missionary action suggests that eventually these larger units might be radically revised to emphasize their own participation in the missionary structure of the whole church. They might be re-constituted to become coterminous with one or more complete zonal structures. But as with other traditional structures, adaptation or re-drawing of boundaries is an inadequate response to the need for appropriate levels of missionary decision.

14. *Inter-denominational cooperation*

In many regions denominations exist side by side. But the present discussion about (missionary) structures in the zone assumes that the whole community of Christians is prepared to participate, regardless of denominational divisions. Practical cooperation about implementing the zonal structure of the church could be an important growing point for unity.

15. *Case studies*

Case studies can be useful as descriptive parables. It is not possible in this paper to publish examples, for such would either be too superficial to be helpful or too detailed to be included here. But urgent attention should be given . . . . to establishing a means of publishing papers about the churches in zones. This would require a central agency, to act as a clearing house and as a means of expert evaluation.

16. *Self-surveys*

Community self-surveys can prove a very useful method of awakening a wider and deeper interest in the area. When a congregation carries out a self-survey, certain problems may be revealed which cannot be solved at the parochial level. This realization can provoke a readier understanding of the wider social framework in which the community is set, and suggests the need for surveys or investigations on the level of the zone. Such wider surveys require the cooperation of the different congregations together with expert knowledge and professional evaluation.

17. *Emergence of regional thinking*

Two factors are encouraging the growth of regional consciousness in the churches. On the one hand are developments in regional, social and economic planning undertaken by government. On the other hand there are already various new forms of missionary work in the course of development which require an awareness of larger or different regions than those included in the existing church organization. As the traditional structures are confronted by these new (missionary) structures, there are considerable opportunities for this zonal thinking to be shared so that its scope is progressively enlarged to include the totality of church structure.

18. *Cri de coeur*

Finally, resistance to change can be expected, but the logic of the argument should support those who have to do battle.

Western European Working Group
Driebergen, March, 1965.

The Cost of Missionary Action

I. At the Yale Consultation on the Missionary Structure of the Congregation Art Thomas described how the little inter-racial congregation in Durham, N.C. which he pastored without the blessing of his local bishop while tending a book store dwindled rapidly when he became active in the (race) demonstrations. Andrew Young, working with Martin Luther King, Jr., testified that in the racial struggle in the South new forms of witness and commitment were opening up and could be characterized only by the word "cost." Here were people willing to give their churches, homes, even their lives, for what they believed.

During the discussion period Gibson Winter said that Andrew Young's declaration of willingness to pay the cost made it clear that we are not really discussing structures, but the cost—even to death—of obedience to Jesus Christ as Redeemer and Ruler of this world. At this point it became abundantly clear that the struggle is not one of mission or structure but of the willingness to pay the cost of missionary action—a cost which might mean our jobs, the structures of the churches as we know them and death of our ideals and theology.

The cost of missionary action becomes clearer when we look at what might happen in various areas of denominational life, if we were to cease entering into renewal as an investment which will pay off with increased membership, financial strength and power. There comes a point at which the church must stop competing with the world on its own terms and begin to examine its life in terms of what God is doing in the world and the points at which he is asking us to stand in judgment and opposition to "powers and principalities." Structures, or the social organization of our churches, must be relevant to the performance of the task we are called to perform in God's mission, not just an imitation of this world or the world of any other century. Form must follow function instead of John Calvin or General Motors. When this happens there is cost because the form itself must frequently die and be discarded.

II. Without making any claims to know what structures or forms are best, I would like to raise some questions concerning the possible cost to the *structures of finance and membership statistics* which may result from serious commitment to engagement in God's mission for the world rather than to campaigns for the sake of bringing men and women into the church.

1. Many suburban churches are intrigued with the possibility of following the executive to his work and engaging in study and discussion of his difficult daily decisions in the light of the Bible. This is a way to strengthen the church. Yet what would happen if the millions of nominal Christian businessmen found that the church is not something which helps to bring him more peace in his private family world, but instead something which invites him to join in a mission which will frequently call him to endanger his job and income. There might in fact be a great loss of membership and of financial contributions, for members brought into the church as a place to find respectability, and help in keeping your wife and children in line, may decide that they don't honestly wish to be part of something which at its heart is disturbing and revolutionary and follows one who "turned the world upside down."

2. Many denominations provide money for church extension by floating three-year loans. Thus they can only invest large sums in congregations which will "pay off." A few experiments are tolerated, but even they are expected eventually to make good. What would happen if the areas of need and tension where God is at work turned out to be the places where large investments had to be made year after year? Where would the money come from? Perhaps from abolishing various denominational agencies which become useless, by ceasing to build new churches in areas of high potential until we find what the mission of the church in our time is all about.

3. Most of the denominations are finally beginning to work on the problems of the racial struggle. But what happens when real involvement means loss of congregations, jobs, financial income?

4. On the local level the world over one of the crying needs is the union of various local churches into one strong church. The cost of this to the denomination and the local membership is obvious from the very fact that seldom do we go beyond willingness to "study the problem."

The list of such problems is infinite. The point of listing these four examples is not whether they are good ideas, but to show why structures for mission involve cost to the existing institutions of finance and membership.

III. An equally long and an even more complicated list can be made of structural difficulties which are met when we begin to assess the cost of missionary action in terms of *ecclesiastical organization.*

1. Problems of ordination are clear from the general confusion concerning its meaning throughout the various denominations, yet are we willing to move ahead and accept the cost of recognizing that a congregation might be stronger and more relevant to its mission in the world if it were led by a trained layman? Or the cost of understanding that boards and agencies are themselves churches and perhaps could nurture, discipline, and equip church executives for their task where they work rather than expecting executives to find meaning in a local congregation which they attend infrequently and with some distaste? Or the cost of seminary communities recognizing that a man is not even ready to reflect on the Bible until he has had at least three years of carefully planned internship in the world?
2. Questions concerning the relevance of preaching and of Christian education indicate considerable cost to the image of the minister as well as traditional structures. Perhaps a minister should preach less and spend more time in local politics if he wants his congregation to see the relevance of God's word to the need for true community. Bible study or house groups force attention away from the pastor to the neighbors and community. They frequently mean that other structures in the congregation such as women's and men's groups have to be eliminated. Serious consideration of Christian education as a sort of in-service training which happens in engagement with the whole church in God's mission may cause many of the publishing agencies of church literature to go in the red.
3. Questions concerning unity and intercommunion are fast reaching the point where the world is going to make us one whether our theology allows or not. A new question of unity has emerged

which requires us to give up the other question. Man in our time cries out for true unity of himself and his world—unity between the private and public spheres of his life, unity between himself and his brother of a different race or class. God's mission is that all find loving community with themselves, each other, and with him. What is the cost of giving ourselves to this battle rather than the one of church politics?

No one expects denominations or congregations to become martyrs just to become martyrs. Yet if we are serious about seeking to see where God is at work in the world and following in his steps, then we must be willing to follow where he leads us, willing to accept the cost to our lives, our congregations, our agencies, our finances, etc. In short, willing to consider all structures as temporary and as expendable in God's mission.

Letty Russell, East Harlem/New York
September, 1963.

Fifth Part

A SUMMARY

The Quest for Structures of Missionary Congregations

The Central Committee of the World Council of Churches, at its meeting at Enugu, Nigeria, in 1965 greatly welcomed the following interim report from the Department on Studies in Evangelism, setting out the general findings to date of its Study on "The Missionary Structure of the Congregation." It commended this to the churches for continuing study.

COMMUNITIES FOR OTHERS

By his Word, God calls congregations into existence. Through his Word, he forms them into missionary congregations. For it is through congregations of his people that Jesus Christ, Lord of all the world, would serve all men. A missionary congregation, like a band of missionaries, fulfils its calling by being present as a servant people among men, for whose sake Jesus Christ has given of himself in full obedience (Philippians 2:5-11). A truly missionary congregation is a community for others.

In every part of the world today, churches are confronted with the urgent quest for authentic missionary congregations, and thus with the quest for their proper structures.[1] This quest has arisen as a fruit of renewal, whereby Christians have gained a new faith in God's Word and a fresh understanding of it.

There has been a renewal of faith in God's purpose for the world and a deepened awareness of his action in the world. On this basis, we recognize a concern lest our churches should become mere islands, isolated from the mainland where a world-wide pluralistic and secular society is in the making. We also sense that our churches are in danger of being unable to point out what God is doing in relation to the movements of our time or what his claims upon them are.

[1]The terms "congregation" and "structure" should be understood in a dynamic sense. By "congregation" we mean any form of Christian gathering. In speaking about "structures" (or shapes or forms) of missionary congregations, we point to the question of "how we organize ourselves so as to turn our eyes outward". The dynamic concept of "structure", over against a static, analytical concept, is best understood when referred to the processes which lie between the "destructurization" and the "restructurization" of a group.

There has also been a renewal of faith in Christ's sovereign, transforming presence in the world. In the light of this, we have been seeking for structures which conform to a life of genuine Christian obedience—structures suitable for our discipleship in all those places where the patterns of contemporary society are being formed and where men are being forced to make decisions, whether great or small. Thus we have come to realize that our disobedience is laid bare in our clinging to structures which we should have allowed to be reformed or left behind. And now we realize, too, that for the most part our congregational structures are no longer appropriate for all those complex forms of human life within which Christ would have the Gospel made known through a servant Church.

There has been a renewal of faith in the Holy Spirit. From this perspective, we see anew that the Church of Jesus Christ cannot endure on its own. The Church is directed to the Word of God, and that Word directs it to the world. It must live in the world, and it must do so in accordance with the Word of God. The Word of God is Jesus Christ himself, and he is, as we have been learning anew through the Spirit's gift of renewal, the man for other men.

STRUCTURES OF MISSIONARY PRESENCE

Especially in recent years, studies have been conducted in many churches concerning the local congregation, the ministry of the laity, and changes in the structures of the churches' life and mission. Often they have arisen in response to a basic issue to which attention was called by the World Council of Churches' Assembly in New Delhi, 1961. The issue was whether, or to what degree, the parish structure of some churches and the local congregational structure of others limit our witness to Jesus Christ in today's world—in spite of the faithfulness of the congregations and their ministers. Herewith it became apparent that we can no longer concern ourselves about true witness without raising questions about proper congregational structures. The studies which have been going on thus show that we are entering into a phase of the churches' experience of renewal in which the concerns of theology are becoming intimately connected with the quest for new structures. For it is in part through the structures of its common life that the churches' response to God's Word is to be seen.

The findings of such studies have received attention in the ecumenical study on "The Missionary Structure of the Congregation," in which the following points of consensus have so far emerged.

1. Our mission is given

Our concern over appropriate structures will be rightly directed only in terms of God's purpose for the world and his action within it, as revealed in Jesus Christ. Every structure must serve God's purpose and action. It has been declared in ecumenical discussion that "There is no participation in Christ without participation in his mission to the world" (Willingen 1952). It is in God's own turning toward the world that the Church is given its mission. Being caught up in that mission, the Church is called to interpret the mighty acts of God in the world, both past and present, and to celebrate them. This twofold task is a single venture, involving the Church's worship, its service and its message as well as its structures. It is a quest for truly missionary congregations.

2. The churches' structures should be flexible

In interpreting and celebrating God's mighty acts, churches must be as flexible as is demanded by the character of God's own action in the world. In recognizing this demand, we must not overlook the once-for-all character of the Gospel and the continuity which necessarily follows from it. At the same time, however, we see that it is precisely for the sake of genuine continuity that the Church must keep changing, under the guidance of the Holy Spirit, so as to meet the changing conditions of human life.

3. All church structures are temporary

No congregational structure is strictly normative. Our insight into this fact results both from study of the Scriptures and rediscovery of the Christian congregation as a witnessing community. One can no longer contend, for example, that the traditional types of the local congregation or the parish are the only structures possible, even though they have been valid for many centuries. Varied and changing structures of Church life are continually developing now as they always have been, through missionary engagement within varied and changing forms of society, in order to meet the real needs of men and to prepare them for new kinds of decision. There has always been a variety of congregational structures within the Church. Today we must learn to look upon every gathering of Christians whose life is nurtured by the Word and sacraments as a Christian congregation. We must also learn the implications of saying that there is no one structure appropriate for a missionary congregation. For in its very essence, missionary congregations exist in different forms in order to meet different situations.

Today we are enjoined to seek for congregational structures which are both *flexible* enough to sustain the engagement of faith with different and changing societies, and *differentiated* enough to integrate particular interests and activities with definite beliefs and values, given the present complex of specialized worlds, and yet *coherent* enough to sustain a firm unity of faith and life among the diversified ministries of the Church.

4. New forms of missionary presence are emerging

In our time, the supposedly integrated and self-contained "world" we once had is rapidly bursting into pieces, forming a highly differentiated urban, technological society. In many parts of the world, our local parish congregations are no longer able to manage within the ever more widely encompassing area of this society and its complex situations—or if so, only in part. This is perhaps not so much due to the faint devotion of the individual member as to the actual structure of the local parish congregation to which he belongs and the importance he is able to ascribe to it. Our parochial structures developed in relation to a form of society which has either passed away, or is vanishing, or leaves but few traces here and there. But now the contours of new structures are appearing. Most of these have emerged in recognition of the varied and special gifts (*charismata*) which the Church has been given in these days. A number of these structures have been either promoted or prepared for within the local parish congregations themselves. And these congregations have experienced a new life.

Industrial missions have been founded in obedience to the call for a missionary presence within the whole widening area of modern economic development and technical research. Ecumenical teams have provided a missionary thrust within the inner city, as, for example, in East Harlem, New York. Others have gone into action in the new cities, as in Port Harcourt, Nigeria, or into new housing developments, as in one of the suburbs of Geneva. "Little congregations" (as they have, not uncritically, been referred to in ecumenical discussion) have been forming everywhere—certain circles, cells and groups gathered for witness and service. In one way or another, these have arisen through earnest engagement with the growing number of new crises and needs of contemporary society. They have formed, for example, for the ministry of counselling the lonely and broken by telephone, or for service to refugees and to the racially oppressed, or for aid to migrant workers, or for the effort toward international understanding and attack on social problems. They have come to life among students, professional people, educators, legislators, and many others. They have formed themselves into house-churches, making possible a human community where it did not previously exist, or into brotherhoods, working parties, fellowships, and orders. They have been conceived, as mission groups were in an earlier day, in hearkening to the call of God to obedience in mission and thereby to an authentic Christian life where they live. The Word of God has made them into "*pro-existent*" congregations, communities *for others*, within the actual social contexts given to them for mission.

5. *New congregational structures need official recognition*

These new forms of missionary presence show the churches how many concrete possibilities they actually have for witness and service within a society from which they have at first recoiled. Many of these new forms often fit uneasily or not at all into the normal ecclesiological categories of the churches within which they have emerged. Despite this discrepancy, the "little congregations" seek under the Holy Spirit to be present in new areas and situations through prayer, proclamation and service, just as parish congregations have sought to do in circumstances proper to their structures. These newer forms must therefore be recognized too as legitimate structures of the Church, as congregations in a proper ecclesiological sense, entitled to the reception and offering of Word and sacrament. Of course, these new forms of missionary presence may represent a certain threat to the cohesiveness of the Church at the local level, and thus the question arises of how this danger can be avoided.

It will only be possible to answer this question aright if the following three problems can be dealt with quite openly: the problem of the doctrine of the Church, particularly in view of the participation of the

Church in the work of God within the world (*missio Dei*) ; the problem of the ecumenical reality of the Church, with particular reference to the New Delhi Statement on Unity ("all in each place") ; and finally, the problem of the new localities in which most of the churches are living today.

6. *The churches are living in new localities*

Reference to new structures in the Church often leaves the impression that a local congregation would be considered superfluous or even misplaced. This impression is mistaken, for such a reference implies the question of where the locality of the Church can be placed today. This question may be rather perplexing to begin with, but its value lies precisely in the way it underlines the importance of the locale.

The Christian congregation has always found its place. It must be able to, for its proper place has always been, in every circumstance, the locality in which men actually do their living. Despite every distinction of church order between congregations, their structures have customarily adapted to this particular place and the tasks which are to be fulfilled there. In Christianized Europe, for example, the parish was an appropriate structure, and other congregational structures have been marked with its stamp. In recent times, however, the nature of the local area has changed in most cases. An area which was once self-contained and cohesive has become an enormously complex structure, which has many different connections with other areas and many quite diverse focal centres (e.g., factories, residential districts, and sports arenas). This is where people's lives are going on, persons very different from each other, persons with a variety of roles (e.g., within the family, in their occupations, in politics, or at leisure) or who represent different sorts of mobility (e.g., older people, wage earners, housewives, and children). It is an area which includes a great many kinds of community, and which has within it numerous possible relations and tensions. If a congregation is really to be a *local* congregation within such an area, it must be adapted to the actual life of that area. That purpose it can accomplish only by having the courage to attain the greatest possible diversity and mobility.

Wherever this task is grasped and affirmed, congregations or other ecclesiastical bodies (dioceses, presbyteries, conferences, synods, councils of churches, etc.) have begun making sociological surveys of their respective areas with the aim of giving new structure to churches in particular localities. Any such new structure is developed according to the character of diversity and mobility within each locality. Congregations are exploring the possibility of closer cooperation with other congregations in their area and with various "little congregations" and movements which are active there. As a result of such activity, the centre of gravity is becoming more widely distributed and the churches' tasks more appropriately divided up, corresponding to the extremely diverse and newly developing "worlds" within which they now live—the worlds, for example, where people have their homes, do their work, make decisions and improve their education. Some churches have been working on pilot projects embodying new structures for neighborhoods lying within new urban areas. They have encouraged the holding of worship services (e.g., for youth), meetings, and projects (e.g., the work of the Evangelical Academies) appropriate for a particular area or several areas, disregarding parish or denominational boundaries. Some local and regional councils have discovered that their task consists not only in the coordination of existing local congregations but in the advancement of larger congregational complexes, appropriate for the large new areas, and the integration of their many smaller components. Many lay institutes, and a few theological schools as well, have set themselves the task of preparing people for various specialized ministries.

7. The local parish congregation is a community of ministries

So that the churches' ministry can become relevant within all these various new localities, the world must be taken seriously within the life of our parishes, in all its breadth and ferment. For this, our congregations need faith, and they need to be informed. The faith of a congregation will show that, on the whole, it is ready, in the face of every trial and difficulty, to take an active part in the Christian world mission. A missionary congregation views the locality in which it happens to exist as a part of that total world which belongs to God and to which his Word is addressed. Information will be made available and will be really given when preaching is at least implicitly dialogical, corresponding to the dialogical action of God himself, and when prayer brings the world as it actually is before him who is its origin and fulfilment. We must discover anew that worship, as a true service before God, can really free a Christian congregation for participation in Christ's service to the world.

We must also take to ourselves the newly rediscovered understanding of the congregation: that it is a gathering of ministries rather than a collectivity of individuals and families, and that ministry is a corporate not merely an individual task. Wherever this view has been gaining ground or has become acceptable, it has been a real liberation for many church members. But it has become more than ever necessary to face the question of the gifts (*charismata*) which God so freely gives, to make room for them, and to develop them. What we need to know about this, and what we need to do, has been indicated clearly enough through recent ecumenical work on the ministry of the laity.

A missionary congregation stands or falls on the issue of its obedience to the task which the Church has received as the Church of Jesus Christ. We have to realize over and over again what an alarming uncertainty prevails in many of our congregations as to the commission under which they have been called to live. Therefore it is continually necessary, in season and out of season, to bring the question of this commission before our congregations. Surprisingly enough, this question becomes all the more insistent as the question of congregational structure arises, as an authoritative answer is demanded, and as in this process the Gospel is heard anew.

WORLD AND CHURCH, CHURCH AND WORLD

The quest for proper congregational structures brings with it a host of difficult and perplexing theological questions. Often these questions have already been outlined in the normal run of theological work, above all in its concern for the authentic witness of the Church. They have come with particular urgency and incisiveness when raised through those new missionary forces and movements of our century which have summoned people to take the world seriously under God, to enter into the tasks he has for them in and for the world, and thereby be open to what the Holy Spirit is doing. These are forces and movements which can no longer abide separation in the lives of churches between their worship and their mission, between their proclamation and their service, between their witness to individuals and their involvement in the movements of contemporary society. And these are questions which point to a biblical understanding of history, to a genuinely historical understanding of revelation and of what God is doing in the world, a proper outlook on the cosmic, world-transforming lordship of Christ, a vital eschatological understanding of this present age, and a theological interpretation of worldwide secularization—in short, they are questions which shatter popular conceptions of the relation between Church and world. In the quest for structures appropriate for the life of Christian congregations in the world, such questions are brought to a focus in the problem of relating the work of theology and sociology.

In the coming years, hard work will have to be done on this problem, in an attitude of openness. It is an ecumenical problem, in its own way, for it concerns not only the relation of churches to each other but also their relation to the *oikumene* as world. Along with the many specialized questions which are bound to arise, the attempt must be made to think through the following questions and to get some answer to them:

On the one hand, how can we move out into the changing forms of human existence in such a way that we avoid losing the necessary continuity of faith, life and order which alone can keep the Church's mission truly Christian?

On the other hand, how can we maintain the true marks of the Church in such a way as to avoid that static conservatism which prevents us from moving out in freedom into these changing forms of human existence as witness to Christ our living Lord?

Bibliography

A Theological Reflection on the Work of Evangelism, WCC, Geneva, 1959.

Report of the Section 'Witness,' in: *The New Delhi Report,* The Third Assembly of the World Council of Churches, 1961, SCM Press, London; Association Press, New York.

Centers of Renewal, for Study and Lay Training, WCC, Geneva, 1964.

CONCEPT Papers from the Department on Studies in Evangelism, WCC, Geneva.

I, March 1962
G. Eichholz, The Meaning of a Charismatic Congregation.
G. W. Webber, Worship in East Harlem.
H. Symanowski, Sunday in an Industrial Mission.

II, (July 1962) February 1963.
The Missionary Structure of the Congregation—Introduction

III, January 1963.
M. A. Siotis, Thoughts of an Orthodox Theologian on "The Missionary Structure of the Congregation."
P. Kraemer, The Urban Church: A Responsible Church?
M. Takenaka, Searching Questions on Structures of the Church in the Asian Setting.

IV, April 1963.
Our Congregation in the D.D.R. A Statement from Eastern Germany.

V, September 1963.
From Letters concerning "The Missionary Structure of the Congregation"
P. H. Vrijhof, W. Eichholtz, M. A. Thung, P. E. Kraemer, Sociological Contributions to the Study on "The Missionary Structure of the Congregation."
H. Chatelain, Notes on Sociology of Religion.
E. Jones, Example for a Regional Study of "Zones humaines."

VI, November 1963.
The Churches in Mission—North American Conference.

VII, May 1964.
Missionary Presence in God's World. Papers of a first World Consultation on "The Missionary Structure of the Congregation"—Bossey, April 1964.
The Call to Renewal in the Churches of Asia. Statement of the East Asia Christian Conference.

VIII, November 1964.
The Esslingen Papers.
The Missionary Congregation in South-West Wales.
Sociology, Theology and the Mission of the Church.

IX, May 1965.
The Driebergen Papers.
P. H. Vrijhof, Mission in Sociological Perspective.

X, November 1965.
Papers on Faith and Order Consultation on "Spirit, Order and Organization."

FLEMING—WRIGHT, *Structures for a Missionary Congregation.* The Shape of the Christian Community in Asia Today, Singapore, 1964.

Institutionalism and Church Unity, Association Press, New York 1963. Cf. *The Old and the New in the Church,* SCM Press, London, 1961.

Laici in Ecclesia: An Ecumenical Bibliography on the Role of the Laity in the Life and Mission of the Church. Geneva 1961.

LAITY Reprints from Nos. 2-6, Geneva 1962.
- 8/1960: Our Call to be a Minority. Considerations arising from the Asian Church Situation.
- 9/1960: Ministers of the Priestly People.
- 11/1961: On the Way to the World of Tomorrow.
- 17/1963: Christ's Ministry and the Ministry of the Church.
- 18/1964: Laity and Missionary Congregations.

MARGULL, H. J. *Hope in Action,* Philadelphia, Muhlenberg Press, 1962.
Evangelism in Ecumenical Perspective (Ec. Review 16, 133-145, 1964.)

A Monthly Letter about Evangelism, WCC, Geneva.
- 5/1957: The Church Becomes Good News (East Harlem Protestant Parish).
- 3-4/1961: J. C. Hoekendijk: On Proselytism
- 7/1961: The Potter's House (U.S.A.).
- 2/1963: Ecumenical Material on "The Missionary Structure of the Congregation."
- 4/1963: Witness in the "Ruhr of India."
- 2-3/1964: Experimental Ministries in the Church (Parishfield).
- 4/1964: The Church with Gas Fume and Bean Soup Smell (Japan).
- 7/1964: The Church in the Apartment Complex (Pillsbury).
- 8/1964: Australian Ministry to a Beatnik Community.
- 9/1964: On the Docks of an African Port.
- 4-5/1965: Michael Mann; The Port Harcourt Project.

WIESER, Th., A New Ecumenical Discussion on the Congregation (Ec. Review 16, 153-157, 1964).

WILLIAMS, Colin W., *Where in the World?,* New York, National Council of Churches, 1963, London, Epworth, 1965.

What in the World?, New York, National Council of Churches, 1964, London, Epworth, 1965.

Evangelism and the Congregation (Ec. Review 16, 146-152, 1964).

YOUTH 10, December 1964: Youth, Complex Society, The Structures of a Missionary Church. (WCC).